CHURCH PASTOR, CHILD TRAFFICKER

CHURCH PASTOR, CHILD TRAFFICKER

The Crimes of Elsa Cueller in a Border Town

ROGER RODRIGUEZ

ROWMAN & LITTLEFIELD
Lanham • Boulder • New York • London

Unless otherwise noted, all photos are from the Elsa Cuellar investigation, courtesy of UISD police.

Published by Rowman & Littlefield

An imprint of The Rowman & Littlefield Publishing Group, Inc.

4501 Forbes Boulevard, Suite 200, Lanham, Maryland 20706

www.rowman.com

86-90 Paul Street, London EC2A 4NE

British Library Cataloguing in Publication Information Available

Library of Congress Cataloging-in-Publication Data

Library of Congress Control Number: 2023951451

978-1-5381-8506-3 (cloth)

978-1-5381-8507-0 (electronic)

♾™ The paper used in this publication meets the minimum requirements of American National Standard for Information Sciences—Permanence of Paper for Printed Library Materials, ANSI/NISO Z39.48-1992.

CONTENTS

Foreword vii

Acknowledgments xi

Note to the Reader xiii

1: Pastora Del Mal (Pastor of Evil) 1

2: Los Solanos de Laredo 5

3: A Ghostly Figure 17

4: Bidi: December 1998—Rio Bravo, Texas 23

5: The Creative Element .31

6: The Hidden Truth 35

7: A South Texas Ranch: June 1998 (15 Years before Cuellar's Arrest)39

8: Angels in Her Path 45

9: The Adoption Defense .55

10: The Chance of a Lifetime 63

11: Evil Crossing 75

12: The Dilemma 81

13: The Older Man: Two Months Before the Arrest of Elsa Cuellar .85

14: El Coco: August 2013 103

15: The Pressure Mounts 109

16: The House on Kearny: March 2013, Laredo, Texas 121

17: The Interrogation 127

18: Revisiting a Murder Case 133

19: The Carnival 145

20: Where the Children's Loyalty Is 157

21: Joaquin: Mexico City, August 1994 167

22: Operation Cabbage Patch: May 20, 2013 175

23: The Fugitive: Monterrey, Nuevo Leon, July 2000 179

24: A Bad Day 201

25: The Psychological Impact on the Victims 209

26: Reflections 215

27: Problems with Strategies to Combat Human Trafficking 223

28: What is Next? 231

29: My Return Home 239

Bibliography 245

Index 247

About the Author 257

FOREWORD

No traditional scholar could ever write this book. These stories in our society just don't make sense. How could these atrocities possibly happen for so many years, to so many children? How could they occur while Elsa Cuellar would reside in a quiet middle-class neighborhood in America?

I first met Roger Rodriguez about seventeen years ago. He was enrolled in my Sociology course at Texas A&M International University (TAMIU). Instantly, I knew he was special, and I expected that I would remember him throughout my career. In the few years I worked directly with him, I was not surprised to see that he would go on to win the grand prize for research at the TAMIU student research conference. Since then, he has become an outstanding college teacher and his books are captivating, always guided by interesting questions. Roger's rich life experience as a writer, trained in Sociology after having substantial career experience working in the justice system allows him to piece together all the parts necessary for us to understand this complex criminal enterprise.

Both of us share a fascination with the culture of "Los Dos Laredos" (Laredo, Texas, USA, and Nuevo Laredo, Tamaulipas, Mexico). I am a New Orleans native and many times, as I hear stories of what goes on in my home city, we say that "truth is stranger than fiction." This can also be said for the border culture of Los Dos Laredos. I wish the stories that Roger shares here were fiction, but they are well-documented truths that have affected countless lives.

Each day, approximately 15,000 people cross the bridge by foot to travel between Nuevo Laredo, Tamaulipas, Mexico, and Laredo, Texas, United States of America. Substantially more people drive across the border. Others cross by illegally hitching onto a commercial train or wading across the Rio Grande. The massive number of individuals crossing makes for a significant challenge in understanding who is or is not crossing in compliance with federal laws. Regardless of their status, many of those people crossing are vulnerable as they enter the United States. They cross the border with no social safety net and nowhere to turn. Therefore, they turned to any good soul offering support, perhaps a church pastor, a doctor, a lawyer, or a midwife. Each time, there was hope for a better life for both them and their children. Elsa Cuellar situated herself in the perfect position to take advantage of many of these people.

Who would not admire a church pastor that opens her home to a young expectant mother with no other resources? For those that have little, the promise of coming to America is so attractive that we simply do not have to ask the question: How could she entice so many of these individuals to cross? There is tremendous power in offering hope to those that have so little. Also, people with education and prestige are honored and trusted by many vulnerable people, whether they deserve that trust or not. Sadly, many people are not who they say they are.

Laredo, Texas is a relatively quiet community and if you carefully look at the FBI's uniform crime reports, you will see that it is a city with index crime rates that are substantially below average in terms of homicide, rape, robbery, and aggravated assault. Some of this low crime rate may be explained by the thousands of trained personnel of the policing agencies at the border ranging from local police and sheriffs to the Texas state department of public safety, of course, Border Patrol, Immigration and Customs Enforcement, DEA, FBI, ATF, and so on. Of course, with all these well-trained guardians available, the obvious question that is posed is: How could these atrocities be carried on for so many years under the noses of these professionals?

A thirty-year veteran of government service once shared his perceived key to having a long successful career. His advice to anyone desiring to fit in a bureaucratic system was to utter three important words: "no problems here." Closing cases, claiming to have the problem solved with a simple explanation, and the belief that most indiscretions are minor, make careers much easier. As Roger points out in this book, simply glossing over unusual behavior and circumstances taken by a simple person in the crowd may lead us to ignore a major issue. The field of social services education and criminal justice deals with the real world. Universities deal with the ideal world. We teach social service providers what to look for, educators how to teach, and criminal justice professionals how to perform their duties in an ideal manner. However, the real world is different. Numerous constraints confound investigations. The Elsa Cuellar case explains why we must continue to strive to be more thorough in our investigations. We often see that investigation of small problems may uncover larger issues.

There were numerous opportunities for people to be suspicious of the Cuellar household, but each unit seeing one unusual action or behavior does not make a criminal case. The "real" world of child protection and public safety deals with finite budgets and overworked staff that rarely have time to thoroughly share intelligence and communicate with other agencies. The "ideal" world calls for complete investigations, full documentation, and constant communication among all those responsible for ensuring public safety. Regardless of how frustrating it may seem that social problems are not completely addressed, and justice does not appear to arrive satisfactorily, we must persist in attempting to carefully follow public safety protocols.

When the teacher is suspicious and calls for a Child Protective Services investigation, they are taking heroic action. It is easier for them to look the other way. However, vigilant teachers and school staff were critical in uncovering this case. Notes and documents from previous small-time police reports were essential to gaining Cuellar's arrest. I am grateful that Roger Rodriguez dedicated years of study to compiling the documents and stories of involved parties to demonstrate the importance of watching out for the vulnerable in our society.

Don't change, Roger.

Dr. John C. Kilburn, Jr.

Laredo, Texas

Acknowledgments

It is not possible to complete a project of this kind without assistance. Leticia Gomez, thank you so much for always being there in support of my writing. I would not have a writing career without you. Investigator Alexander Rodriguez was critical in steering me in the right direction. Without his assistance, it would have been very difficult to know who to speak to and where to find them. District Attorney Isidro R. "Chilo" Alaniz, took the time to visit with me during his busy schedule. I appreciate you penciling me in, it means so much to me. Jose Angel Almazan and Jesse Perusquia were at the center of the incident that is the subject of this project. Thank you so much for meeting with me during your work hours. Your expertise gave me clarity in this case. Thank you! Those who were so close to the case that they preferred to remain anonymous, including some of the family and victims. Thank you for taking the time to visit with me. I know it was not easy to relive some of these events. Your help was of great value.

Author Carlos Nicolas Flores has been a great inspiration and an exceptional mentor and friend in my journey to become a writer. Your knowledge, passion, and road trips along the Rio Grande Border served as an unprecedented ingredient to this project: *Mil Gracias*! Along with these wonderful people, Dr. John Kilburn has been at my side and a co-pilot on my journeys for nearly twenty years as I flew through my college years into where I am now. Thank you, Dr. Kilburn. Your support is unique—your friendship is priceless. I never thought a childhood friend could someday contribute to my passion for writing, but this is the case with L.I.S.D. Police Chief Doreen Hale. Thank you so much Doreen for taking the time to speak with me. You have always been a great supporter and I hold a special place for you in my heart.

Attorney Al Greene has a remarkable legal mind and an unprecedented resume to go with it. Thank you for helping me understand the legal process for child placement. Last, certainly not least, the fine people at *En Frecuencia*. Their journalism uncovered information about this case I never would have found on my end of the country. Thank you!

Note to the Reader

One of the most important things the reader should understand is how difficult it was to put this project together. Finding victims was extremely difficult for several reasons. First, Elsa Cuellar was so dexterous in her manipulation of others, that many did not see themselves as victims at all. To them, Elsa Cuellar was the only mother they ever knew and not even proof through DNA testing would change their mind. Second, some of the stories shared by victims or members of the victim's families were in fragments. These fragmented accounts were put together to get a broad understanding of their experience; the rest had to depend on theory. Third, I was faced with having to confront one extreme over another. Elsa Cuellar operated for many years, so on one hand, many of the victims were already over the age of eighteen; many had married, moved away, and had families of their own. Other important people in the case had passed away. On the other hand, I dealt with many officials who still had the same position since Elsa Cuellar's case was investigated. Logically, they were afraid to overshare and risk their careers so close to retirement.

Some of the stories related here happened to me personally working with border families as a counselor. Years later, I wonder if they were somehow victimized by Elsa Cuellar in a time when I had yet to hear about her. Although we will never be able to know if they were victims of Elsa Cuellar, nor will I suggest they were, readers will be able to appreciate the remarkable similarities in the experiences these families had to share. It would be great to learn how these families are doing today. Unfortunately, having worked with hundreds of families in a seven-year span as a counselor, I am today only in contact with one of those families.

One of my initial concerns during this investigation was having readers adopt a misconception of the victims. Elsa Cuellar had a specific type of target readers will become familiar with as they read the story. They will learn that low IQ in their victims was a critical component if her operation was to be a success. Therefore, great caution should be taken when considering perceptions about how easily some of these victims were manipulated. The vulnerability factor was essential in the personality type Elsa Cuellar hunted, and she knew very well how to find them. For this reason, many of the interviews conducted with Cuellar's victims remain anonymous. It is necessary to protect the identity, safety, and comfort of those deemed incapable of fully understanding the full scope of this case.

Finally, all readers must understand this is not a school district issue. This is an immigration and border security issue our country must face. The United Independent School District is highly committed to the safety of all students. Identifying false documents created by an experienced professional is outside the scope of U.I.S.D. employees' expertise and job description. Amazingly, they were able to discover what they did and create a whirlwind that would turn Elsa Cuellar's criminal career upside down. Every person and agency mentioned in this project should be applauded for their efforts in this case. There is no such thing as a small role in a criminal case of this magnitude.

For the safety and privacy of the many individuals involved in this case, some names, locations, and details have been changed. In addition, the subject of this book has used many aliases during her lifetime. To avoid confusion, this research will only be using the name, Elsa Cuellar. The subject of this book was never charged with any other crimes outside the ones mentioned in this project.

Pastora Del Mal (Pastor of Evil)

In December 1998, I was working for a program that counseled at-risk youths between the ages of seven to seventeen in the South Texas border town of Laredo. I had not been working there long when ten-year-old Leslie Marie Cuellar sat in my office waiting for me to get there. "Hi," I greeted her. I was not expecting to see her there. I usually visited my clients at their schools. She acknowledged me only with a slight smile and a reluctance to look at me. She was not very clean for someone who was supposed to be at school, but other than that, I did not notice anything so unusual about her. Leslie had always been quiet in previous meetings, and she always mentioned her family being poor. "So, why are you here today, Leslie, aren't you going to school?" I asked.

"No, my mom doesn't want me to."

I found this to be very unusual. Her mother was nowhere to be found and family sessions were always more productive with parental involvement. As quiet as she was, Leslie had been referred to my program for peculiar conduct in her school. She would pull her hair out in class and play with it at her desk. It was difficult to make a breakthrough with her because she always responded that her mother did not want her talking about "private home things." Since most behavior in children is a product of the home environment, understanding her well enough to help proved a difficult task. The case was not court-ordered, so I had no legal basis to make her talk and after consulting with Child Protective Services I learned that being reserved about their domestic life did not merit CPS investigation. I had no options other than to do some activities with Leslie and wait for her to open up voluntarily.

I found it unusual that her mother was waiting for her in the car. Most parents I had dealt with wished to participate and learn more about what was going on with their children. Leslie's mother demonstrated no such ambition and sat in the car reading the Holy Bible. I walked Leslie over to her mother and said, "Good morning," and she only smiled. I invited her to our next session hoping for a compassionate response. What I got was a gentle suggestion to never ask that again. "I'm not the one who needs counseling," She answered coldly. Leslie and her mother drove off and were gone as mysteriously as they had arrived that morning. I would not know until twenty-one years later that I had just met Elsa Cuellar: one of the most notorious child traffickers to ever set foot on American soil.

I was not experienced enough at the time to have seen the signs and often wonder how Leslie turned out twenty-four years later. She should be around thirty-four years old now and hope she has had a good life. Reflecting on those things I should have been able to notice, I came to realize that it is not only within the individual that the most obvious warnings can be found. Instead, it is best to examine society as a whole. The environment must contain specific ingredients that make human trafficking possible. Laredo, Texas, contains these ingredients making it a viable option for such a lucrative business. These ingredients will be explored in an investigative approach to the case of Elsa Cuellar. In essence, *Church Pastor, Child Trafficker* is a sociological perspective in identifying social characteristics that contribute to, cause, or facilitation of human trafficking.

Being able to identify the different social traits that may allow communities to understand human trafficking is one thing; having them understand them is an arduous task on its own. The reason for this has to do with the current social mindset of human trafficking. First, the idea of human trafficking has been glorified by the film industry and social media as being something that is exclusively happening on the United States–Mexican border. This ideology undermines the journey that some trafficked children, men, and women take to get to the United States from other parts of the world. Secondly, there is a misconception by many that this form of organized business is something new. One must consider that slavery and the treating of people as property was once a legally accepted practice. Because of this, this behavior was never recorded in history as a crime against humanity. Instead, it was seen as a profitable business. In addition, before the invention of the printing press, children were not classified as minors or underage. To the common farm owner, they were people able to work and contribute to the demands of running a business: they were nothing more than smaller people. After the invention of the printing press, the distinction between children and adults could be made with the speed at which they were able to achieve literacy.

Almost every society in the history of the world has practiced slavery in one way or another. Few societies, such as the aborigines in Australia do not have slavery recorded in their history, but as Philip D. Morgan suggests in *Origins of American Slavery*, this could be owed more to the exclusion of this part of their history and not so much the absence of the practice (51). Excluding slavery from a culture's history is not necessarily a flaw in academics. It reveals that there were people in earlier societies who felt there was a sense of immorality in the practice. For them to rather not have slavery recorded as part of their history suggests compassion for victims of slavery. These societies were minimal. Most other cultures had followed the lead of more respected societies because they were convincing in their approach to enslaving humans. Literacy was a strong indicator of a society's progression; by the time the Spaniards had arrived at the Aztec Empire, Europeans had already established a sense of culture. They were well read in theology, philosophy, art, law and had explored the world extensively. Few would make a connection between this and the practice of slavery, but powerful empires such as the Greeks and Romans used their interpretation of the law, religion, and philosophy to justify slavery. To them, it made sense and was a constituent factor in a successful society. At that time, it was a difficult principle to reject when scholars such as Aristotle claimed that some people were "slaves by nature."

Philosophers were not the only ones who had a powerful influence on how society perceived the enslavement of humans. Many used biblical references to justify slavery. During times when political practice relied heavily on the word of God, it makes it difficult for people to refute something the Almighty himself approves of. Arabs along with their Muslim partners were the first to enslave black Africans from Sub-Saharan regions. By the seventh century, they had established long-distance partnerships that flourished well into the nineteenth century. White people were also enslaved by Muslims because the Quran and Islamic law did not recognize any distinction between races. Although it is documented that black Africans seemed to be treated with the most hatred and it is believed that the attitudes toward black Africans were injected into the fabric of other societies encountered through the trade routes.

Elsa Cuellar is not Greek, Roman, or Muslim. She does not belong to a time period that any kind of justification for her actions would be seen as anything less than immoral. Still, she encompasses some minor aspects of what history tells us was the mindset at that time. She does not rely on religion to justify her actions; however, she uses her role as a pastor and her deceitful religious nature to create a smokescreen for who she truly is. Like the Romans and Greeks, she uses her ability to read and more advanced education to manipulate and groom the less literate and desperate citizens of Mexico. To them, she is a God, an extremely educated woman. To enhance this misconception, she has passed herself off as a doctor and a lawyer making her credibility more sustainable. Much like the sub-Saharan kings who would enslave their own black people for profit, Elsa does not care that she is tearing into the soul of her own culture. She has little concern for the contribution she makes to the stereotypes that have polluted the image of a struggling nation, but unlike the Sub-Saharan region which was very unpopulated with few to stand up for human rights, she belongs to a society that is doing what it can in efforts to combat human trafficking. Why she never saw a day in prison in her entire life is not something this project can answer, but it will explore the malicious deeds she has committed and bring to light the many atrocities that are occurring in the dark corners of our society.

2

Los Solanos de Laredo

THE ABILITY TO CROSS THE INTERNATIONAL BORDER FREELY IS A CRIT-
ical part of the process. Many have argued that the United States needs
to tighten its immigration policies and security while screening more vig-
orously for criminals. These are arguments posed election after election.
The truth is that many politicians are looking in the wrong place. Those
immigrants coming the traditional way by train, *coyotes*, or by simply
taking their chances by swimming across the river are not likely to be
those who are committing the most deplorable crimes. Most of them are
not criminals at all; their true intention is to try to find work and survive.
Consistently, we ignore the science of sociology. Human behavior tells
us that wealthy people do not generally like to get their clothes dirty. So
how do they do it? The answer is much simpler than one would expect;
they walk directly through customs at the international bridge. Yes, some
of these trafficked children are simply walking into the United States
with a smile on their faces and holding their "mother's" hand.

This brings to light the question: "Why are US customs officers
allowing this?" In their defense, they are not allowing it; they do not
know. Elsa Cuellar is a master at her craft and there are many like her.
She is one of the most prolific creators of counterfeit documents that the
world has ever known. Having gotten her experience with various drug
cartels, it was not difficult for her to obtain the resources she needed
to create flawless documents. So is it immigration policy that needs to
be amended or the security in the documents required to cross into the
United States that we should be talking about? It is not as commonsense

as some may believe. When someone is as gifted as Elsa Cuellar at creating flawless documents and birth certificates, she often avoids authorities feeling there is a reason to examine the paperwork any further. Most children being brought into the United States through the international bridge aren't aware at that time they are being trafficked, so their behavior does not raise red flags either. In most cases, children are being brought into the United States with the false pretense of a new beginning with glorious happy days ahead. In essence, one of the necessary ingredients to successful child trafficking is mobility, that is, the freedom to cross to and from Mexico without fear of deportation.

This is not enough. The business of human trafficking is an organization that requires help from different directions and various settings. Where does this help come from? During my investigation, I came across some people willing to speak to me on the condition I do not use names; however, I was given some flexibility in discussing some aspects of their organization. For them to allow me to do this tells me they are not afraid of being caught. I am talking about the ghosts of Laredo, Texas—*Los Solanos*. In other words, they are "solo" as in they do not belong to any one specific organization. They are not involved in the cartel (which is one of the first focuses of law enforcement) and they are not affiliated with anyone under the scope of law enforcement.

At the time of this project, I am also working on a true story about a former Mexican mafia member titled "Black Pearl of Mexico." While researching this project, I found myself among some of the most dangerous men on the border. I must admit there were times when I was not sure if I was going to live through one more interview. It did not matter that one of the most notorious of the men was working very closely with me (*El Viejon*). The organized crime world does not work that way. Had he been given an order to "take care" of me for whatever reason they found justifiable, then that is what he would have to do. It was a risky undertaking—one my wife did not care for me to take. She was not happy about it at all. Those close to me who knew what I was doing saw the potential for serious risk; I saw an opportunity.

As an English major and writer, my heart was set on completing the book. The sociologist in me saw an amazing opportunity to gain an inside perspective on what takes place on both sides of the border in a more elaborate way than simply reviewing the existing literature. The more I associated with the group of people I came to know as "Los Solanos," the more I realized how much sociologists, law enforcement, and the government do not know. There is a world of underground work taking place from one side of the border to the other that serves as a powerful foundation for the things law enforcement does know. The problem is that at the point where the government and law enforcement have a good understanding of what is happening, it is already the tail end of the process. The number of large businesses involved in helping organized crime fulfill their trafficking goals is higher than anyone can imagine. Companies that specialize in pet products have special formulas that are not available on their store shelves. It is a very expensive formula mostly purchased by the wealthy to keep their dogs and cats off expensive furniture. It does more than that; it keeps dogs off millions of dollars of drugs and humans coming into the United States via Mexico. It is an interesting product that is highly valuable for anyone looking to get past law enforcement. Very few can afford this product outside drug traffickers and of course those contributing to their business. Sadly, I am unable to disclose the specific name of this business.

Loads of marijuana, cocaine, and trafficked humans can get from the Laredo, Texas, border to Lake Charles, Louisiana without a problem. It cannot be stopped, and the business will never die. This is because American authorities have their eyes on the wrong place. Where are they looking? At Los Zetas? The Gulf Cartel? Are they looking into the local American gangs who work with the cartels distributing? Perhaps after many years of looking at these same groups, there needs to be a realization there is a reason the war is being lost. Those doing the real work are ghosts. The men and women working to help organized crime achieve their fullest potential belong to no one organization with the reputation for trafficking drugs or people. They are *Solanos*, that is, *"solos"*: the Spanish word for "alone." Where are they? Where do they come from? What role do they play in society and how does it work? Most importantly, will they ever be caught?

The short answer to the last question is "no." They will never be caught because before that happens, law enforcement and the US government would first have to know who they are. Without having one single street name, nickname, real name, friend, relative, date of birth, or any other proof they even exist—How does one go about arresting them? They are ghosts. They will remain ghosts never to be seen by the eyes of the law in any capacity. Some of them are lost among the faculty of the public school systems while others work for their city: yes, on the American side of the border. It was a profound joy I felt as a sociologist to see these ghosts. I spoke to them, I mingled with them, I ate with them; they showed me things I never would have seen in my life without them.

My first visit with *El Viejon* (for the moment, he prefers I not use his real name though he promised I could reveal it when he thought it was a better time) was a few days after Thanksgiving 2021. I was given an address on San Francisco St. in Laredo, Texas, as the meeting place. This is not where the meeting would be held but rather where I would be picked up and taken to where the meeting was going to be. I was asked to step into a van; *El Viejon*'s presence always made me feel at ease, but he did not come. While he remained close with his associates, he had closed the chapter on that life and was a different man outside of prison. He asked me not to tell him of anything I saw. He didn't want to know. I must admit this got me very nervous. We drove for almost an hour to a small ranch around what I believe to have been San Ignacio, Texas. This, of course, was only speculation. I could not ascertain with any satisfactory validity where I was since they placed a cover over my head. We arrived just in time. I was getting car sick in the back of the van with no ventilation and not being able to see where we were going. Ten minutes more and I may have thrown up all over myself.

The worst part was driving down the dirt path off what I believe to have been Zapata Highway (I'm still not sure). I had tried to feel the direction we were going, but the driver took paths that greatly confused my sense of direction. Whether this was done intentionally as part of their routine or if it was an accident, I never knew. The dirt road was bumpy and obviously off the main highway. About six miles into the South Texas mesquite wilderness, we finally came to a stop at an old house and the hood was removed. When I stepped foot onto land, I felt very dizzy and nauseous. I hid this well by acting as if I had done this before. I was escorted through an old house. Some of the sheet rock was broken and the home could easily have been mistaken for being abandoned if it were not for the fact, it was not. As they guided me through the torn-down halls, we passed a room where I saw a nude man sitting on a chair with his hands tied behind his back and his eyes covered. It was obvious he had been beaten at some point before my arrival. I quickly looked away; I did not want anyone there thinking I was interested in their private business. I only wanted information that could help me finish my story with as much detail as possible. Several thoughts had gone through my head. First, I have heard it said many times before how much I resembled *El Viejon*. I feared being mistaken for him by someone resentful that he no longer worked in the trade. Secondly, I thought I would be a great replacement kill: the kind that would make the enemy think my contact had been murdered. I got calmer by telling myself I needed to stop watching so much Netflix.

I sat in a small room where artwork hung. I recognized some of the paintings as work that *El Viejo* had done. He used his time wisely at the Coffield Unit and learned to paint. In that same room, a man was doing a tattoo on another as they spoke in Spanish about their families. They never addressed me or looked me in the eye. I wondered what it was I was waiting for. As it turned out, the man I was waiting for was the same one who was doing the tattoo. He was the person in charge: *Solano Uno*. That is all they would ever be to me—a number. *Solano Dos, Solano Tres*, and so on. There would not be an exchange of names, history of things that are ongoing or talk about each other's origins. I was very nervous until Solano Uno began to speak. He was polite, welcoming, and treated me better than some committees I faced for job interviews. I was very impressed with their cordiality and manners. Solano Uno was all about respect; he demanded it in both forms: as a recipient and deliverer of it.

"*Eres gente del Viejon?*" he asked me if I was family to my contact. At this point, I had to take the chance that saying yes was not disadvantageous. I acknowledged that this man known on the streets as *El Viejon* is indeed my cousin and did so with conviction to show some kind of pride in being able to say that. He embraced me with both of his hands on each of my shoulders and showed me a handshake he had me swear never to show anyone. I promised him I would not and intend to keep that promise (I later learned there was no such handshake and that they were "bullshitting" me. They probably joke about it to this day). Not even the law had held me to such standards of respect and swore to myself never to break a promise to any Solano I met. We sat and he passed me a drink. I did not dare to tell him that I did not drink alcohol, so I took it. It did not taste like alcohol at all. It was a very delicious fruity, citrus drink I never had before. I could hear a blender in the far-off kitchen as if they were in the process of making more.

"So, what do you want to know?" It was that simple! The process was nothing as I had imagined in my head. There was no interrogation of any kind forcing me to spit out some bogus confession about what I was doing there. I was not tied up and tortured until I spoke the truth. I simply went to meet them; they asked me what I wanted to know: perhaps I had been watching too much Netflix indeed. "Tell me about the avocado orchard. Why was *El Viejon* sent to kill such a defenseless man?" (This is a question that was asked for my other project and will be answered when that book is released). I got the information I needed. For an hour, we spoke and were given great detail (Some so detailed I was asked not to write about it.) When the hour expired, Solano Uno called out to Solano Tres to take me home. They covered my head again, but the ride home seemed much shorter for some reason. When the head cover was removed, I was already blocks away from San Francisco St. where *El Viejon* was waiting for me. We went to have some dinner at a family-owned place on Saunders Ave. and set an appointment for the next meeting.

The next adventure was about a month later on December 16, 2021. This location was also on San Francisco Street at the corner of Lyon. There is Zacate Creek Park where *El Viejon's* artwork is displayed on the back brick wall. Large butterflies throughout the long cinderblock wall decorated the declining park and overshadowed the gang graffiti on the playground. Ironically, the area was swarming with real butterflies. It was from here we left for the next meeting site. The excursion from the park site was bittersweet. On one hand, I was not blinded by a cover on my head which made it difficult to breathe and more tasking to avoid motion sickness. On the other hand, we crossed the border into Mexico which I was not prepared to do. It was frightening enough the first time being on the American side. We drove for about two hours before getting to a place called *Colonia La Joya* where I was given a bag and told to change. I opened the bag, and it was a Santa Claus costume. At first, I thought I was the chosen one to be made to look like an idiot, but when I got out of the van, everyone in the group had changed into Santa Claus costumes. They gave me a bag filled with toys. Some of us handed toys to the children in the *colonia* while others handed money and food to the adults. A van that had arrived there before we did had boxes filled with cash to the rim with armed men standing beside it. It was not a scenario I expected to see. I saw destitution at a level I had never witnessed before in my life. One of my first career jobs after obtaining a BA in psychology was working with at-risk youths along the border for an agency called S.C.A.N. I would do home visits in some of the poorest homes in Laredo, Texas daily. After visiting this *colonia*, I witnessed firsthand that the American perspective on being poor was very different than that of Mexico.

From that point, the trip once again put into place its privacy criteria. I was hooded once more. To be honest, I am not sure what purpose it served. I was so lost geographically and so unfamiliar with the territory, that I would not be able to return to wherever they were taking me even if I tried. When I got home later, I Googled *Colonia La Joya* and realized there were so many that went by this name I would be unable to accurately say which one I was at. Some, I was able to eliminate because they were much too far in the interior of Mexico and we had not driven that long, but the number of possibilities for *colonia*s that went by that name was a few. Still, I had to play by their rules and this trip was still about two hours from where we left, and the motion sickness kicked in as I had expected but not as severe as the first time. When they finally removed it, we were still driving, but it was a farm, dirt road in the middle of nowhere. The environment suddenly changed and what looked like a desert, South Texas mesquite land transformed into a tropical paradise. Palm trees, green grass, lakes with blue water, and animals of all kinds roamed the area. I saw zebras, rhinos, and elephants. One of the men turned to me and said: "You know your cousin did a painting of those elephants."

I smiled with pride knowing *El Viejon* had such an amazing talent. We continued the drive until we got to a very well-paved area that led to an amazing house. Heavily armed men walked the entire area, and the van came to a stop at a tall gate with large silver angels hanging from them. To get to the gate, one would have to drive across a small bridge over a river. I was told there were crocodiles in there, but I did not see one. However, I did see amazing spider monkeys and exotic birds on trees inside the compound I was entering. As we got deeper into the property, I began to feel vulnerable. My Netflix experience began to take charge of my imagination again and too often I had seen characters on narco series-type films get murdered unexpectedly. I did not want to be one of those victims, but I wanted to complete my book so badly and needed all the material I could get. I eased my mind by talking to myself in my mind: *What possible reason would they have to kill you? What threat can you even pose to them if this isn't even your world? Why would they target you after allowing you into their world? You don't even own a gun.*

At the gate, I faced the most terrifying thing I could imagine. A short distance away, there were a group of both men and women very formally dressed. It was within their company I was asked to drop my pants—including my underwear. I remember weighing my options: *Should I just identify myself as D.E.A so they can shoot me right then and there?* A chubby, middle-aged man like me had no reason not to feel insecure about his body, especially in the presence of women. I chose humility over death, closed my eyes, and dropped everything. When that trial was over and we began to walk into the house, a woman about my age wearing a bright-yellow dress and holding a margarita smiled at me flirtatiously. She made me feel better about my body and felt more confident as I walked in, yet she got me nervous. I knew better than to get caught gawking at a woman who could potentially be the current or ex-girlfriend of a cartel member. I decided to try my best to flip my eyeballs completely around to be looking toward the inside of my head and not out.

I was escorted through a living room where several people were socializing. We walked past a dining area where what appeared to be a serious meeting was taking place. One of the men told me that it was a conference between some very important men. One of those in attendance was the cousin of someone known by the world and law enforcement but asked me not to write or speak of his name to anyone—another promise I intend to keep. We kept walking until we came to a narrow corridor. At the entrance, there was a long table where everyone had to leave their weapons. Hundreds of handguns were on the table, and none could be loaded. During times when very high-level men were in the building, no loaded guns were allowed in the house. Every gun on the table had to be unloaded and as a gesture of faith that everyone would comply, those entering had to pick up a random weapon, point to their head, and pull the trigger.

This ritual is one that made me very uneasy. I had made up my mind to refuse the gesture and take my chances. As it turned out, I did not have to do such a thing. My cousin *El Viejon* had a reputation for taking the shot for anyone he had invited. He picked up two guns, pointed to his head, and pulled the trigger on both guns, taking my shot for me. He did not hesitate to do this, and it frightened me. How would I explain to my mother that my cousin blew his brains out on my behalf? This was her sister's son we were talking about. Luckily, it did not come to that. We entered the next room, and it looked like a fancy restaurant inside. I was never told officially who the owner was; whoever that might be, he had exquisite taste. He flew in chefs from France and Italy, musicians from Spain, and his Colombian security team who watched closely while the chefs cooked everything. I did not want to ask, but I imagine the owner would have his fair share of those who would want to poison him.

I ate a little bit of everything and met people as if I was at a family affair. For a minute, I forgot where I was and who I was with. It was one of the most beautiful settings I had ever seen. When I tried to think of something more beautiful, only buildings I saw in Paris, France, in my younger days came to mind. I doubt in my lifetime I will ever know anyone personally who could own a more magnificent structure. One of my textbooks for a sociology class I teach at Texas A&M International University referred to this as *narco-architecture*. That may be true of many places owned by cartels, but this mansion was not it. The building was not lacking in sophistication, culture, or beauty. It was eloquent in its most aggressive form and nothing about its design could be mistaken for anything else but class. While I could never survive the lifestyle of organized crime, I can certainly understand its appeal. If I did not know where I was and who I was surrounded by, I would incline to believe I had entered heaven.

The day ended. I had enough lobster, jumbo shrimp, and fine Mexican cuisine to last me a lifetime. I felt as if I could not possibly get hungry for the next three weeks. A hand came from behind me and touched my shoulder. I braced myself and turned to see the last person I would have hoped it would be—it was the woman in the yellow dress. Fortunately, *El Viejon* interfered immediately. He asked me to follow some men who took me back to the van. My cousin did not come with us. It was getting late and as the sun set, I was able to see the tips of mountains from a distance. Perhaps I was somewhere near Monterrey, Nuevo Leon (I don't know). It was dark already and maybe this was the reason I did not get a hood to wear at the beginning. We took a dirt path off the property in a very different direction than where we came from. About three miles off the main mansion, we drove past a compound where other men were. I saw they had three men bound by their arms and legs against a post. I thought of the man I saw in the previous interview spot and wondered if this would be his eventual fate if it had not been already. I must have done a poor job hiding my fear because one of the men looked at me and said in Spanish: "Don't worry, that's not where we're taking you."

He was a nice man; it is a difficult thing to conceive of someone holding an M4 Carbine. I tried to remind myself that my very own cousin lived this life once and he had a story behind it. The man reached into his pocket and extended something he took out toward me. I took it: a piece of Mexican candy. I was already very full, but I did not want to offend him and tried it. The taste was delicious: "*Revolcadita,*" he explained. I was not very familiar with Mexican candy outside the *Mazapan*. Now I understood he may have been wanting to distract me from the sounds of the distant gunfire that went off. The men tied to the post had met their fate; I pretended not to hear and continued to dissolve the candy in my mouth looking away.

Shortly before getting to the end of my journey, we came across a small red house. It reminded me of my grandmother's two-bedroom 1,100-square-foot home in Laredo. There were hundreds of children, men, and women in it. They were packed under very unsanitary conditions. It was not until much later I realized these were possible victims of human trafficking who thought they were on their way to America for a better way of life.

After another hour and a half of driving, we came to a ranch area where someone had to open the gate. It was already dark outside, but here, they proceeded to place a hood over my head once again. An hour later, we were at another gate where I could see through the hood that one of the men was speaking to a man in uniform. It was dark and with a hood over me, there was no way to ascertain who it was they were talking to, but I was able to see the image of the person getting into an official unit and leading the way through some very isolated areas. We stopped again and with only highway lights in my favor, I could see the images of the same two men speaking. The person driving the van gave this official something, but I could not see what it was. I realized at that point we were somehow in the United States. The car that drove off was either a Rodriguez County deputy, a border patrol agent, or a D.P.S unit. It was unmistakably a law enforcement vehicle.

I did not share this with anyone because most would want more information. There are always people wanting to get inside information on corruption in our society, but I simply could not see anything and there was nothing more for me to share. At this point, I was a little more familiar with the territory. We entered Zapata Highway somewhere before San Ignacio, Texas, and were taken to Rio Bravo where one of *El Viejon's* friends picked me up and took me back to Zacate Creek Park. I'm not sure why, but when I got home, I was overwhelmed with a need to cry. My emotional constitution had somehow been compromised by what I experienced. Although I was in the absence of any real threat or danger, the temporary lifestyle change did something to me on the inside.

I do not believe I will ever be the same after working on this project. I realize now that what I have seen on television is Hollywood and the fear of actually being there can never be felt through the camera lens. I am asked all the time if I developed a "soft spot" for the people I met. I think long and hard about that question but can never muster up a conclusive answer. Still, whenever I come across media showing the violence credited to the drug wars, it helps me to reflect on that one special moment when these same men were enriching the young lives of children during Christmas. When I see that a major arrest had taken place and agencies inform the public about the major dent they made in the drug trafficking industry, I smile and say to myself: "Not even a scratch." I am sure somewhere not far from me, the ghosts of the underworld, *Los Solanos*, were thinking the same thing.

Solanos hold meetings in the basement of a downtown building. The location changes every three months. I was not allowed to go and was advised by one man not to ask. I was shown enough and as he told me in Spanish: "If someone lets you lick a little frosting off their cupcake, don't ask for a bite." The point was well taken and was satisfied with my experience, but reflecting on everything I saw, I understood how support from such a mysterious group could be a valuable asset to someone like Elsa Cuellar.

For this type of partnership to exist, there must be a collaboration between people with the mobility to move freely across the Mexico-United States border. It is known that Elsa Cuellar has enjoyed this type of freedom for many years and whether her documents to do so are legitimate was never ascertained. Through interviews with law enforcement, I was able to trace Elsa's freedom to simply walk across the international bridge back as early as 1998—the year I first met her.

3

A Ghostly Figure

MOST WOULD AGREE ELSA'S STORY BEGINS MUCH SOONER THAN ANY research will ever be able to trace. Sources close to her reveal a deadly beginning to the terror she would cause later in her life. This occurred when two of her church brothers along with Elsa were taken to a remote part of Mexico where both men were murdered. It is not known whether Elsa witnessed the executions, but she was certainly in the vicinity. We know this because she revealed to the source that she saw both men were forced to dig their graves. Why she was spared is left to speculation, but whichever organization allowed her to live, must have found merit in her professional ability to produce false documentation. This was a critical moment in Elsa's early years because this association with higher and more dangerous criminal organizations led many authorities to believe she was working for a drug cartel. This may have been true, but she was not trafficking children for them; she was only producing false documents. Trafficking children was an opportunity feasible to her design because she was most likely to be feared if people believed she was working for a drug cartel.

Elsa's actions predate much of the research that has been done on human trafficking especially acts against children. Her methods also predate the procedures that would later be used by future traffickers. Throughout this project, the question "How could she do this and never be caught?" came up very frequently. My answer was always: "Because she did everything right." It would make every nerve in my body tremble when I found myself giving credit to someone who brought so much harm to others, but Elsa was not an obtuse woman. This is why when she passed herself off as an attorney, a doctor, or a nurse, people would believe her. Her *modus operandi* was so difficult to replicate that those who trafficked after her had to implement much less sophisticated ways to succeed. From there, others followed with the more common practice of human trafficking because it was easier. This was problematic for the academic world which began to research the more common ways humans were trafficked leaving Elsa Cuellar's process much too unique to explore and much too tedious to research.

To complete this project, I had to read through thousands of pages on the subject. Many books, peer-reviewed journal articles, and documentaries. One night, I woke with an apnea-type disturbance after having a nightmare about Elsa taking children, I read about in these books with their ambilocal cords wrapped around their necks. I gave the nightmare a lot of thought for the next several days and concluded that it may have been because of one recurring word I would see in every piece of human trafficking literature: the word "force." Most, if not all, definitions concerning human trafficking had the word "force" as part of the way they defined the crime. Elsa defied this definition because she did not force even one of her victims to come to the United States with her. By definition, then, she was not a trafficker. In 2009, there was only one organization that did not use the word "force" in their definition of the crime and instead narrowed their definition to the jobs a trafficked person "could be forced to do" (DuPont 9).

Without using methods that met any definitions that had been put in place for human trafficking and without organizing her crime activity with drug cartel involvement, Elsa Cuellar may have been one of the very first "Solanos" to ever exist. She was a ghost to law enforcement and certainly to her society. Most importantly, she was a phantom to her victims who saw a completely different person than the one law enforcement would come to know. For there to be any chance of exposing Elsa Cuellar for her crimes, something not likely to happen, an unexpected phenomenon would have to occur that could throw a sheet over her body and expose her ghostly figure to the world. In 2011, this is exactly what happened at an elementary school in United Independent School District in Laredo, Texas.

LAREDO, TEXAS, 2011 U.I.S.D

Being a police officer anywhere can be dangerous; being one along the Mexican American border can be life-altering. The majestic echoes of Mexican culture resonate thunderously across the Rio Grande, penetrating American city streets like a plague. Before long, these streets are now part of Mexico, no matter what Google map reads, and incidents that are more likely to occur on the other side, or *"El Otro Lado,"* as it is said by the locals, begin to parallel what is going on in schools along the border on the American side.

When U.I.S.D police officers responded to a complaint at an elementary school, they never imagined that they were responding to anything else other than a parent wanting to press charges because a child put gum in their daughter's hair or two boys fighting in class for a dispute over who had the strongest father. Instead, they would be facing Bobby Diaz, a young elementary school child who was threatening to murder his teacher. The young, disgruntled student was only five years old and demanded to be placed in the same school as his brother. The idea of a new environment was appealing to the responding officer, but one question baffled him instantly: *"Why does he have a brother close enough in age to be in the same school attending a different campus?"* It was easy to surmise Bobby may be caught in the middle of a parental dispute or divorce. According to Very Well Family, there is a 16 percent increase in the probability that a child in a divorced-parent setting would have behavioral issues (2022). This statistic was collected in children ages 7 to 17 and Bobby was only 5, but with a brother on a different campus, it was not an unlikely reason for such aggressive behavior. Looking for Bobby's brother was ideal for campus police to learn more about the family's dynamics; it was here law enforcement and the district run into a problem.

Bobby Diaz did indeed have a brother on another campus. However, he had a different last name and was the same age. Ironically, according to school records, they also had the same date of birth. With different last names, the two boys were probably not twins nor did the responding officer believe they shared much of a resemblance. The only thing left to do was to call in their mother to explain the information on file. It took her three days to respond, but Elsa Cuellar was before Director of Admissions Jose A. Almazan having had plenty of time to prepare her story. I was very curious about what Elsa had to say, so on May 22, 2002, I traveled to Laredo, Texas, and two days later met with Almazan and his attendance specialist Jesse Perusquia. Student files are usually confidential, but Elsa Cuellar's case was already a public record and it had appeared in the local news. Almazan recalls Elsa using herself as a scapegoat. "She claimed to have had an affair and was embarrassed about it, so she used her last name for one child and put the other in a different school."

Both Almazan and Perusquia laughed a little as we finished our lunch at a popular local eatery in North Laredo. I understood their amusement immediately. Having had a child with another man would not explain why the boys were the same age. For the first time in probably more than the thirteen years we know of her, Elsa Cuellar was against the ropes. It was not a government agency, the local police, or any government agency affiliated with border protection that placed this sheet over such a dangerous ghost—it was the police at United Independent School District and the admissions team who ignited a cycle of investigations that most likely saved the lives of future children.

This is not to say that other agencies should have been aware of what Elsa Cuellar was doing. Investigating child trafficking is not an easy thing to do especially when someone is using irreplicable methods not many could get away with. In addition, laws passed to help combat human trafficking will almost always have flaws that make it easier for traffickers to escape the clutches of the American legal system. For example, the Victims of Trafficking and Violence Protection Act (2000) was put in place to fight against sex labor; however, Elsa Cuellar never used her victims for sex labor in the traditional sense. Instead, she used a private, domestic setting that created a familial atmosphere to manipulate her victims into believing they were part of a family. In essence, an exploration into whether the word "manipulation" or a phrase such as "false pretense" is underused when defining human trafficking.

Today, recent laws continue to merit amendment and re-evaluation. This is especially true of other countries which should be working together with the United States to find commonalities in the reasons why countries of origin and destination nations fight against human trafficking. If the laws in one country do not partner well with the laws of another, the impact of amending local legislation is weakened. For example, as of 2015, South Africa remained an active country of origin for human trafficking and still has no database or an area of law enforcement established exclusively to combat these activities (Mollema 40). It is doubtful that Elsa ever worked with people in South Africa, but the systems in place in Mexico are likely just as primitive when it comes to statistics, databases, and organized task forces that dedicate to this specific area of law enforcement. The unstable political blueprint in Mexico along with the fight against corruption and drug wars does not allow much room for the establishment of these resources.

Elsa may not have had statistics available to her, but she was a smart woman with access to two countries she understood the social structure of intimately. Ideally, in American society, women are more commonly seen as victims of human trafficking and not the heads of the operation. Even in scenarios when women are arrested for their involvement in human trafficking, they are usually part of the recruitment phase. In many cases, they were victims of trafficking themselves and they recruit to purchase their own freedom. Some of these victims are lucky enough to get paid for finding other girls to introduce to this underground world. The United Nations has referred to this phase of the trafficking pyramid as "happy trafficking." Certainly, there is nothing joyful about this crime, but the word "happy" comes from the illusion recruiters create for their victims to believe they are very prosperous and successful abroad (Aronowitz 53).

Most of the research shows that victims are groomed and disillusioned with a promise of a better life in another country. The reason these methods are widely published is that this is usually how it is done. Cuellar, however, was much different. She never approached her victims; they came to her. She was meticulous in her system by using herself as bait. By posing as a doctor, a counselor, an attorney, and very often a religious pastor, Cuellar qualified herself to be of assistance to any person who might be in need. For example, she would pass herself off as a doctor if the young girl she had her eye on was pregnant and alone. Logically, a teenager with no home or money in Mexico would love to get to know a doctor with such a "generous" and "giving" soul. It was the perfect design for Cuellar, and it worked every time.

Research shows that victims of human trafficking are usually from the same ethnic background as the perpetrator (55), but this demographic can be seriously flawed because people within the same region will by default share similar ethnic and cultural backgrounds. For example, Cuellar's victims were mostly Hispanic girls, but this is to be expected for someone operating out of Laredo, Texas, where, as of 2020, the population was 95.5 percent Hispanic in a city of over 255,000 people (and it is probably more). This would leave very minimal opportunity for Cuellar to have found an Asian, African American, or Anglo victim. It can be argued then, that rather than looking at the ethnicity of the perpetrator in relation to the victim, the focus on geography and accessibility to one particular ethnicity may be more appropriate for learning more about trafficking activity. Had Cuellar been Anglo, but still lived in Laredo, her victims would certainly still be Hispanic because that is what she has access to.

4

Bidi

December 1998—Rio Bravo, Texas

A CASE WORKER I WILL CALL CHRISTINA WAS ASSIGNED TO THE CASE. No one wanted to take it. Few wanted to deal with Bidi Mata. She was, by most people's description, an eccentric woman. She called on a local organization that serviced at-risk youth to help her get her son Anselmo to go to school. According to Bidi, she had tried everything, but he would not come out of his room. He was eleven years old and was already absorbed by heavy metal music, which he listened to all day.

When Christina arrived, the music was blaring from the boys' room. When Bidi answered the door, she was thrown back by the woman's appearance. She had been told so many stories about the woman; she expected to see an older unattractive female on the other side of the door. Bidi was quite the contrary. She had beautiful, long, jet-black hair, neatly polished fingernails, and perfectly applied makeup. If anything was repelling at all about the woman, it was how she carried herself. She wore a long white night gown and walked slowly, creating a ghostly image of her. Something about the way she carried herself was frightening, but Christina felt she was able to conceal her perception of Bidi successfully and moved on.

Immediately, Christina felt it was in her best interest to consider Child Protective Services. The apartment was in complete disarray, there were cat droppings throughout the home, and there was a plate of food on the table so old that it was growing maggots. There did not appear to be a father in the household, so Christina did not ask. Instead, she inquired about the son.

Bidi vanished into the bedroom where the loud music was playing to let Anselmo know that the case worker was there. Christina heard an argument begin to emerge. The little boy sounded very disgruntled and disrespectful. The case was going to be difficult and was going to require a lot of patience. After a few minutes of arguing back and forth, the radio lowered, and the mother came out. Once again, the woman explained to the case worker that her son would not come out of the room. Christina agreed to try and contact him at school away from the home environment if the mother agreed to make sure he attends at least one day. The mother agreed to try and get him there.

Christina had never stepped out of her boundary in her job. She was always known as a hard worker who followed the guidelines as requested. On this day, she did something that she would never have done if she did not believe it was in Anselmo's best interest. She asked to use the bathroom, not because she had to go, but rather to check the medicine cabinet to see if Bidi may be taking anti-depressants or pain killers. The state of the house worried her, and she was still battling with the decision of whether Child Protective Service was appropriate for this case.

It was not uncommon for homes near the border to use shower curtains for doors when the original door was missing. Even if the families had the money to replace it, they would most likely prefer to use their money for something more essential to their survival. Christina closed the shower curtain and pretended to use the restroom. She waited a minute and ran the faucet as if she was washing her hands. She opened the medicine cabinet and found what she had expected. However, she could not ascertain who the anti-depressants were prescribed to because it appeared as if they were obtained illegally from Nuevo Laredo, Mexico. This was a common practice among families who did not have insurance or could not afford much-needed medication. It was a dangerous practice, but it was common. She opened the cap to see how many were inside the bottle and saw that she was down to her last couple of pills. She may be taking them more often than is good for her.

Christina was careful not to make noise. She snapped the cap back on the bottle carefully and was slow to return the bottle to where she found it. She closed the small door to the medicine cabinet. Once it was closed, she was startled to see in the reflection of the glass window Bidi standing behind her where the shower curtain was once closed. She stared blankly at her guest, with her black hair dropping down to cover part of her face. She stood motionless, giving Christina a feeling of an internal horror that shook her entire body. Christina apologized and told Bidi she was looking for medicine for a headache. Bidi did not react, nor did she appear upset.

Christina avoided any further explanation and assumed Bidi was simply not in the frame of mind to understand what her guest was doing in the bathroom. The counselor reminded the mother to have her son at school the next day, left the home, and decided to drive to the Child Protective Service office. On her way to the car, a neighbor stopped her and appeared a little upset. She did not know who Christina was but told her that people should leave Bidi alone. The case worker tried to explain she was there because Bidi herself had called for services to get her son to school, but the neighbor laughed and told Christina that the woman she just visited did not have a son. It was known by all who knew her well that Bidi tended to pretend to have a child. The argument Christina heard was Bidi arguing with herself. It was difficult to imagine that she could create the voice with such deception, but it had already been thoroughly investigated. The story Bidi tells is that her baby was stolen from her in Nuevo Laredo. She had been in such despair that she had begun to keep her child alive in her mind. Sometimes, the child was already an adult. In her mind, he had been with Bidi since he was born and was now a young adult. She would cook his dinner and leave it on the table, waiting for him to eat it. Of course, the food remained there, waiting to be consumed by a figment of Bidi's imagination. It was a horrible scenario for any mother to experience. Christina felt the woman would benefit from receiving help. The following day, she returned to Bidi's residence. Her program did not provide adult services but wanted to let her know that help was available for adults through another agency. Communicating with Bidi was much easier the second time around. She was dressed differently and in a completely different state of mind. She was happy to see her looking better and wanted to ensure she was aware of adult assistance.

NUEVO LAREDO, TAMAULIPAS OCTOBER 1992

Bidi Mata was part of a minority in Mexico. She was born into an unseen wealthy lifestyle. As far as Bidi knew, her father's fortune was not earned through corruption or organized crime. Instead, he had done well for himself in constructing *maquiladoras* (factories) that created jobs for many people. Once established, he began to toy with the real estate business and began to grow from there. It was a remarkable accomplishment for a man born to a father who never managed to get out of working the fields for cantaloupe and onions. He was a very disciplined man and believed in honor. He was considered incorruptible and not afraid to let it be known.

With his family, he was no different. He expected everyone in the household to always conduct themselves with proper etiquette. The degree to which his expectations had to be followed were especially true of the women in the house. His wife and two daughters had to act like proper women and tend to domestic obligations as they would when he was growing up. His son would have to demonstrate skills that were worthy of inheriting his empire one day. This is why when his oldest daughter Bidi got pregnant, it felt as if the world around her had fallen apart. Her father would never pardon this.

Her pregnancy was not entirely an accident. She had discovered love at the age of nineteen and like many women before her, had been promised to be taken care of and a promise of a good life. Her boyfriend, Ricardo Tijerina, was an ambitious young man. There was no doubt in Bidi's mind he would someday amount to something great just as her father had done. Ricky, as she referred to him, was her way out of the house that had been suffocating her for years. In the town of Reynosa, everyone knew Bidi as a beautiful girl, but they also saw her as a meal ticket out of poverty. Her father had always warned her about being alone. Abductions by the cartel for ransom were common. Still, Bidi was convinced that her father was less interested in her safety and more committed to avoiding ever having to part with his fortune.

Rick was a simple young man. He was kind, hard-working, and gentle. His mother was in a wheelchair, and his tender heart would never allow him to abandon her. As much as it appeared he needed financial help, Rick never asked her for money, and this was very assuring to Bidi that he was interested only in her and not what her family could provide. They had made plans to get married and work together toward a bright future, so when she learned she was pregnant, she was not worried about her stability. The only concern she harbored in her heart was the fear she had of her father. It made her heartrate get out of control every time she thought about telling him the truth. It was, for this reason, her mother was the first to know. She was much more understanding and, for a moment, had an excited look in her eyes. The thought of having a grandchild and a baby in the house fascinated her. Once she had a moment to think about how her husband might react, the level of excitement evaporated into a gas of fear and concern for what he might have Bidi do.

She concealed it for as long as she could, but there came a point in the pregnancy when it became more difficult to hide the truth. Her body was changing, and she was experiencing morning sickness. The excuse of having eaten something bad the night before can only work once. After that, the explanation would have to be more creative. While she waited for the right time, she and Rick made many plans for the baby. They thought of names together, the best place to raise a child in America, and the pre-planning of birthday parties. Together, they bought baby clothes and a crib for his house so his mother could spend time with her grandchild. When Bidi was not thinking of telling her father, it was a joyous moment.

The time finally came for her to confront her father. The physical changes her body was undergoing had become too much to conceal. Together with her mother, they told him the news. As expected, he was outraged. It was the angriest she had ever seen her father. The mother was also at the receiving end of his wrath for having known and not told him. To him, it was the ultimate deception and a trait of an unfaithful wife. When his temper subsided, he gave Bidi until the morning to leave the house. Her mother was in the most depressive state Bidi had ever seen her. She cried uncontrollably and offered to go with her; Bidi would never have her mother leave the comfort and protection she currently had.

The mother hugged her daughter tighter than she had ever hugged any of her children. Despite the outcome of her father hearing the news of the pregnancy, Bidi felt a sense of relief. It was as if an enormous weight had been lifted from her shoulders. The truth was out, and the fear that had been consuming her the months before had let her breathe more clearly now. She arrived at Rick's house with a suitcase in hand. Rick knew exactly what she was doing there, so he did not ask. Bidi had nowhere else to go.

When the mother arrived rolling in on the wheelchair, she had a large envelope containing all the documents. Her warm smile melted Bidi's heart. Her kindness reminded her that she was no longer in a house of luxury but had come to a place of compassion and acceptance. Even in her wheelchair, Rick's mother was very helpful and caring for Bidi. Besides her mother, she had never known a kinder woman. Time passed, and it was soon time to have her baby. They woke Rick up in the middle of the night. His mother yelled with profound excitement that it was time for the baby.

Bidi's contractions were getting stronger, and she was moaning in pain. She was comfortable and able to walk herself, but Rick was taking too long. The contractions were coming fast, and in the middle of a scream, Rick entered with an unsettling announcement. He told his mother their car tires had been stolen. Bidi was very scared at the announcement, but she had to be brave with the car unable to move. Having the baby naturally was not an easy process. It was very painful, and without an actual doctor present, it was very frightening, which did no favors to her stress levels. Suddenly, she heard the crying of a newborn, and her heart warmed her entire body. Rick's mother assured her that she was experienced as a midwife and that she would be all right.

Bidi held the baby firmly against her chest. It was impossible for her to love anyone more than the love felt for her new son. She could never understand how someone could love a stranger so instantly, but there she was doing it. Suddenly, everything Bidi went through with her father was worth it. Bidi suddenly began to feel dizzy and felt as if she was going to faint. She was not sure if it was in her mind or not, but she thought she saw Rick's mother washing the baby standing on her own two feet. In the morning, Bidi was so tired and very sore. Her vision was cloudy, and the room was extremely bright. When her vision adjusted, the new mother realized she was in the hospital. Bidi did not remember being taken there. She had been examined and cleaned. When the nurse went in to check on her, the confused girl inquired about visitors and her child. The nurse assured her that when they found her outside the hospital, there was no one with her. The nurse said something that suggested that maybe the young girl had been conned in some way. Bidi genuinely believed this to be true. When released from the hospital, she hurried to Rick's home, but there was no one there. Rick was gone, and his mother's wheelchair was folded and placed in the corner of the room. She saw the large envelope on the table and looked inside it. Her baby's birth certificate was gone along with Rick's papers to cross into Laredo, but her documents were still there. *Could they have gone ahead of me and are waiting in Laredo?* She did not know exactly where to go, but when she saw the car was still outside and that the tires had not been stolen, she began to think of the unimaginable.

After an hour of uncontrollable crying, she thought American authorities would be more helpful. It had been hours since she left the hospital, and no person in law enforcement had shown any interest in asking her what she had done with her baby. Even if they did, they would only believe that she aborted her child. That ideology had already been planted in their minds by the person who called. She now believed the callers to have been Rick or his mother. That is if the woman truly was his mother. Rick could have been hired for human breeding. Now that she had papers to cross, she could at least inquire on the bridge if anyone matching their description carrying a baby had crossed into the United States recently.

She was thinking about her baby so much; she did not have time to get nervous about being in a foreign country her entire life. She wanted to be brave and strong for her baby. She did not care much about being a single mother. If Rick had turned out to be a con, she could have raised her baby without him. She was determined to find her son but came across a serious obstacle at the bridge. The customs agent seemed upset and serious. They took Bidi into a room. Could it be that Rick and his mother left her name at the bridge, and they were asked to inform them when she arrived? It was a type of wishful thinking that would not play out that way. She had been informed that her documents were false! Now, she had a legal battle with the American government to worry about along with the possibility of being banned from ever getting a passport. It was all part of the plan and Bidi would never see her son again.

Had Christina just met one of Elsa Cuellar's victims? If she had, this would be the earliest record of Cuellar's work. In my research, I had never known Cuellar to play sick to get a child, but if this was her victim, it would have been back in 1992 when she was still experimenting with ways to operate. Bidi's child would be thirty years of age at the time this project was being researched with no way of knowing anything about the biological mother. Christina was overwhelmed by Bidi's experience and decided to stop by and visit her whenever she could. On one occasion and without warning, Bidi suddenly vanished. Christina became worried for her friend. There was nothing she could do. The phone number in her paperwork was not in service, and no emergency contact was listed. She went back to the complex two months later, asking if she had ever returned to inquire about her belongings. She had not. To many, she was a crazy woman. As far as Christina was concerned, there was nothing crazy about loving your child that much. She prayed for Bidi every night. That was all she could do for her. She never saw her again.

5

The Creative Element

IF THERE IS NO UNIVERSAL CONSENSUS FOR DEFINING "HUMAN TRAFFICK-ing," those in the business will always find creative ways to circumnavigate legal definitions. Bidi's story bares strong similarities to Cuellar because of the use of illegal documentation. The trafficker had to have known Bidi's documents were just flawed enough for her to get caught. With no record that the baby even existed, there was no way involvement by authorities could produce any results. After all, who is it they would be looking for? Cuellar's process had always been methodical. By having Bidi get caught at the International Bridge, her privileges of getting a passport would be revoked and she would be blacklisted. She would be the only one who could go into the United States and know who she was looking for.

The woman claiming to have experience as a midwife parallels Cuellar's passing off herself as a nurse in later years. Still, the strongest indication that justifies speculation that Bidi had fallen victim to Cuellar was how the trafficker got the child. Authorities believe Cuellar used her husband to father children with the young girls she managed to lure into the United States. These babies would then be sold under the belief that the adoption was legal. Miguel Alvarado Rivera was arrested later, but not for the sexual abuse of a child. Instead, he was arrested in connection with Cuellar's false documentation scheme—a charge that would soon allow them to be free. If anything at all came out of Miguel and Cuellar's arrest was that authorities were able to trace Cuellar's activities two years sooner than I had previously thought. Her activities then were far more sinister than I had expected.

Miguel Alvarado Rivera was a significant accomplice in Elsa Cuellar's actions.

WARRANT OF ARREST

THE STATE OF TEXAS
To any Peace Officer of the State of Texas, Greetings:

You are hereby commanded to arrest

ELSA CUELLAR ALVARADO

DOB: 5-23-58
416 MANOR RD.
LAREDO, TEXAS 78040

if to be found in your County and bring him/her before me, a State District Court Judge
in Webb County, Texas, at my office at 1110 Victoria, Ste 304, 49th District Court,
Laredo, Texas in said County, immediately, then and there to answer the State of Texas
for an offense against the laws of said State, to-wit:

Count 1 :   **Tampering with Governmental Documents, Felony 2**
Count 2 :   **Tampering with Governmental Documents, Felony 2**
Count 3 :   **Tampering with Governmental Documents, Felony 2**
Count 4 :   **Tampering with Governmental Documents, Felony 2**
Count 5 :   **Tampering with Governmental Documents, Felony 2**
Count 6 :   **Tampering with Governmental Documents, Felony 2**
Count 7 :   **Tampering with Governmental Documents, Felony 2**
Count 8 :   **Tampering with Governmental Documents, Felony 2**
Count 9 :   **Tampering with Governmental Documents, Felony 2**

of which offense he/she is accused by the written Complaint under oath or affirmation of
Alexander Rodriguez (attached herein and made a part of this warrant), filed
before me.

Herein fail not, but of this writ make due return, showing how you have executed the
same.

Witness my official signature, this 28 day of _MAY_ . 2013

Jose A. Lopez, 49th State District Court Judge, Magistrate
Webb and Zapata County, Texas

Bond $ 100,000 per Count
Total $900,000 —

Arrest warrant was issued for Elsa Cuellar. By the time of her court date, the number of charges had been drastically reduced. Details of that arrangement are not known.

6

The Hidden Truth

WHEN ELSA CUELLAR WAS ARRESTED ON MAY 30, 2013, BY UNITED Independent School District Police, she was charged with nine counts of tampering with government documents. After the behavioral issues with young Bobby Diaz, the numerous problems with her documents came to light. Miguel Alvarado, her husband, was only charged with one count, but the investigation also led to questions concerning the welfare of the children. Cuellar told officials she was ill and needed surgery to remove a tumor. My research led to two groups of people, those who say she never had a medical problem and surgery was never done while a second group of sources confirms that she did indeed have a procedure to remove a tumor. Still, whether Cuellar was ill at the time was not as relevant as the outcome, that is, she was free on bond after having spent hours in jail. Cuellar somehow managed a $900,000 bond.

While Cuellar admitted to having falsified birth certificates, social security cards, and medical records for children ranging from elementary to high school, she never conceded to any wrongdoing with the children. Those doing the initial investigation found evidence to the contrary. Guns and knives within children's reach, chicken feces, and an unsanitary environment were enough for Child Protective Service involvement. More than one agency suspected Cuellar of child trafficking and after considering all the evidence, six children were taken into CPS custody and four others were sent to federal protective custody in San Antonio, Texas. At the time of their removal from Cuellar's Del Mar area home, the children's true age, date of birth, nationality, and real parents were not known.

A few weeks later, Judge Paul Gallego ordered DNA tests to be conducted. Perhaps it was the realization that such testing would prove the children were unrelated that compelled Cuellar to alter her story. Now, she claimed that the children who were not biologically related had been abandoned by their parents and she took them in. As unrealistic as this sounded to law enforcement, there was no way to prove it differently. Cuellar had been so meticulous in her calculations; she left no stone unturned when it came to having an answer to every question asked of her. One official reported that "It was as if she knew what was going to be asked before they asked it." This proved to be critical at the hearing; the defense team had a field day with several questions that could not be answered. In speaking to a CPS officer being questioned, the defense asked: "So, if these children are in danger, were they kidnapped, sold, or simply given away?" The only response was "We don't know." CPS officials were also asked, "Was there any indication the children had been mistreated?" Of course, the answer to that was also a "no."

The issue, in this case, is not how law enforcement, the school district, or CPS officials handled the case. The problem was that Cuellar was far more experienced than anyone had previously believed. To some of the law enforcement officers on the investigative team, Cuellar's experience did not fool them. United Independent School District police investigator Alexander Rodriguez looked far deeper into Cuellar's past. His instincts as a retired crime scene investigator with the Laredo Police Department were confirmed by an email he received from an assisting federal agency. This agency has asked we keep their identity confidential, but their assistance was critical in understanding how sinister Cuellar truly was. Not only was she a suspect in human trafficking, but she was also known by other agencies to have been involved in a murder of a fourteen-year-old boy years before her arrest in Laredo.

Delete Prev Next Reply/All Forward/Inline Open Inbox 129 of 129   Go to   Move Copy Ir

Date: Tue Apr 23 15:37:15 CDT 2013
From: ▮▮▮▮▮▮▮▮▮▮▮▮▮▮▮▮▮▮▮▮ ► Add To Address Book
Subject: Case
To: "▮▮▮▮▮▮▮▮▮▮▮▮▮▮▮▮▮▮▮▮" ◄ ▮▮▮▮▮▮▮▮

Some of our queries have the female involved in a homicide out of the Valley area. In addition she has prior convictions for the same thing in the Valley. Thanks for letting us assist you with this case. I am available to assist you in anyway (video recorded interviews, evidence collection, surveillance, search & arrest warrants, etc.). In addition when any ▮▮▮▮ assists another agency with a case Austin Headquarters Crime Lab usually expedites evidence needing to be examined. We also are able to go anywhere in Texas and the US in general when we assist anyone on a case. (flying to another city or state with lead investigator to further obtain investigative leads).

I will collect and turn over all evidence to you as I obtain it. Thanks again and look forward to assisting you with this case.

Border Security-Joint Operations Intelligence Center

Office: (956) ▮▮▮▮▮
Fax: (956) ▮▮▮▮▮

This email to police with United Independent School district reveals Elsa Cuellar was not your typical school mother.

7

A South Texas Ranch

June 1998 (15 Years before Cuellar's Arrest)

EL RANCHO ESCONDIDO WAS USUALLY QUIET. THE SOUTH TEXAS SUN would shine just enough at the break of dawn for the deer to see the clear water from the natural pond at the very center of the property. On June 19, 1998, the natural tranquility offered by the South Texas wildlife was disturbed by the many United States Border Patrol agents, Texas Troopers, and Webb County Deputies. They canvased the area not far from where the deer would have been drinking at this time in the morning. Without the timely investigation, the shallow grave serving as the resting place for fourteen-year-old Juan Valentine Alonzo would never have been discovered.

He was an innocent child, having owed nothing to society outside of skipping a few classes at Lamar Middle School. Further investigation led officials to believe he was nothing more than an example being set for the actual person who owed the debt to the wrong people—a street thug he did not even know. Still, it was Juan's young, cold body that was placed in a black plastic body bag carefully placed on a light green bedspread on the autopsy tray at the medical examiner's office. The bedspread was torn and dirty with distinct blue and white stripes. That 8x8 tear exposed the child's upper chest, right elbow, and left shoulder. For the examiner, it was no longer a meaningless mass wrapped in torn fabric. It was now a young life that had been taken. He hoped that at some point, the killer treated

39

the corpse with the least bit of courtesy the remains of such a young man are owed, but he doubted it.

The body appeared to have been positioned with the face down, and the bedspread was pulled to the back of the body. It may have been used to drag the victim to his grave rather than wrap him in it. The right arm was flexed upward and across his neck. The left arm was extended down alongside his body. The lower portion of the body was tensed upward with the left foot resting against the buttock and the right foot on top of the left ankle. A dry lump of brown blood, skin separated from the body, and a small twig was stuck to the mid-anterior region of his chest. The bedspread was finally removed from the body. Small pebbles and crusty dirt fell to the floor. The bedspread and everything that fell from it was retained as evidence. The left eye was covered by gray duct tape. The tape was folded forward, exposing the gray side of it. The body of Juan Valentine Alonzo had nothing more than a pair of white boxers soaked in decomposition fluid. The body had already begun decomposing to some degree. The skin across the right hand was already mummified and rotting.

It did not take the medical examiner long to find the three gunshot wounds. One of them was on the upper left anterior of the chest midway between the nipple and the shoulder. A second bullet was at the apex of the left shoulder. The third bullet was on the left lateral back behind the heart. It was a disturbing case for the lead investigator, whose first job was to learn more about the property. "What do we got?" His name was James Dugan from the Texas Ranger's office. He terrified the other members of the task force put together to learn more about why the young man had been murdered.

"The property is under the name Elsa Cuellar."

Dugan's jaw tightened as if he was trying to crack walnuts between his teeth. He took out a handkerchief and blotted off the beads of sweat on his forehead.

"A woman?"

"Yes, sir," said a young officer.

"I suppose it could have been a woman. The choice of a .22 would make sense for a girl. Is the ranch only under her name?"

"Yes, sir."

"Any known associates?"

"Looks like she was previously charged with tampering with government documents in the Valley about two years ago. She was arrested with Vicente Guerra and Rogelio Tobias."

"Let's talk to both men and the woman."

It took about three more months before Dugan and the task force got anything solid concerning the whereabouts of Elsa Cuellar and her associates. They finally got a break in the case when they arrested a small-time drug dealer from Roma, Texas, who was believed to be the brother of Rogelio Tobias. Dugan's large square frame towered over the dealer's small body. The rim of Dugan's cowboy hat produced a shadow over the man's face.

"Are you Rogelio's brother?"

"He's my cousin, sir."

"Where is he? I'd like to meet him."

"He's gone, sir."

"Look, you already got one boot in the snake pit, son. I'd be lying to ya if I didn't say I'm getting ready to stick your entire head in it unless you work with me here."

"I'm not lying to you, sir. He was murdered about two months ago."

"Murdered, you say?"

"Yes, sir."

"What about Vicente Guerra?"

"They were murdered together, sir. They were both buried at the same time. They even made them dig their own graves."

Dugan took out a toothpick from his shirt pocket and put it in his mouth. It helped kill the craving for one of his midday Cohiba cigars. He looked over to the officer serving as a witness in the room. "Looks like Elsa Cuellar doesn't leave witnesses."

"That lady scares me," the young man said. Dugan had already made his way to the door, but he instantly reacted to the comment and came back.

"You know her?"

"Yeah, she's the pastor at my church."

"What church is that?"

"*Hermanos del Siglo Nuevo.*"

Dugan took out a pen and asked the witness officer for a sheet of paper. "I'll tell you what you're gonna do, *amigo*. You're gonna write down the exact address of this church without any bullshit, and if I go to this address and find out it's a vacant lot, I'm gonna come back and put my boot where one wouldn't think it'd fit."

The young man was quick to comply with Dugan's requests. The Ranger's demeanor never left much room for negotiation. "And write neatly!" He made one last request. The scared young man handed Dugan the paper. He held it away from his face enough so that he could read it. The ranger looked at the young man curiously and crumbled the paper and threw it at the detained man. The address was in Nuevo Laredo, Tamaulipas, Mexico. It was well out of the jurisdiction of local authorities. Although law enforcement knew Cuellar was responsible for the young boy's death, not enough evidence could be found to charge her for it. Once again, Elsa Cuellar was one step ahead.

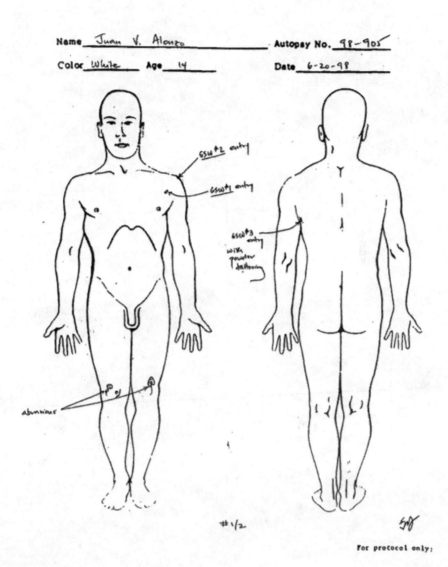

Autopsy report for 14-year-old Juan Valentine Alonzo.

8

Angels in Her Path

MANY OF THE AUTHORITIES INVOLVED IN THIS CASE I HAD THE PLEA-sure of meeting appeared to be very frustrated with some of the victims for not turning on Elsa Cuellar. At first, I felt the same way; but after delving deeper into the secret life of this wolf in sheep's clothing, I came to realize that Elsa had a specific kind of victim that was instrumental in her success as a child trafficker. While it is easy to judge the victims for seeing Cuellar as their biological mother, one must keep in mind that even under any deplorable conditions these children may have been kept in, the environment continued to be much better than what they would have in Mexico. While in the United States, we would consider the conditions these victims faced as unacceptable; it was a luxury they would never believe they would have in their life.

Cuellar knew this; she also knew how to keep the conditions just slightly better than these girls would have in Mexico. It was the incentive for remaining under her roof. Cuellar was very familiar with the environment these victims were once part of so her home on Manor Road. in North Laredo had two kinds of children: those who saw their environment as favorable when compared to where they came from, and the children who knew Cuellar as the only mother they had ever known. With this dynamic, what child would turn on her? This mastermind understood vulnerability very well. Her cunning ability to draw victims to her versus her chasing the victims is problematic for organizations trying to obtain a more accurate number of victims being trafficked. This project took me to many different figures and statistics that were continuously inconsistent with other findings from alternative sources. At times, the number of children being trafficked into the United States was different by the hundreds of thousands, so in the end, I left these figures out of this study for lack of reliability.

Again, Elsa Cuellar may not have been a statistician, but she was very knowledgeable of the profiles that fit a trafficked child and ensured to create the appearance that countered that profile. She did this with herself, which is why no evidence was ever found on her for the kidnapping and murder of Juan Valentine Alonzo. When children, or adults for that matter, are being brought into the United States under the pretense of a better life, they are entering voluntarily. In Cuellar's case, she would bring them with documentation that appeared so authentic, she was never questioned. Because of this, it is impossible to add these trafficked individuals to the figures being recorded because there is no knowledge of them having been brought into the United States under Cuellar's deception. US customs agents are unable to look at a person and visually know that a human is being deceived. Therefore, the statistics rely heavily on the number of trafficked victims that are found.

Currently, most organizations are limited to a "rights-based approach" when it comes to promoting laws intended to stop child trafficking (Duger 121). In essence, many laws and policies are limited to identifying human trafficking as being against the law and morally wrong while at the same time acknowledging that children from all nations have rights that should be respected. While we need these forms of acknowledgments to be in place, they are heavily flawed when dealing with someone like Elsa Cuellar because she never violates a person's rights as part of her process to get her victims to the United States. Of course, one may argue that lying to the victims is indeed a violation of their rights; however, this is not something detectable by border security from a visual standpoint.

The vulnerability in children can be measured in many ways. Most definitions created to identify what constitutes vulnerability tend to be Americentric because they are established based on the American social variables that make a child more likely to fall victim to any form of abuse. Other countries, however, may not have the same social structure and less than ideal living conditions, in Mexico for example, it may be more of the norm for a child than a form of abuse or factor for vulnerability. Once again, Cuellar was an intelligent woman who knew this, so it was no surprise to many authorities that she had chickens throughout her house—a common practice in many parts of Nuevo Laredo, Mexico.

LAREDO, TEXAS, 2011

Alexander Rodriguez, a veteran United Independent School District Police Investigator, got to campus early on the last day of school before the Christmas break. A student sat in the nurse's office across from where he would fill out his paperwork. She was crying uncontrollably. "You okay?"

"She thinks she's in trouble. I've already told her she wasn't." The nurse interfered. She was new to the campus, but she had made recent discoveries that hadn't been detected earlier in the school year. There had been a sudden increase in the number of students with lice being reported, and the nurse believed it might have begun at the home where the little girl who was crying lived.

"What makes you think it started with her?" the officer asked. The nurse walked over to the little girl and lifted her arms for Investigator Rodriguez to see. She had hundreds of small bite marks all over her arms.

"My goodness! Any idea what did that?"

"Not sure. It could be bed bugs, lice, or flea bites. I'm not sure, but I can't imagine the mother not having noticed."

The officer leaned gently in front of the little girl.

"What's your name?"

"Samantha Nuñez."

"Samantha, I'm a police officer with the district and want to help you. You wanna tell me what made those things on your arm?"

"Chickenpox."

"Chickenpox?"

"That's what my mom calls them."

The officer looked up at the nurse. She shook her head as an indication that they were not chickenpox. It was apparent to the officer, who was more familiar with the law than with medicine, that Samantha did not have chickenpox symptoms. He gave her a gentle smile and left her alone. On his way out, the secretary at the front of the school caught up to him.

"Officer!"

"Hi, Becky."

"Sir, there is a State Trooper waiting to speak to you in the principal's office. He said it was kind of important."

The officer went back into the school. He was surprised to find the Texas State Trooper in the principal's office alone. For some reason, he did not want to discuss the matter in front of school officials. The man stood erect and clean-shaven. The trooper's boots were so shiny that the officer saw himself on them as he walked into the office. It didn't look like he wanted to smile, but Rodriguez's demeanor always brought out a smile in people. "Investigator Rodriguez?"

"Yes, sir, what can I do for you?"

"I needed to ask you about a student you called Child Protective Service about when you were with the Laredo Police Department."

"I can try and remember. Should the parents be here?"

"This isn't a school matter, sir, and I don't need to talk to the girl— for now."

"Who's the student?"

"Martha Nuñez."

Alexander found it very coincidental that the trooper was there for a case that involved the sister of the girl he had just visited with mysterious health symptoms. He had not recalled ever having to deal with Martha as a street officer, but as it turned out, the young girl was already ten years old, and he responded to her home while she was still an infant. He was curious to know what use his information would be.

"Martha is still in elementary. This is a middle school."

"Yes, well, the question is more in line with her identity. Child Protective Service has nothing on her, but your report describes some issues that should have appropriately been managed by CPS. Do you remember why they didn't take her case?"

"No, I don't recall. Once I did my report for CPS, the crimes against children unit would take over. I was never called for court or anything. Can I ask you what this is about?"

"Apparently, Martha's mother applied for some kind of health insurance benefits for her. When she applied for these services, she used a deceased person's social security number out of Terrell, Texas. The state is very interested in why she did that."

Investigator Rodriguez describes himself as someone who had always been good at thinking ahead. His peers and fellow officers knew him as someone who thought outside the box. Working for a school district had not changed this in any way. He did not want to reveal that he had the sister of the student he was looking into in the very next room. Rodriguez was getting ready to uncover what he suspected was a child trafficking ring. Still, if he revealed too much, the Trooper could compromise a serious charge of trafficking for the lighter sentence of falsifying documents. He hated to keep information from other law enforcement agencies, but he was thinking bigger than using dead people's social security numbers.

"I wish I could be more help, sir. I just can't recall the case well enough to be of any use to you. My last run-in with that student was when she was just an infant."

"Okay, well, thanks for your time, but if you think of something later, give us a call."

Rodriguez was sure the trooper knew better than to believe he was going to get a call. For now, the investigation into the confusing paperwork was going in a different direction. Still, the trooper's visit was not in vain. Since Martha Nuñez was still with the United Independent School district, she was within Rodriguez's reach. He went to visit Martha at her middle school. The young girl had grown into a beautiful young lady. There was no way for her to remember Rodriguez from his street officer days. She was merely an infant. He slowly began to remember the case. Child Protective Service had been called to her home because the neighbors were very concerned that the children had been playing out in the street for almost two days. Rodriguez was called in to perform a welfare check on the children.

When he entered, he saw the infant Martha in her playpen. Several other children were in the living room. All of them had a full diaper. Their stool must have been there for days because the excrement on the side of their legs had become dry and crusty. The children showed signs of being malnourished; they were very thin. The house had a foul odor and was without electricity. "Where's your mother and father?" Rodriguez remembers asking. There was no father in the picture, but the little girl said her mother was in the bedroom sleeping. The house felt like an oven. How could someone sleep in the overwhelming South Texas heat that is so prevalent in the summer months? The foul odor got much stronger as Rodriguez approached the bedroom. "Hello? Laredo Police Department!"

There would be no answer from the young mother sleeping on her back. Her skirt was lifted to her waist, exposing her private area to anyone who entered. A large pickle jar with money and crack was on the end table next to the bed. The heroin needle was still stuck to her arm. It must have become part of her body as the woman hardened. The investigation revealed that she would prostitute herself to the men on the street. If she was passed out, the men knew to leave either drugs or money inside the pickle jar while they finished having sex with her. There was no way of telling how many men got to her for free, but the autopsy revealed she died of an overdose. Interestingly, she also had AIDS. It was the kind of case Rodriguez could never forget, but to remember Martha as the infant at the house was impossible. This, however, raised a question in Rodriguez's mind that he could not let go of. *If Martha was an infant when her mother died of an overdose, how could she have a younger sister?*

Rodriguez began his questioning there. Martha had a look on her face as if she feared the world. It was a demeanor that had become part of her, and it revealed her outlook on life. She was so young, yet she had a story to tell. It had not been told to anyone. Her experiences had blended in with the thousands of other little girls who were born into unfortunate circumstances. Having a police officer in front of her seemed so natural. She must have wondered: *What do they want to know now?* Rodriguez gave her a Snickers bar and bottled water. Her eyes got wide with the chocolate. It seemed like a natural everyday thing to so many kids. For many others, it was a rarity. "Martha, I understand your mother took you to get some medical attention recently?" The little girl looked as if she wanted to open the candy, but she was unsure if she was allowed.

"Go ahead. You can eat it." She began a very slow process of pealing the wrapper off. "Yes, she took me for some ointment."

"What kind of ointment?"

"For this."

Martha pulled her sleeves up. She appeared to have the same specks on her arm as her sister Samantha, but they seemed to have healed already.

"Do you know how these got here?"

"Chickenpox."

Rodriguez decided not to push her too much on that. He knew they were not chickenpox, but he wanted to move on to her relationship with Samantha. "Martha, can you tell me about your real mother."

"She's at home."

"She's at home?"

"Yes."

"Can you remember ever living with anyone else?"

"Not that I can remember."

For Rodriguez, the case seemed to have taken an unusual direction. Wouldn't Martha have known at some point that she went through Child Protective Service? She must know that she had to go to a foster home. It had been a long time, but he called the CPS officer who arrived at the scene that night. Her name was Leslie Ortega, and she was now a schoolteacher for a private school in a small town about an hour from Laredo. She was still a pleasant woman with a childlike tone to her voice. "Investigator Rodriguez! It is nice to hear from you. How did you get my number?"

"I'm an investigator," he said, laughing. She laughed with him. Leslie had always had a kind heart. That was the most likely reason she left CPS. Watching so many children suffer was far too much for her kind character to take. "Leslie, do you remember that case we used to call the Barbie case? You know that beautiful mother with a Barbie face who overdosed on Bismark Street?"

"Yeah, I remember that well."

"Do you remember anything about the children and what happened to them?"

"Well, I suppose it's okay to tell you since I don't work there anymore."

"I'll keep your name out of it anyway. I could use your help."

"The young boy Carlitos died already."

"He died?"

"Yes, he had AIDS, like his mother."

"He must have gotten to his mother's needles."

"Maybe, but he had signs of having been sexually assaulted as well. Maybe one of the men who would do business with her. We'll never know."

"Any word on the infant?"

"An aunt showed up almost immediately and claimed her. She knew someone in the courts that allowed her to take her while they did the paperwork. I left before those proceedings took place, so I don't know what happened."

"Do you remember the aunt's name?"

"You won't believe this after all this time, but I do. I remember her name because it's the same as my grandmother's: Elsa Cuellar."

It wasn't surprising for Rodriguez to hear this name. He now understood that there was something very wrong with the family under Cuellar's roof. The only way to know for sure what was going on was to get inside the home. To do that, he would have to learn more about the children. A judge would never approve a search warrant without cause. For now, he photographed Martha's marks and took photos of Samantha's as well. During the next month, he gathered enough information to get some attention. Eleven children were registered under the same address and as having the same mother. He's heard of large families before. He once visited a home for a child who was truant from school frequently. He had fifteen siblings. This case was different. The paperwork made no sense. Two sisters: Angie and Elizabeth Ibarra, were sisters, but their birthdays were only three days apart. Andres and Rolando Tejada were listed as twins. They had the same date of birth, but the country of birth was different. Bobby and Guillermo were listed as twins as well, yet they were not the same age and were born in different counties. It was too much for it to have been attributed to clerical errors. Elsa was an expert. Rodriguez was aware of her having been investigated in the valley some years back for false documentation. With so many kids in different schools, there was no way for the school district to compare. Investigator Rodriguez felt responsible for Martha having lived her life with Elsa even though he had nothing to do with her placement. Still, he was determined not to fail the little girl again.

At the time of this investigation, Investigator Alexander Rodriguez had no idea the pecks on the girl's arms were caused by actual chickens. When US Marshalls entered Cuellar's home in May 2013, chickens were discovered running inside and outside the home. A source who preferred to remain anonymous and worked for CPS at that time claimed she was aware of the animals in the home but had been threatened by Cuellar with her life if she pursued the matter further. Because of the misconception that Cuellar was working for the cartel (a rumor that favored her throughout her career), the CPS officer thought it best to secure her safety. No one can blame someone for looking out for their safety. Cuellar had found a new weapon by threatening officials, thus giving her more freedom to victimize the angels in her path.

9

The Adoption Defense

THE DECISIONS THAT MANY YOUNG GIRLS IN MEXICO ARE LEFT TO MAKE can be very challenging when it comes to family. In a country plagued by drug wars, poverty, and an unstable political system, all that remains is a predominantly Catholic nation that still holds expectations for young women to adhere to Christian values. The combination of social and family pressure can make a young woman vulnerable to the kind offers Cuellar made. At times, what she promised was far too appealing to reject. Throughout this investigation, I could not help but wonder if Cuellar ever did her research that would assist her in maneuvering her actions around the law. If she did, I could not help but consider that she may have come across the loopholes faced by South Africa when dealing with matters of adoption.

The situation in South Africa makes it easy to avoid the legal process when it comes to removing a child from their country. The intention is to serve the best interest of the child, but once that child is removed from the country, the jurisdiction of the case is lost, and the child's legal rights are left in "limbo" (Moodley 146). The manner in which Cuellar operated mimics this concept of creating scenarios that are not easily dictated by law. Her expertise in creating false documentation facilitated her process and made things more difficult for law enforcement and school officials. To compound the problems for law enforcement, Cuellar had implanted herself into the fabric of Laredo society as a respected member of the community. To many, not only was she raising abandoned children but was also a pastor of a local church. Functioning as a woman of God was critical to the success of her manipulation of others.

JENNIFER—LAREDO, TEXAS, 2008

Like many other seventeen-year-old girls, Jennifer Ortega was naïve about many of the realities that embody a person's life. It is not always because they are doltish. Sometimes growing up in Mexico's most impoverished areas can create false illusions about what the United States has to offer, especially when someone makes you a promise. So, when the charming side of Ruben Ibarra mesmerized Jennifer with his glowing face and masculine facial features, she was immediately taken in. He was an American citizen who made the arrangement a yet more attractive scenario. It was everything Jennifer had always been told she could never have. For a moment, she thought she had found it. Instead, she was now a single illegal immigrant hiding among the many others in Laredo, Texas, due with her first child any day now.

One of the many places Cuellar preached. Cuellar should not be the face of this establishment. Many good people attended service here.

She was not completely alone. Jennifer had the support of Elsa Cuellar. She was the newest person in her life to have demonstrated any form of compassion for the young girl. There she sat at the back of *Uncion Fe Y Poder Ministries* while her new sister, known as *La Pastora*, resonated her voice through the walls of the building with the thunderous words of God. She commanded the stage as if she knew God personally, and the message she delivered came directly from him. This was the impression for most whose life *La Pastora* touched. Jennifer needed her now more than ever. She felt like a foreigner with no one to go to. When Elsa Cuellar approached her at the free clinic, she added herself to the list of people who had made this young girl a promise. Unlike Ruben, Elsa was more convincing. She was passionate and delicate in her speech. The promise of citizenship, a healthy baby, and employment was too much for Jennifer to turn away from. God had sent her this angel to ensure that everything was going to be fine.

During the service, Jennifer began to feel what appeared to be the birthing process. Elsa noticed immediately and ended her sermon early.

"Let us go sweetheart; the Lord is ready to deliver your child."

"Is the hospital far?"

"Oh, no *mija*. Your child will be born naturally at home like Jesus. You'd like that, wouldn't you?"

"Is it safe?"

"Of course, it is—even safer. Why do you think doctors are always getting sued? Have you ever heard of a midwife being sued?"

"No."

"You see, now let's go."

Much to Jennifer's relief, her child was born into the world. She named him Joshua as she had always wanted to do with her firstborn son. It was not long after holding him for the first time that Elsa had the midwife take the baby back so that Jennifer could sign some papers. Her husband Miguel was usually quiet and submissive to what Elsa requested and was ordered to bring Jennifer some food and water. "Here, sweetheart, sign here."

"What is this?"

"You want your baby to get checked by a doctor, don't you?"

"Yes, that would be great."

"Well, honey, you can't take Joshua yourself. They will deport you."

"No, please! What do I do?"

"Not a problem, my angel. You just sign here giving me the authority to take over your son. I will take him to get checked, and there will be no questions asked. In a few weeks, I will have your papers ready, and you will be able to take your own son to the doctor in the future."

"Thank you so much *Pasotra*, for everything."

Jennifer never realized why, but she had slept for almost two days. She woke up very sore and tired but managed to get up. The morning sun was beginning to pierce the darkest part of the sky, and the birds were singing to a new day. Jennifer felt a sudden burst of energy and inspiration for a new day. She felt strong enough and ready to be a mother. The house seemed very quiet that early in the morning, but she soon heard the distant sound of a baby crying for its milk. Jennifer was eager to nurse her child for the first time. She got to the kitchen to find another woman she had never met breastfeeding her child.

"What are you doing?"

"Oh, it was time for little Robert's feeding?"

"That's my son; I named him Joshua. Who are you?" Her question was interrupted by Elsa Cuellar as she came in from the other room. "His name is Robert now, but we can call him Bobbie—little Bobbie even, at least until he gets to be a man."

"*Pastora*, why did you rename my son, and why is this woman feeding him?"

"You're just a little girl, Jennifer. Besides, you signed custody over to me."

"I did no such thing. I just allowed you to take him to the doctor."

Elsa's demeanor changed entirely from what Jennifer was used to seeing from her. The lines on *La Pastora's* face began to take a more sinister form. She was no longer the compassionate sister Jennifer thought she had found. "The document I have says otherwise, and if you continue to insist or give me problems, I will have you sent back to Mexico. Maybe you don't know this, but I am also an attorney, and you legally gave me custody of your child. If you care for him, then you will stay quiet and enjoy your time with him here."

Jennifer decided she did not want to make a scene. For now, she was content with seeing Joshua whenever she could. Sadly, she had to wait until the days of worship because Elsa never made the child available to her during the week. She was asked to perform domestic duties and tend to other children during the week. Her payment was being able to attend the Sunday sermon and have Joshua sit on her lap. This was the highlight of Jennifer's days. As far as she was concerned, she only lived one day a week.

Jennifer's contentment was short-lived. She was happy to be able to see her son once a week. She thought to herself that perhaps one day she would be able to simply escape during one of the most intense services. It was an ideal design she would never get the opportunity to orchestrate. Sometime before Christmas, Jennifer was curious as to why she was being given the week off. For the first time since having been under the current living conditions, she was not obligated to engage in any domestic responsibility. While the rest was welcomed, Jennifer feared it was a plot to not earn time with her son at the end of the week. Perhaps Elsa noticed the natural joy a child could only feel with his biological mother and feared losing control of the conditioning the child was undergoing under Elsa's plan. The best thing was for her to confront Elsa.

"*Pastora*, may I speak to you?"

"Of course, sweetheart. I am always here for all my children."

"Will I be able to see Joshua . . . I mean little Bobbie this Sunday."

"Of course. Haven't I been kind so far? He's sat on your lap every service since he was born."

"Yes, *Pastora*, but it is a right I usually earn with work, but I have not been given any chores this week, and it is Thursday."

Elsa displayed a look of remorse. She had been sitting behind a desk covered in paperwork and boxes. The room smelled like animals, and Elsa appeared to be sweating more than usual. She removed her reading glasses and took great care of her next choice of words. "Jennifer, I have been waiting for the right time to tell you, but you need to rest."

"Rest?"

"Yes, sweetheart. You see, the hospital had been trying to reach us for some time, but they just now found me. It appears there was a problem with Bobbie."

"Oh, my God. Please, *Pastora*, tell me what kind of problems. Is he okay?"

"Well, no, Jennifer. They learned that he has an illness that he got from you."

"From me? But I am fine."

"This illness doesn't have symptoms right away."

"What is wrong with us?"

"I am so sorry, Jennifer, but doctors found you have AIDS."

Jennifer was in complete disbelief. She cried uncontrollably with Elsa Cuellar at her side to console her as best as she could. Her large frame embraced Jennifer with the care that a mother would give her child. She walked her through her ex-boyfriend's experiences and assured her that she had contracted the disease through him. It was not difficult for Elsa to convince Jennifer the best thing for her is to get treated in Mexico. "You cannot take the chance of being deported here. Do not worry about little Bobbie. You signed him over to me so that I can manage his healthcare here in America. He will be fine, and we will all be together again soon."

"How will I come back to the United States?"

"Do not worry. I will take care of all that for you. Right now, you need to focus on getting better."

It was with extreme reluctance Jessica returned to Mexico without her son. She wanted the best care for him and knew he was in much better hands with American doctors. Mexico had some well know doctors but none that she could afford. She convinced herself that it was the best option. By the following day, Jessica was in the medical office of Lazaro Vargas. He had seen her when she was a child and trusted him with the secrecy of her condition. Jessica was very embarrassed to have AIDS and wanted to keep it from everyone she knew.

The test was made very quickly, and Dr. Vargas was very caring and nonjudgmental with Jessica. She had to wait a few days for the results; the young girl was now faced with the task of having to survive with nowhere to go. She found food and shelter at a local church, but the services were not consistent since funding often led to a lack of provisions. The days leading up to the results were very difficult for Jessica. She explored her own body for signs of the progression of the disease. This was done without being familiar with what to look for, but she was scared. After a few days of sleeping on benches and eating one meal a day, Jessica returned to the doctor. He invited her into his office, and she was terrified by the look in his eyes. The scared, young girl could not help but interpret his face as having worse news than she expected.

"*Mija*, who told you that you contracted the AIDS virus?"

"My church pastor said that the hospital in Laredo informed her."

"I can't imagine they could make such a mistake, but I cannot find any indication there is anything wrong with you."

"What do you mean, Dr. Vargas? My pastor assured me I had the disease and gave it to my son."

"I am sure your son is fine too, Jessica. Even if you did have AIDS, there are ways to reduce the risks of the child being born with it. I really don't know what else to tell you, but you are not in need of any treatment."

Jessica was arriving at the sinister motive behind Elsa's intentions. She provided a convincing reason for the young girl to return to Mexico without any legal means of getting back. She was stranded in Mexico once again—this time, without her son. Jessica was certain she would never hear from Elsa Cuellar, the trusted pastor, ever again. Her son's fate rested with the most sinister woman she had ever known.

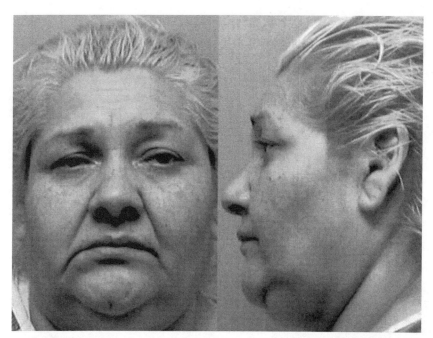

Elsa Cuellar's mugshot.

10

The Chance of a Lifetime

·

LAREDO, TEXAS, IS HOME TO SOME OF THE BEST FOOD I HAVE EVER HAD. Every time I return to this culturally enriched environment, I make sure to take full advantage of their street tacos. It does not matter so much where I go, the competition is stiff, and the locations are plenty. On May 25, 2022, my colleague and author Carlos Nicolas Flores offered to drive down to Zapata, Texas, with me to visit with the Executive Chief of the Zapata County Sheriff's Office. Flores has a beautiful house in San Ignacio a short drive south of Zapata overlooking the Rio Grande River. I will revisit our trip to Zapata later in this book but wish to mention Carlos treated me to lunch at a makeshift taco stand on our way out of Webb County.

Once the customer stepped into the eating area, the ambiance changed; It was as if we simply walked into Mexico. The Rio Grande River was not far behind the establishment and the Mexican breeze coming in from Tamaulipas created the illusion it was going to rain. Both Flores and I knew better than to think it was going to rain again. It had stormed the night before and more rain in Laredo was unlikely. I did not know of many places that sold *tripa* anymore, but this place certainly did. It was Carlos Flores's idea, and it was a good one. So good that I did not want to go home before going back myself to get some to go. My colleague did not know this at the time, but his lunch suggestion created one of the most unlikely chances of a lifetime. I was already walking back to my car with my food when I heard a voice. "Mr. Rodriguez?"

"Yes," I asked curiously. I had not ventured into South Laredo in quite some time. The number of people I knew there were few and those who remembered me even less. "I'm Carmen De La Rose. You used to be my daughter's counselor many years ago."

"Oh yes," I was not faking. I remembered Naomi De La Rose instantly. She had fallen in with the wrong crowd and had developed a kind of aneurism in her head when a friend of hers told her she could achieve "the ultimate high" if she crushed an aspirin inside a cigarette and smoked it. She could have died, but Carmen said she was doing fine, living in Houston, and working as a certified nurse assistant (CNA). She had five children already and lived with a sister because her husband was in prison on an armed robbery charge. It was not the ideal situation for Naomi, but it was much better than most with her background. "So, what are you doing here, did you move back?" she asked confidently. I was reluctant to tell her because I usually keep my projects quiet until I am prepared to release them, but it was so good seeing her, and wanted to keep the conversation going. "I'm actually doing research on a woman named Elsa Cuellar."

"Aye esa señora, ahora que eso?" "Oh, that woman, what did she do now?" was what she asked me. I was silenced by her response. "You know her?"

"Oh yes, she ruined my sister Dolores's life." I smiled to myself and thought *Thank you, God!* "So, Carmen, are you eating here? Can I eat my tacos with you?"

"Yes, that would be great!" She was excited to have company. I did not want to bring it up, but I knew her husband had been murdered outside a Nuevo Laredo bar when Naomi was only seven years old. Naomi was in her thirties now and Carmen was in her fifties and know the poor woman had been through so much in her life. Her frail frame took time to find a comfortable position on the exact same table Carlos Flores and I had sat on just days before. I waited for her to order her meal and we both had an *agua de piña.* The large foam cup covered half of her face and once I saw she was relaxed enough, I straight out asked: "So Carmen, how exactly did Cuellar ruin your sister's life?" The straw from the large cup divided her face in a way where each of her eyes was on opposite sides of the straw. She looked directly at me with a look of grief, and this is what she told me.

LA SANTISIMA MUERTE
Nuevo Laredo, Tamaulipas, Mexico, 1992

Pedro Maz sold what he could to provide for his family. It was not much of a stand, but it was a stand, nonetheless. Oranges, peaches, bananas, coffee, and various nuts were among his inventories. His wife Dolores questioned him daily about how he managed to erect such a business. It was small yet still beyond their means. She had suspected, for some time, that Pedro had gotten involved with a questionable group. For some time, he left Nuevo Laredo for days at a time without coming home. He was evasive with his explanations as to where he was and reluctant to continue any dialogue having to do with his activity.

It was early December one morning at 3:00 am. Nuevo Laredo's streets were quiet, with the distant sound of the Rio Grande's current keeping people asleep with the beautiful sound of nature's music. Dolores loved to sleep to the sound of the Rio Grande on nights when there was no commotion from the Border Patrol on the American side. On this early morning, it was the sound of a door closing that woke her. She stepped out into the cold flooring of her third-floor apartment. She wrinkled her toes to withstand better the rigid, aging wooden boards that creaked with every step. She walked over to the window and looked down to the corner of *Calle Tomas Urbina* and saw a black Navigator parked on the curve next to the building. The emblem of *La Santisima Muerte* frightened her. She could not see clearly through the dark tint but knew Pedro was in there. It was nearly an hour before he emerged from the back seat. The Navigator sped off, and Pedro returned to the apartment without disclosing any details concerning who those men were or what the nature of their business was—and he did not expect to be asked.

Dolores did not push the issue by asking Pedro what kind of exchange he had with men of questionable character, but it was less than a week later that the stand of produce was opened. Could a produce stand have generated the kind of income that would explain the changes Dolores would soon see in their lives? A new carpet was laid over the cold wooden floor, and some of the old furniture was replaced with new. Their son had more toys than they ever imagined he would have in their lifetime. It was an unexpected Christmas for Dolores, but the joys of the festive season went as mysteriously as they had arrived. On New Year's Eve, Pedro entered the home in a very disturbed state. He insisted that it was an excellent time to move. Dolores could not understand the timing for a relocation just after making such a mass investment in their home renovations.

"Pedro, you want to just pick up and move?"

"Why are you so surprised? Come on; you know how we've been doing here." He said this while gathering their son's belonging and placing things in big black garbage sacks.

"I thought we were doing fine, I mean, you fixed the place and everything." Pedro did not answer and continued his packing in a hurry.

"It's New Year's Eve. Can't we take our time and look for a good place?"

Dolores's suggestion fell on deaf ears. She could not understand what had provoked her husband to lose his senses. While his intentions were honorable, his design was irrational and without careful planning. An inexplicable fear pushed against Dolores's breast. She had reserved her concerns for a time like the present and was certain Pedro's recent circle of associates was a significant factor for why he was running. Dolores was not an educated woman, but she was not so slow as to not be able to understand these things. She did not have to see the rats; she only had to examine the bite marks on the cheese. The evidence was clear. Her husband was in danger, and she was afraid.

The panic in Pedro's demeanor was obvious. He rushed down to the street, where he began to clear out the produce from his stand. He was proud of his business, so only something drastic would compel him to leave it behind. It was against her better judgment to begin a conversation about what was transpiring with her husband. She knew it was a discussion that would take more time than they had. Although she did not know precisely why Dolores was afraid and found herself moving as quickly as Pedro in getting the essential things together. It was almost midnight, and the family would be able to escape under the cover of fireworks. The eyes of Mexico would be on the sky. The eyes of the panicked family would be on a new future. She took her young son by the arm, lifted him over her shoulder, and carried some belongings down with her free arm. There was much that would have to remain behind. Material possessions were never something Dolores lived her life worrying about. At this point, her family's safety to precedence over all other matters.

She got to the bottom of the steps and realized how late their intentions began to unfold. The navigator was already in front of the stand where Pedro cleared his produce from the crates. At exactly midnight, as the fireworks began to illuminate the night sky, gunfire erupted from within the dark vehicle, spraying Pedro with rounds throughout his body. Dolores dropped her garbage sack and buried her son's face in her chest so that he would not watch his father endure such a tragic fate. She used her free hand to place over her mouth in hopes of resisting the natural inclination to scream in grief-stricken horror. She dropped what she had and ran back up the stairs, and triple-locked the apartment door behind her. Dolores knew better than to think that would be enough should the men decide to pursue her. After a few minutes, locked in the closet, the time came for the now-widowed mother to assess the environment. Could she safely leave now? Should she bother calling the police? Dolores bravely walked to the window and looked down. The navigator was gone, and a crowd of people had already assembled around her husband's body. It rested in a pool of blood. Many of its internals were stuck to the wall behind him. What remained was an empty shell of a body drenched in its own blood beyond anyone's recognition. Not even those closest to Pedro nor those who knew him well could discern his features with accuracy. Dolores felt as if her soul had stepped outside her body and was standing next to her. For those around the lifeless body, the scene's familiarity was becoming more of an expectation than a shock. It is a horrible direction for any society to take, but for now, Dolores had to endure the harsh reality that her husband had contributed to the rising statistics. At the risk of feeling selfish, she was suddenly plagued with the immediate concern for the welfare of herself and her son. It was difficult for her to simply dismiss her husband's death and move on to the next chapter of her life, but the risks that came to her and her child without Pedro were impossible to deflect. She was not an educated woman; she was not a working woman. The hands of poverty were reaching out to her. Dolores knew that once those hands reached her and her son, the clutches of its palm would be so tight that loosening the grip would be impossible.

The stains of her husband's blood would forever mark the driveway of *Calle Thomas Urbina*. The blood-soaked gaps in the cracked pavement absorbed the now black fluid as if it was an intentional paint job. It will no longer be a reminder of the loss of life in a few short days. Instead, it will become part of the street. The permanent mark will become lost among the many reminders that are left on Mexico's pavements. People will continue to take those paths to the market and step on the blood with no name. No memorial will be erected. No plaque will be screwed to the wall. There simply is not enough room.

Now, having had to endure this tragedy at the beginning of the month, Dolores was aware of the limited time she had before the landlord would request the rent. She was a woman without a country now. Mexico often forgets about those in need, not because it lacks people who care; instead, it is deficient in assisting those who need it. Resources are often unavailable as are those qualified to provide them. She had no alternative but to seek refuge in the most likely place to find someone with a caring nature. The desperate mother walked into the sounds of singing and dancing. Everyone looked happy as they praised their Lord and Savior. Their hands were raised high toward the sky, and the tears flowed from their faces as if every disgrace they had ever experienced was exiting their body. Dolores and her frightened son walked past the large sign that read *Hermanos Del Siglo Nuevo*. She had not spoken to anyone yet felt a sudden sense of belonging. The woman on stage commanded the room with an instinctual demand for attention. Her frame was corpulent by nature, and the shadow of her smile reflected off her portly cheeks. The passion in her eyes was evident, and the fire in her sincerity illuminated from within her. Not one person in the room had their eyes somewhere else as the echo of her words vibrated through the interior walls. Dolores instantly felt as if there was no other place she would rather be. This was the place that would help her out of her current dilemma.

After the sermon, the woman was quickly enclosed by a large crowd wanting to praise, touch, and talk to her. It was an amazing display of the utmost veneration that could be offered to a single person. It took nearly an hour for the crowd to clear enough for Dolores to be visible to the *Pastora*. There she stood with tired eyes and falling cheekbones. Her countenance was in obvious disarray and her spirit broken. Her appearance alone was enough to lure the holy woman towards her.

"Why are you so sad, child?"

That question was all it took for Dolores to break into a fit of tears. The woman quickly called out to someone named Miguel.

"Miguel, please take this woman to my office. Bring her some food. I want to talk to her."

The kind host gave Dolores some time to compose herself. The tired woman ate her meal slowly, but her son ate as if he hadn't eaten in weeks.

"What a charming boy. How old is he?"

"He is four."

"What a wonderful age. What is your name?"

"My name is Dolores, and this is my son, Christian."

"What a wonderful name for a boy."

"Suppose you tell me what brought you here in such a condition."

Dolores related her story carefully. The *Pastora* was obviously moved by what she heard, but she seemed specifically concerned with how Dolores ended her story. In the weeks leading up to her husband's death, Dolores learned that she was once again pregnant with their second child. She had intended it to be a New Year's surprise—one she would never get the chance to deliver.

She was known simply among those who knew her as *La Pastora* because Arlene Jasmine Elsie Alvarado Cuéllar was too much for any person's tongue. For Dolores, Elsa Cuéllar was enough, and she quickly became a regular at the *Hermanos Del Siglo Nuevo*. The first few weeks, Dolores and her son Christian became regulars, but when the lease to her apartment finally expired, Elsa opened the doors of the church to her. It was a very small room to the rear of the building, but the now destitute woman and her son had everything they needed and did not have to pay rent. Dolores did chores around the church and kept the place neat. Elsa was very impressed with the work being done, and the two became close. Both women became so fond of each other that when Dolores reached the sixth month of her pregnancy, Elsa offered the vulnerable woman an opportunity to improve her life.

Dolores was resting her swollen feet while Christian played with toys Elsa bought for him. In fact, she had showered both Christian and her mother with various gifts during their stay at the church. The kind woman empathized with the road Dolores would have to travel in raising two children. She sat next to her and placed her aging hand on her shoulder.

"Your feet must be really hurting you."

"I'll be okay. I worked much harder when I was pregnant with Christian."

"You might have, but you're older now. You have to think carefully about what you want for your children."

"There is little I can do, *Pastora*. You know how difficult things can be here in Mexico."

The woman looked carefully around her and slid closer to Dolores. She looked around a second time. "I might be able to help you, Dolores."

"Help me?"

"Yes, I have good friends in America that can help you have your baby there. It will make a big difference if you try to become a citizen and have an opportunity at a real life."

"*Pastora*, that sounds wonderful, but I cannot cross legally to America. I do not have papers."

"Don't worry. I can help with that too. You just meet me here Friday morning, and we will take care of everything."

"Do you mean I will be going to America on Friday?"

The woman embraced the hopeful Dolores as if she was a sister. She smiled at her like an angel and assured her. "Dolores, on Friday, your life will change more than you can possibly imagine."

LAREDO, TEXAS, 1993

Dolores was very nervous. She saw the United States Customs agents standing with authority at the station all going into America had to go through. She did not have to learn to say "American citizen" without an accent. According to the documents that *La Pastora* arranged, Dolores had permission to go into Laredo, Texas, to work. She knew the papers were false even if she did not admit this to herself. There was no way anyone could have arranged legitimate paperwork in the time frame *La Pastora* had acquired them. Still, the desperate woman was excited about having her child in the United States. She would speak to *La Pastora* later about possibly remaining in Laredo without ever going back to Mexico. She was certain she could find work as a maid and get paid in cash. She had many friends who had done that.

The agent had a shiny nameplate that had the name Gamez on it. For some reason, Dolores always believed that federal agents were only white. Close up, it was obvious that agent Gamez was not a white man and not all that intimidating. There was an unpleasant smell about him, and he did not seem to want to be there. His boots were not as polished as the military band before the annual Christmas parade in Tamaulipas. The bands in Mexico were always well represented. His shirt was stained, and there was nothing attractive about him. In a way, it made Dolores feel more confident about crossing. Agent Gamez examined that paperwork and looked over it closely.

"Where do you work?"

"I work for a family. I take care of their children."

That is what *La Pastora* told her to say. They did not ask for anything more. They did not care to know what family. In minutes, Dolores was in the United States. A few blocks from the international bridge, Dolores leaped into *La Pastora*'s large frame and embraced her. She was so grateful for the help. So many illegals go through some of the most hazardous environments to get into the United States. Dolores simply walked across without fear of death. She had never felt so free. The excitement was heightened by the fact that her child would be born in the United States. Her son Christian poked his head out of *La Pastora*'s vehicle. Dolores was delighted to see him. She had never been apart from him. "How did you get my son here?"

"Do not worry; everything is going to be fine, sister. Let us go."

Elsa Cuellar had always been good at dodging questions. She was fast to deflect Dolores's curiosity and quickly got her into the car. They arrived at a beautiful home in central Laredo. The neighborhood was not new, but it was affluent and on a much larger scale than Dolores would ever think she'd see. She was enamored by the paved streets and the tall trees. The neighbors had luxury vehicles, and children played on the streets without the fear of random acts of violence. It was a beautiful sight, and Dolores thought it was the perfect place to give birth to a child.

"*Pastora*, do you think I will be able to stay here?"

"We have plenty of time to talk about that later, sister. First, let's get you something to eat."

Dolores was provided with meals she had never tried before. She had known no red meat outside fajita but tried sirloin steak and shrimp for the first time. There were other children in the house, and Christian was making new friends. His birthday arrived during their stay, and Elsa had a big party for him. Many children were there, and Dolores felt happy. Christian's happiness meant the world to her, and to see that he was coping with the loss of his father with laughter and a new environment was pleasing. She could not thank her new friend enough for everything she had done. Finally, the day came for her to have her baby. She was very excited and prepared herself to go to the hospital.

"Will I be asked anything about my citizenship at the hospital?"

"Hospital? Oh, no sister, you will be having your baby here. We don't want to ruin this opportunity."

"Here in your home?"

"Do not worry, Dolores. The doctor coming to meet you here is very qualified. You are in good hands."

Dolores was skeptical at first, but she had no reason to doubt *La Pastora* in all this time. She had been kind, nourishing, and helpful. Without her, the living conditions she and her son would have had to endure would have been deplorable. She smiled and agreed to have her baby at home. The labor was smooth and clean. Dolores gave birth to a beautiful little girl. She did not expect it to go so well, but she could not seem to recall the birthing process.

"My daughter?" She asked.

"You rest, sister. Your daughter is healthy and beautiful." Elsa Cuellar was always soothing, and her voice was calming. Dolores was very disoriented, but she could not understand why. She was confused for some time and, in a moment of realization, noticed that she was on her feet and walking toward the front door.

"Where are we going?"

"Do not worry, sister. You ask too many questions. We need to have you checked."

Dolores was unsure why she could have her child in *La Pastora*'s home but had to get checked somewhere else. If giving birth in a hospital could get her deported, then it would be reasonable to believe that a doctor's visit of any kind could also have her sent back to Mexico. They walked her to a large, black SUV. She was terrified at the sight of the *Santisima Muerte*. It reminded her of the night her husband was murdered. Further observation of the vehicle revealed something more sinister; it was not just the same saint on the vehicle—it was the same vehicle! Before she could fight her way out of getting into the car, Dolores's drowsiness became a complete loss of her senses. The next thing she saw was the pure absence of any color.

She had not realized it, but Dolores had woken up a day later in a hospital bed. She called out to a nurse who was very kind and attentive to her. She had always imagined no one in the United States spoke Spanish, but the nurse clearly had the language mastered. Dolores asked to see her baby. "I'm sorry, I just started my shift. I didn't realize you had a baby. Let me check with the head nurse."

"Thank you."

It took nearly an hour before the head nurse came in place of the kind lady who had responded to Dolores's request.

"How are you feeling?"

"Much better. I would like to see my baby."

"Ma'am, when you were brought in here, you were left alone. You didn't have a baby with you."

"Can you please call the pastor of my church? She will bring my baby."

"Yes, of course. Do you have a number for him?"

"Um, no. It's a woman. She never gave me her number here in America. I only know the name of her church in Tamaulipas."

"America? Ma'am, you are not in America. You are here in Nuevo Laredo, Tamaulipas."

"That cannot be, *señora*. I went to America to have my baby."

The head nurse was in complete confusion. Dolores had become irate and inconsolable. She was sedated once again so doctors can ascertain whether she had given birth. Dolores had become hysterical before the hospital could even get her name. She was never formally admitted as a patient. She was simply dropped off by a stranger in a black SUV who claimed he had found her in her current state on a bench at *Parque Viveros*. Dolores did not have anything that could prove her identity. Her work permit, her identification, and what little money she had were gone. She had no way to return to the United States. She was now a woman without a country, without a husband, and no children.

It was a difficult story to hear. The loss of a child is too much for a mother to take at times. Today, Dolores lives in Matamoros, Mexico, nursing an amputated leg owed to diabetes. Carmen lives just across the river from her in Brownsville, Texas, and was in Laredo only to celebrate a relative's high school graduation. The entire family wonders about Dolores's little girl, what she had become, if she has any recollection of her mother, or if she is even still alive. It is a difficult uncertainty to live with, but sadly, Dolores was not the only one of Cuellar's victims who had to live with these questions. It was pointless to attempt to answer them—as pointless as trying to decide whether the wind floating above the Rio Grande River is Mexican or American.

11

Evil Crossing

THE DEBATE CONCERNING IMMIGRATION ISSUES IS ONGOING AND MAY never see a nationwide consensus on the best practice for combating illegal crossing. One of the misconceptions regarding border issues is that it is a new social issue. While social media has created the illusion that this is a new problem because of the rate at which it can deliver information, the truth is that illegal residency has been in place for many years. World War II brought an influx of migrant workers into the United States from Mexico with the American government's consent.

With many American men fighting in the war, the shortage of labor in domestic farming was a concern for the local economy. Many petitioned the government for some kind of temporary labor assistance. The most logical solution was the importation of Mexican labor. The nation's capital responded with the Bracero Program in 1942. The program's outcome was so favorable, that the American government agreed to import more Mexicans to work on the railroad. In 1943, twenty thousand more Mexicans were brought across the border to work, the following year, fifty thousand more workers were imported and in 1945, seventy-five thousand more immigrants were crossed into the United States with permission to work. The program would grow to develop a strong commitment to bringing in more workers from Mexico, especially during wartime. Manual labor was cheap and kept the American economy afloat. But the adverse effect was the embedding of the idea that to prosper, one would have to cross into the United States. Even those who were not drafted into the Bracero Program rushed to the northern states of Mexico for an opportunity to cross into America. As Ganster and Collins note: "This wartime flow of labor north to the U.S. border states and beyond marked the beginning of a massive influx of Mexicans to both the Mexican and U.S. border states" (99).

The early seeds planted in the minds of Mexicans that prosperity could only be achieved on American soil continues to this day. While opportunities are more abundant, success in the United States is not guaranteed and often produces hardships difficult for illegal immigrants to overcome. This is what made Cuellar successful in her endeavors. She took the strong perception that success is available north of the Rio Grande and eliminated the factors that would create hardships for unsuspecting victims. She did this by creating the illusion they had no reason to cross illegally through false documentation. Still, it is worth noting that many illegals crossing into the United States are not destitute and are looking for a different kind of opportunity on American soil that is far more sinister. In an interview with the U.I.S.D. police investigator overseeing much of the Cuellar case, Alexander Rodriguez, I learned this continues to be an issue. "I see illegals crossing through the ranch all the time while I'm hunting. Some of them appear to be armed and dressed in tactical gear, so I'm always careful to carry my weapons with me." When asked if they have ever confronted him, Rodriguez says "Not really, sometimes they just look back a little."

LAREDO, TEXAS, 2012

The year was nearly over. With only a few weeks left before the Christmas break, a U.I.S.D. police investigator Alexander Rodriguez set out to the home he had been so curious about. He was surprised to have found the address to be in such a nice part of town. The Del Mar area had always had respectable neighborhoods and got little attention on the local news. The district officer used the upcoming break to open communication with whoever answered the door. He was a tall clean-cut male. He was lean and muscular but did not appear to be all that strong. His speech was lazy and his posture feeble. *It's too early for him to be drunk, isn't it?* The investigator thought to himself.

A camera at one of the ranches where Investigator Alex Rodriguez captured this group of men crossing in from Mexico.

"How are you, sir? I'm with the U.I.S.D. police just following up on Samantha and Martha. How are they feeling from the chickenpox?"

"Fine."

Rodriguez got a much better idea of what the girls meant by chickenpox. Although he was not invited in, he could see the home was in complete disarray. It was messy beyond belief, and inside the house, there were hundreds of loose chickens.

"May I ask who you are, sir?"

"Tomas."

"Are you the girl's uncle?"

"I'm there, brother."

The age gap was unusual. Rodriguez had no reason to interrogate the young man, but he believed him to be in his thirties.

"Nice chickens. Are they dinner or pets?"

The young man only gave a mild response to the joke. He did not appear coherent enough to understand humor at the time. Perhaps he had just woken up. He did not engage much, and this made it difficult for the investigator to initiate further communication. He was suddenly called by a voice from within the house to come inside. Someone needed help with something.

"Well, let your mother know we're here to help if the kids need anything."

"Okay."

Rodriguez did not get much out of his visit, but his luck changed as he walked back to his unit. A beautiful young lady in her mid- to-late twenties arrived with what appeared to be breakfast. The first thought in Rodriguez's mind was that this woman could be a model or an actress. She approached with great concern. "Officer, is everything okay?"

"Oh yes, nothing to worry about. I was just checking to see how Samantha and Martha are doing."

"Oh, much better. We've told them a million times not to play with the chickens."

Rodriguez was much too experienced to believe the chicken pecks on the girl's skin were an accident. After all, chickens were common in Laredo; many people had them. He knew well that one peck from a chicken would be enough to keep anyone from handling a chicken. No one would endure so many random pecks. Still, he went along with it.

"Well, you know, kids. They're curious."

"Yeah," she laughed.

"Hey, I spoke to a young man. I know he's not a student, but is he okay?"

"You mean my brother, Christian, yeah. He's just a quiet type."

"No, I spoke to Tomas." At this, the woman became more restless and unwilling to continue talking. She looked up as if she had made eye contact with someone who was looking out from within the house. She seemed to have become uneasy after this; Rodriguez could see her efforts to get back into the house without further discussion. He did not fight it and wished her a good day. Something was not right. It was time for law enforcement to take a much closer look.

Investigator Rodriguez could not sleep that same night. He woke early to go fishing. It was the one place he felt human. The stress of life refused to follow him there. The biggest decision he had to make the next morning was whether he wanted his eggs scrambled or over-easy. Still, Christian or "Thomas's" face would not leave him. There was a familiarity to his countenance, and the fact that he was in Cuellar's confirmed address, made his suspicions that much more valid.

The Dilemma

MUCH LIKE INVESTIGATOR RODRIGUEZ, MANY OFFICIALS INVOLVED IN Cuellar's case were left with much to think about. The problem for law enforcement and the United Independent School District was not that they did not know what was happening; the real issue was actually proving it. For her entire career, Cuellar had learned how to walk a tightrope when it came to what was defined as legal or illegal. Much like she did to claim adoption or justify the taking over of a child with consent from another country, there were also loopholes to the issue of child placement. When a child is "placed," they are typically relocated to a residence where they can be socialized and live in a comfortable environment. Elsa provided this environment and manipulated her victims into believing they would be deported if they were to ever express any dissatisfaction with how they lived. This would not be likely. Elsa Cuellar was smart enough to provide a setting that was favorable to conditions many of these children would have in Mexico.

Another dilemma faced by authorities was the question of when the right time to arrest Cuellar would be. Ultimately, they had no choice but to act on the tampering with government documents, but the idea was to hold out as long as possible to prove child abuse or endangerment. The problem with patience is that if they were correct about the abuse taking place at the Cuellar residence, it stands to reason it was taking place as they worked to gather evidence of it. It seemed counterproductive for law enforcement to prolong the children's exposure to danger while trying to prove it at the same time. So how much evidence do law enforcement agencies need? I learned that it is necessary to have enough evidence for the case to be held up in court. In my interview with the director of admissions Jose Almazan, he highlighted some of the issues with possible trafficked kids, that is, many domestic issues mimic the symptoms of a trafficked child.

The director related a case to me of a child who had not eaten in four days. He was attending school appearing dirty, tired, and malnourished. When the school investigated the domestic situation, it was learned the mother had been displaced by her husband to make room for another woman. This left his wife and son in a small place with no electricity or clean water. She was doing what she could for herself and the son but being alone and unable to afford childcare made things difficult. There was no abuse taking place, but the current lifestyle the mother and child were living created symptoms that paralleled a household in which child abuse was taking place. This was not an uncommon scenario in Laredo, Texas, nor is it unusual for many communities on the border extending as far west as California. So many different border lifestyles and domestic issues could easily create signs of abuse or trafficking in the absence of any wrongdoing. The symptoms become so common that they eventually become part of an impoverished culture. For this reason, signs of children being endangered are often dismissed as minors in a low-income setting. It is, for this reason, law enforcement was careful not to make any mistakes with Cuellar that could jeopardize any charges they may want to bring against her later.

The best thing that could happen for the district and the police was to continue to have incidents with the children that would give them probable cause to investigate Cuellar's home more carefully. Like Rodriguez, the district had questions about the older men living in her home and the case of Imelda Cuellar did just that. This was a blessing because Imelda's well-being was now becoming time sensitive. There was no way to know what could be happening or what would happen in the near future as the investigation moved forward. Already, there was an overwhelming concern for the little girl's psychological state.

With her mental health in mind, this brought another dilemma that can easily be overlooked as an important factor. The language in the social service system is very different from that of the legal. Knowing what the appropriate language was to use in this case could make a very significant difference in whether the matter was seen as an international crime, neglect, child abuse, or even nothing. Was the language to be used in Imelda's case one that would merit a prison sentence for Elsa Cuellar or parenting classes? How could the best interests of the young girl be served if it came to be known she was not a legal resident? How much additional evidence would need to be collected if Imelda continued to fail in understanding that crimes were being committed in her domestic setting? Considering her IQ, would what Imelda has to say even matter in a court of law? For law enforcement, these questions were very difficult to answer, therefore, complicated to act on.

13

The Older Man

Two Months Before the Arrest of Elsa Cuellar

THE NUMBER OF CHILDREN ENROLLED WITHIN THE UNITED INDEPEN-
dent School District who had Elsa Cuellar listed as their mother began
to grow as the investigation unfolded. In one short day, that number grew
by at least one more when a concerned teacher made a report that got
the attention of the district police. For several days, Imelda Cuellar had
been attending class without any regard for covering up her "hickies."
Her homeroom teacher was concerned since Imelda had only celebrated
her thirteenth birthday the week before. She thought her to be much too
young to be involved in a relationship that consisted of physical conduct.
It further worried her that the class was for special education students,
and many of those in her class did not have the intelligence level to make
decisions about relationships. After class, Mrs. Cantu asked her to stay
behind.

"Hi, Imelda."

"Hi, ma'am."

"Thank you for staying behind Imelda; I wanted to talk to you about
something."

"What about?"

"I'm worried about the marks on your neck. Can you tell me how
they got there?"

"My boyfriend put them there. He said he wanted to make sure no
other man looked at me." The little girl said this shyly as if it was a good

thing that her boyfriend marked his territory. She spoke with a prideful tone and, in her mind, felt as if she had impressed her teacher for already having a boyfriend at her age. On the contrary, Mrs. Cantu was becoming more concerned.

"Does your boyfriend come to this school?"

Imelda giggled as if that was a ridiculous question. After a few giggles, she was laughing hard.

"Of course not, ma'am. He is already twenty years old. He's too old to come here."

"Twenty? Isn't he a little too old for you, sweetheart? Does your mother know about this boyfriend?"

"Oh yes, ma'am. My mom introduced him to me. He even sleeps with me at the house. She told me, *que no hay pedo*, ma'am."

Mrs. Cantu understood this to be a Spanish slang term for *There's no problem.* The experienced teacher was not committed to believing whether the mother knew about this or not, but she had been teaching long enough to know that these things had happened. She escorted Imelda to the principal's office to get some advice from her superiors. Reporting to Child Protective Services was often a complicated thing. If it was not something the state will act on, the school prefers not to ruin relationships with parents.

The principal was engaged in a district meeting but had the fortune to have seen an officer taking a report on another student in the front office.

"Officer, can I speak to you for a minute?"

She explained the situation to the district officer. Whether it was owed to sensitive intuition or to how much the Elsa Cuellar case had engulfed the department in recent weeks, he did not know, but he thought he would check Imelda's file. "Give me a second, Mrs. Cantu." It was no surprise to him that upon opening the file, the name Elsa Cuellar jumped at him as the girl's legal guardian. With every passing day with the district, this woman began consuming every ounce of moral being in the district's soul. He remembers serving the warrant and wanting to end the case by shooting her and releasing all the children from the burden of her existence. However, he was able to embrace the law and moral code he had always lived by and restrained himself from doing anything that could compromise the case against her. Although he did not express it at the time, the officer knew exactly what was taking place. And now, with the little girl Imelda's testimony, the officer was able to put together the articulate manner *La Pastora* was operating.

It was already known that she was an expert at falsifying documents. For over twenty years, she had been successfully falsifying documents of all kinds and for many different reasons. Her connection to the cartel was a strong indication that she was used to creating illegal papers for dealers to cross into the United States to manage their businesses. The purpose for getting on the American side of the border would range from dealing drugs to establishing money laundering businesses, such as car washes, slot machine establishments, strip clubs, and restaurants. Other times, their duties were more sinister: crossing illegal immigrants and even murder. It was with the crossing of illegal immigrants that Elsa Cuellar found her road to underground success. Using the sheep's wool of religion to keep the herd around her from knowing she was a wolf, Elsa would harbor many of these illegal women with the promise of naturalization, prosperity, and a comfortable living for their children. Since many of these women were so uneducated that they could not read in either English or Spanish, it was very easy to convince them to sign any documents that were supposedly explained to them.

Law enforcement authorities did not necessarily attribute this to a skill that Elsa had. It did not take much effort to falsely explain a document in a different language to a woman in a strange country who is hungry, desperate, and pregnant. It took very little effort. The documents could serve numerous purposes. The design of the forms could have surrendered a child's rights to Elsa, falsely claim the unsuspecting immigrant was now an American citizen only to have her deported after the rights of the child were given up, or could have claimed Elsa as a legal guardian who was related. Still, the sinister woman's ambition did not stop with taking these women's children. She would often raise these children and have any one of her alleged husbands have sex with them for no other reason than to get the young girls pregnant. From here, the options were numerous, and the extent of the damage that could be done to these young victims had no limits. It could very easily be decided that the young girls would give birth dangerously at home without proper medical supervision for not having that child's existence anywhere on record at a hospital. She could sell these children, tell the obtuse young mothers that their child did not survive the birth, and the world would never know the difference. A life with no country, no identity, and no honest history is brought into the world through this woman's work, and they would never know the difference.

Sadly, having the child sold was often the best-case scenario. The idea, after all, was to make money. If time elapsed and the child appeared to be getting older, the blueprint for Elsa's actions would take a more sinister route. It made sense for her to have an alternative plan. She would not want to spend the rest of her life raising a child that was not hers at her own expense, and few people care to buy a grown child on the black market. It is here that it was decided to make the right connections with underground black markets for organ selling. In one of the many properties where it could happen, she would hold gatherings that were in the eyes of the children nothing more than family time. They had no way of knowing that the real motive for getting together was more of a ritual than a celebration. Children were being murdered and burned in one-hundred-gallon barrels but not before their organs were removed. The US Marshals knew that this was probably what Bobby saw when he said he saw a boy get stabbed. This had to be it! Too many children had gone missing under her care. This was more than a coincidence. In America, parents often get massacred by social media for losing one child. District police could not help but wonder: *How can this one woman get away with so much undetected right under the American flag?*

Now, with Imelda coming forward, the police were convinced that a hidden suspicion they had was now coming to light. Some of the kids were found to have sexually transmitted diseases and further testing for HIV had been requested by the court. Many were suggesting the obvious sexual abuse, but authorities believed it went much deeper than that. They had always felt the girls were being pimped at some point. Imelda's story did not confirm this theory; however, it gave them an idea of how she was doing it. If an adult male paid for sexual services with a minor, the business arrangements were concealed under the blanket of deception through the mother's alleged approval of the relationship. Little did Elsa know that things did not work that way in the United States, and it was still considered statutory rape.

It had long been suspected that many of those girls had been sexually abused, had children in their homes that no one knew about, or were fooled into believing that an older man was interested in them. Elsa knew exactly how to manipulate people and understood the vulnerability of a special needs child who relished the very thought of having a romantic involvement. It was all fabricated! There was no relationship. It was nothing more than someone else's sexual consent. It made school officials sick to their stomachs to come to terms with the realization that their theories were on a road that led to a different place than they would if they had solid evidence to prove it. The District Attorney's office would need more, and the police were not sure how to get it.

The officer looked into Imelda's dark little eyes. She was eating a cookie the teacher had given her. Her tiny dark pupils and clueless smile made him feel a sense of sadness. The entire life the young girl had lived was no more real than a whisper. Her boyfriend, her guardians, the concept of right and wrong, and her life, in general, were not real.

LA HISTORIA DE IMELDA (IMELDA'S STORY)
The Valley Near Pharr—San Juan Alamo, Texas, 2000

The group of illegal immigrants had been housed in a warehouse in McAllen, Texas, for three days before Juan Arredondo began to complain. The man responsible for their safe crossing was a different man than the one responsible for taking them to their next location. The tired group had been promised jobs, a ranch to stay, and documentation confirming legal status in the United States. On the day they had arrived, the group was told that food delivery would be in an hour. An hour passed, and there was no food. Instead, they were visited by a mysterious woman. She prayed with the group and made them feel welcome. She went over the plan with them and explained the process. They were overwhelmed with joy and hope. For the first time in their lives, they had experienced the prospect of stability. The thought of someday owning their own homes and doing something with their lives was too much for them to contain. The woman was so skillful in relating this wonderful news to the group that they instantly liked her. She was skillful at her craft and could lie to the devil and get away with it.

Her manner of speech was so convincing that they did not doubt that her words were as good as a written contract. She was aggressive yet gentle. It was evil in its most concealed form. Through the angelic sound of her words did they come to respect and trust this woman with their children after she recommended moving them first. She took great care not to suggest such a thing until after she delivered her prayer and speech. If she did, it would be like putting poison on the outside of the cupcake. This woman knew much better than that. The poison goes inside the beautifully decorated pastry. It was to be found under the tasty frosting and the beautiful sprinkles that added to its appeal. She made everything sound as if it was the right way to do it. Speaking to people in such vulnerable states made her design much easier to execute. She convinced them all that because of the size of the kids, it would be much more feasible to move them first. She also assured them that they would be able to move the adults to the ranch much faster if they did not have to carry children. They assured each parent that they were prepared to care for their children with professional nurses. The parents were excited and trusted the woman without any degree of indecision about her character. The woman carried a small Holy Bible that she handed to one of the women to read to her group. She assured them food was on the way, and in two more days, they would be reunited with their children.

A group of neatly dressed men and one woman entered the warehouse and collected three babies who were not a year old yet. The mothers blessed them with the sign of the cross and thanked the woman for being so kind. The babies were taken, and the last thing they saw was the dark figure against the sunlight coming in through the main door of the warehouse. The woman's large frame left nothing more than a golden outline of her obese figure in the doorway. Suddenly, the warehouse was dark again as the door closed behind her. It would be the last time anyone in the group would see the woman. More significantly, it would be the last time any of the parents would see their children again. The woman got to the outside, where her husband waited. "Make the call," she told him. It was not a call to have the group picked up and taken to any ranch. It was not a call to have food and water brought to them. It was a call to the United States Border Patrol to report a warehouse filled with illegal immigrants.

If any truth at all had come from the woman's mouth, it was that there was a ranch somewhere near Zapata, Texas. Their plan was always to have only the children transported there. Nothing could ever be learned about the two of them, but the woman decided to keep one of them for herself. She became enamored by her and arranged for all the documentation needed to prove the baby's existence. It was a little girl with dark-brown eyes and tiny dimples that few could resist. She fed the baby and played with her until it was time to put her to bed. She used the evening to prepare all the paperwork needed to prove the baby's existence. She gave her the name Imelda and prepared everything that would prove her to be her child. Who would know any better? Who had evidence to contest the woman? Before that moment, Imelda Chavez Cuellar did not exist.

Her childhood up until she got to be a teenager had been all but a suitable environment for Imelda. Whether it was owed to an unconscious feeling that she was not in the right place or if it was how Elsa Cuellar raised her will never be accurately attributed to the young girl's mental capacity. It appeared as if her body had continued to grow while her mind remained steady since she was seven years old. She was a playful girl who understood and embraced life in a constant childlike manner, but she never developed the cognitive capacity to think logically. Not only did this separate her from classmates taking regular courses, but it also prevented her from discerning between right and wrong as well as an illusion from reality. Perhaps it was intentional; after all, it was a great benefit to Elsa that Imelda lacks in these skills.

Everything in Imelda's life had been molded into accepting why things were different for her than for other children. It appeared they were only Jehovah's Witnesses when it was her birthday or Christmas. When it was Elsa's birthday, there seemed to be something else that allowed the celebration. She never fully understood the presence of so many children and how they became her siblings. Children who do not understand the world at the same level as most normal people don't question these things. Very simply, it becomes their reality. When enough time passes, they come to accept it and become comfortable with it to a certain extent.

All human beings have the capacity to acquire a dislike for something no matter their intellectual level. Imelda did not like eating at the same table where the chicken feces had not been cleaned off. She never liked having chickens in the house. No one would ever feed them, and when they got hungry enough, they would start plucking at the children. They occasionally plucked at her too, but the day she complained, she learned to sympathize with the animals and never filed a grievance with Elsa again. The plump woman listened attentively to Imelda as if she cared about the pain she endured when being plucked by these hungry beasts. She took her by the hand and escorted her outside. The woman kneeled to be at eye level with the little girl and asked her to identify which of the chickens had plucked at her the night before. Of course, with so many chickens being housed on the property and few having any distinguishing features that would separate them from the rest, Imelda pointed to one randomly.

Elsa took the chicken and began to pet it. "Is this the one that bit you?"

"Yes," said the little girl unconvincingly. Elsa asked Imelda to follow her into the kitchen. She took her cutting board, placed the chicken on it, and used a butcher knife to decapitate it. Imelda jumped back in fear, not fully understanding what lesson was to be achieved with such an act. Elsa looked at her with a blank stare as if there was nothing else that should be said. She handed the head to the confused little girl and walked away. Imelda never complained again and went to school with the "chickenpox" that many of the other children in the house went to school with.

The problems for Imelda did not stop with the unsanitary keeping of animals in the home. She was often repelled by Elsa's husband. She never questioned why they never referred to him as "father," "Papi," or "dad." He was always Miguel or Elsa's husband. Imelda would listen to kids speak about their "fathers," and it confused her as to the role the men in her household played. As the years went by, she would see more men enter the house. Sometimes, these men would stay for days. She never said anything to Elsa or the other girls in the house, but one night she saw a man leave another girl's room in the house. When the man left, the girl was crying, and she was nude from the waist down. Imelda was not sure what to do. In her indolent mind, the girl was crying because she did not want the man to leave.

The most challenging thing for the young girl was living in a home with so many children and never actually formulating any kind of relationship with any of them. When she saw the strange man leaving, she was not comfortable asking the girl what was wrong. In the past, she had always been told to mind her own business. She recalled having school projects in elementary school where she was asked to list her siblings and things that she liked about them. She did poorly on the assignment because she did not know the names of all of them. As she got older, she had memories of children in the house that were no longer there. *Where did they go?* She would ask herself. As slow as she may have been, she knew that her mind did not conjure up the memories of these children. She remembers seeing them, touching them, and playing with them. For some reason, Elsa always limited their interaction. While most parents encouraged family unity, there was always something distant between the people in the house.

The food portions were always small, and meals were not appetizing. It was not the traditional home environment in a Mexican American household where the mother has dinner ready at a specific time. When most other kids got home to school with the aroma of freshly made rice, beans, and *picadillo* with freshly made flour tortillas, often, she would have to settle for whatever was left. Usually, it was nothing more than a small can of Vienna sausages, which she thought were disgusting. On a good day, she would find something sweet that she could have with a cup of milk if it was not expired. In all, Imelda recognized there was something very different about her home situation, but she only knew this by comparison to how her friends lived. She did not know why the difference was there or how to articulate any domestic issues that would be of interest to Child Protective Services. Her inability to differentiate between what was socially normal and what was normal in her home contributed to her suffering. For Imelda, society had one set of rules to follow, and her household had another.

It was not until Imelda, along with some of the other children in the house, began to experience a sudden infestation of lice in their hair that educators and campus police began to want to learn more about the girl's well-being. Before that time, Imelda had never been questioned. The school district's interest in Imelda's well-being could not have come at a better time. The month before their concern, Imelda's life had taken a sinister turn.

She was slowly being groomed by Elsa and some of the older girls in the house. It was not typical behavior for someone who had mostly been alone in a full house her entire life. So, when the signs of kindness from others were displayed, Imelda felt an acceptance she had not felt in her entire life. For the first time since being born, the simple-minded girl felt as if she had a birth mother and true sisters. They combed her hair and showed her how to apply makeup to her face. They counseled her on ways to stay looking young even when she got older. It was a joyful time for Imelda, who did not understand the sudden generosity but did not have the frame of mind to question it. She was much too young, too innocent, and too slow to understand the truth. The sweet girl was not being made over for no other reason than an advertisement.

The day a new man came into the house, Imelda was not surprised. Men had come and gone from the home many times. The more unusual thing was that she was allowed to mingle this time and got to speak to the company. "What is your name?" The man asked. He was tall, thin, and muscular. Imelda thought he was frightened at first because his tattoo-covered arms made him look mean. Once she heard him express himself, her impression of him changed enough for her to let her guard down.

"My name is Imelda."

"That's a beautiful name, Imelda. Hey, you think your mom will let you go for an ice cream?"

"An ice cream? Really? Me?"

"Yeah, sure, why not?"

Imelda looked over to Elsa, who watched over the conversation with sincere interest. She had a large smile on her face. Her oversized cheeks caved in at the top with a joker's expression. She held her thumbs up to Imelda, indicating that she had something good going there. Imelda had never held the interest of a man before and was flattered by the invitation. Before that week, she was a little girl attending a middle school getting attention from her peers for her chicken bites, lice, and dirty fingernails. On this day, she had clean fingers with press-on nails, newly applied make-up, and a new dress Elsa's husband bought her. Now, she was on her way to her first date with a thirty-six-year-old man. Of course, Elsa told the little girl he was twenty and that it was fine with her. "If he marries you, Imelda, he will only be twenty-seven when you are twenty. No one is going to mind that."

"Marry? Me?"

"Why not? He is a grown man with a job and money, and you are a beautiful girl."

"But me?"

"Yes, now go on."

The man gave Elsa a large amount of money and left with Imelda. She had never had the logic to question those things, but on this day, she had the mind to. "Why did you give my mom money?"

"Oh, that is a Mexican tradition, sweetheart. I give her my money, and she knows I would never leave with you without coming back. She's just trying to protect you."

"Oh, okay."

Later in the evening, Imelda got home with something of a frightened look in her eye. None of the other children were anywhere to be seen. "What's wrong, Imelda?" Elsa asked. Imelda explained that she had a very good time. The man she knew only as Luis was very nice to her. He bought her food, and ice cream and got her a nice bracelet. He told her he loved her and thought she would make a beautiful wife. It was a night of glamour for Imelda and one she never thought she would experience in her lifetime. Toward the end of the date, her level of comfort had changed. He parked at a nice spot overlooking the Rio Grande and got comfortable. He began kissing her on her neck and lips. She liked it at first, but he started touching her between her legs and breasts. Having experienced it for the first time, she was not against how it felt. She thought that was the normal course to take on the first date. After all, she was a woman now and wore make-up to prove it.

As the sunlight began to fade and the last streak of sunlight melted into the Rio Grande River, Luis began to make his intentions clearer to the young girl. She never saw him lower his pants, but at some point, while they were kissing, he had moved her small hand onto his bare penis. Arousal was new to Imelda. She thought that the natural physiological stage she was experiencing must be love. To her, that is exactly what she was feeling, making her actions appropriate. He forced her face to his penis and demanded oral sex from her. This type of foreplay continued for over three hours until he was ready to take it a step further. The final step was to be taken in a bed. Unbeknownst to the foolish girl, Luis had paid for the service and was not going to experience it in a car. Now, the young girl was home and looking frightened at what Elsa might say to the man's idea of going inside the house for the night. To her surprise, Elsa was in favor of it. "Of course, *mija*, bring him in."

"Really? But he wants to be with me in the room."

"Well, he might be your husband, no?"

Imelda smiled at the thought of being someone's wife. The level of discomfort that she felt engaging in sexual acts with a much older man evaporated with Elsa's approval. If one's own mother sees a positive side to a certain action, likely, so will the child. That night, Imelda lost her virginity. It hurt her at first. She screamed so loud, she thought Elsa would be going in to see what happened, but she never did. In the morning, Luis was gone, and when the young girl got up for the day, she saw that her bed was covered in blood. It scared her at first, but she remembered having seen the other girl go through a similar experience. Now she understood why she was crying. Unlike her, the other girl's man may not have wanted to be her boyfriend after all. Imelda did not cry. Why would she when her man wanted to marry her someday?

Time passed, and the man continued to see Imelda regularly. Every time he would go to the house, he would give Elsa money. Imelda would assure Elsa that she did not need such security because Luis would never run away with her. "He is a good man," she would tell her. Elsa would smile without giving her an answer or acknowledging that she even received any money. Finally, the inevitable happened. The child began to show the obvious signs of pregnancy. Elsa removed her from school, telling the girl's campus that they would be moving to Nuevo Laredo, Mexico, and Imelda would continue her studies there. Instead, she kept Imelda home with no formal education for the duration of her pregnancy. As slow as she was, the little girl did ask why she never went to the doctor.

"I cannot take you to the doctor, *mija*."

"Why not? Don't I need to make sure the baby inside is going to come out?"

"Well, the truth is something I am ashamed of, but I never told you."

"What is it, mom? Please tell me."

"When I had you, we were still in Mexico. You are really still a Mexican citizen. If the doctors were to find out you are an illegal, they will inform the authorities and send you back to Mexico without your baby. You wouldn't want that would you?"

"No, mom, please don't let them do that. Luis would be so mad if we didn't start our family."

"Nothing to worry about, my angel. We're going to have the baby right here in the house, and everything is going to be just fine. You do trust me, don't you?"

Throughout the pregnancy, Luis never showed face, nor did he visit Imelda. She often asked for him, but Elsa assured the young girl that with the baby on the way, he would have to work longer hours to support a family. Not only did Imelda believe this, but she was excited to have a hardworking husband to look forward to. She could not wait to have her baby. She thought of many names for both genders, picked out colors for the room, and started looking into where she and Luis could possibly live. For Imelda, it was a dream come true. In her mind, she would return to her middle school as a mother and be the other students' and teachers' envy.

The pregnancy proved difficult. Imelda was often sick and lacking in the many vitamins that are essential while carrying a child. To Elsa's relief, the time came close enough for her to inject Imelda with what she needed to induce labor. Imelda would not know this was going to happen. She would be induced while she slept and wake to the pains of delivery. It took nearly nine hours, but Imelda gave birth and passed out. She was given a sedative by a nurse from Mexico Elsa hired to tend to the young girl. By the time the young woman would wake six hours later, she would no longer be a mother.

"Why mom, what happened?"

"I am so sorry, Imelda, but your baby died."

"Died?" she asked, crying. "But why?"

"These things happen, my angel. I've lost babies too."

"You have?"

"Oh, yes, of course. You were supposed to have a big brother before you, but it died at birth."

"And then you had me after?"

"Yes, and you know what that means?"

"No."

"It means that you too can have a baby after losing one."

Imelda smiled and was very happy to have heard this. She hugged her mother tightly and thanked her for making sure she was okay.

"But what about Luis? He's going to be sad."

"Luis is just fine. He said he would be coming to see you as soon as you [have] recovered, and things will continue with you two as it was before. I told you, everything is going to be just fine."

"He really said that?"

"Of course he did. He would be dumb not to come back for an angel. Now you try to get up and take a shower. We have to get you ready to go back to school soon."

While in the shower, Imelda heard the door open. The other kids were supposed to be in school, so the sound of the door opening scared her. She opened a small crack in the shower curtain to look out and saw Natalie and Valerie standing in the doorway.

"I'm sorry, did you need the shower?"

"So, how's your baby?" Natalie asked.

"It died."

"Was it a boy or a girl?"

"Mom said it was better not to know. She said it would make me feel more sad."

Natalie and Valerie looked at each other, and Valerie looked back at Imelda with a look of pity. "Yeah, we know. That's what she told us too." They closed the door and allowed Imelda to finish her shower and think about what they had just told her. They trusted Imelda would understand, but she didn't.

Luis continued to give Elsa money and would visit Imelda regularly. The lopsided union was love for one and sex for another. The design's authors thought it would be prudent for them to protect Imelda, so they gave her birth control under the little girl's assumption they were vitamins that would prevent her from losing her next baby. Still, evil minds are not exempt from errors, and the true nature of the relationship would slowly become undone.

When Imelda returned to her school, Elsa explained their return by stating that things did not work out in Mexico. It was not uncommon for families along the border to experience some degree of imbalance, and many of them often fought for stability from one country to the next. While the economy was a better fit on the American side, many had their relatives, friends, and true comfort in Mexico. Eventually, the need for income played a more significant role in their well-being, and they would return. So, when Imelda returned a year later, no one thought anything of it. There was no way to know that at twelve years old, she had given birth. Now thirteen years old, she was at risk of many other dangers that got her teacher's attention.

The warning signs began early during Imelda's return. She would continuously stop by the office to ask if she could use the telephone to call her father. The practice became so frequent that staff began to wonder what needs the child had that would justify having to call her father on such a regular basis. It wasn't until shortly before the Christmas break that an alert secretary overheard a sexual conversation between Imelda and whoever she was talking to. She reported what she heard to the administration. Imelda did not admit that it was Luis she was calling, but the principal knew it was not the father. While questioning Imelda, the principal could not help but notice how much the little girl would scratch what appeared to be her private area.

"Imelda, are you alright?"

"Yes, ma'am."

"Why are you scratching so much?"

"I'm just itchy."

The principal sent her to class without ever having learned that the alleged boyfriend was twenty-six years old. Throughout the next two weeks, Imelda began to be a problem with her peers and her teachers. Mrs. Cantu had also noticed how much she would scratch her vaginal region, but they had no cause to have her checked. Anytime a school gets involved with something so private, the risk of liability increases. It is a chance few districts are willing to take with good reason. Soon, Imelda began to show signs of disrespect, aggression, and sinister overconfidence she had never displayed before. When the administration restricted her phone use, her behavior became even worse.

Elsa and her husband were called numerous times. Instead of forcing Imelda to get tested, they suggested to the mother that the little girl go to a doctor for an examination. The parents always gladly agreed to do so, but they would never actually take her to the doctor. Imelda continued to scratch. The opportunity for Mrs. Cantu came with Imelda arriving at school in an aggressive fashion. Restrictions on using the phone had taken her behavior to a different level. Mandatory district involvement became necessary when Mrs. Cantu noticed the young girl scribbling suicidal ideologies on a piece of paper. This also allowed the teacher to question the "hickies."

"Is that how you feel, Imelda?"

"Sometimes."

"Why?"

Imelda would simply shrug her shoulders. Little did the district know that she was not being evasive. She did not understand why she wanted to die. Her desire to not live was a battle between what she felt in her heart was right and wrong and what she was raised to believe. Something inside her must have told her that she was in someone else's world and that somewhere in Mexico, a mother who loves her and laments her loss daily wept for her while she slept. It was during this conversation that Mrs. Cantu learned of the supposed boyfriend's age. She used the history of Imelda's lice to justify Child Protective Service's involvement in forcing her to get checked by a physician. A week later, it had been confirmed, Imelda had a sexually transmitted disease.

Now, the police found themselves in a very difficult predicament. They have proof that Imelda was involved with an older man and that Elsa, her legal guardian, had given consent. Her permission was not enough to justify the statutory rape, but it was not enough for police to prove what they suspected all along, that is, that many of the girls inside the home were being pimped out to older men.

Sent Mail > View Message

Note: This message has been marked urgent.

↩ reply | ↩↩ reply all | ↪ forward | ! report misuse

From: ▮▮▮▮▮▮▮▮▮▮▮@unitedisd.org
Sent: Thursday, ▮▮▮▮▮▮▮▮:06:04 PM CDT
To: ▮▮▮▮▮▮▮▮▮▮▮▮▮▮▮▮▮▮
Cc: ▮▮▮▮▮▮▮▮▮▮▮▮▮@unitedisd.org> ▮▮▮▮▮▮▮
▮▮▮▮▮▮▮
Subject: ▮▮▮▮▮▮▮

Delete | Move to Folder | Junk Mail | Mark as Unread | Flag | Print View | Close   Next ►

This is to inform you that student ▮▮▮▮▮▮▮▮▮ was in my office at 1:00pm and asked to call her father. I noticed she called him and hung up and began dialing other numbers. I asked her who she was calling and she said her father. I told her I gave you permission to use the phone once. I called her dad and explained that she was not feeling well but did not have a fever. He said for her to stay in school unless it was an emergency. I sent her back to class. Ms. ▮▮▮▮▮ checked her phone log and there was the number again. The number that belongs to her "boyfriend." I called her in to my office and questioned her but she denied it. I told her that she would no longer have the privilege of using the phone. I told her that from now on an school employee must dial the number and speak to whom ever she wants to call. I informed ▮▮▮▮▮▮▮ who in turn asked me to notify her mother. I called her mother and advised her. Mother stated that she has been have trouble with her behavior but thanked me. I advised her mother I would be notifying her counselor.

Nursing is compassion

School Nurse
▮▮▮▮▮▮▮▮▮▮▮
Laredo, TX ▮▮▮

Delete | Move to Folder | Junk Mail | Mark as Unread | Flag | Print View | Close   Next ►

This email is in reference to "Imelda's" behavior in school.

14

El Coco

August 2013

LAREDO, TEXAS, IS MORE OF A FASCINATING CITY THAN IT IS GIVEN
credit for. When looked at closely, it is also more beautiful than many
realize. The Rio Grande slithers its way through the edge of the state
and promotes glorious wildlife to neighboring ranches. In the right spot,
at night, one can see the dancing lights from the Mexican side of the
border illuminating the edges of International Bridge 1, showcasing the
artery that brings the sister cities together. The inviting Mexican culture
survives in the food, music, and language that defines the people who live
in the city. They are festive people who embrace the traditional Jalapeño
Festival, Washington Celebration, parades, and the annual carnival that
brings it all together. They are passionate about the Dallas Cowboys and
San Antonio Spurs and take local high school football seriously. It is a
wonderful place to be a Hispanic and an even better place to preserve a
heritage.

Yet, amid all this beauty lies the conflict that exists between those
who don't care to embrace the beauty of the city. They prefer to contribute to the stereotypes that often plague border cities, no matter how
untrue they are. Some traditions slowly became exploited and used for
something more sinister than they had been intended for. Sunday night
on San Bernardo Avenue, the cars lined up for miles cruising the strip
for no other reason than keeping a self-inflicted tradition alive. There
was nothing special about the strip. There are no large buildings, famous

clubs, or beautiful sites. Yet, it was a practice of community unification and cultural awareness. For many, this awareness included alcohol, as it did for Luis Alistar Ramirez, who had already been drinking before deciding to join the convoy of vehicles on San Bernardo Avenue.

On any other day, he would have laughed it off or taken his frustrations out by shooting the other car the finger. On this night, he was much too drugged to maintain rational faculties and lived up to his name "El Coco" by taking his distaste for having been cut off on the cruising line.

"*Orale*, What's your problem, *pendejo*?"

"*Calmate*, you don't know who you're talking to *ese*." This was the reply from the car that cut off El Coco. Not to be shown up in front of his friends, the short-tempered Luis took out a gun and pointed it toward the car. Once he saw the weapon pointed at him, the driver sped off in fear, since he was unarmed at the time. El Coco only meant to scare him off and laugh about it with his crew, but something inside him went off. He enjoyed the look of fear in the driver's eyes. He basked in the warmth of triumph he felt and the humiliation he was able to expose the driver to. So, he began to chase after the vehicle. They both swerved between the many cars in the cruising line and through streets of people crossing from one end to another. It was a dangerous predicament for anyone who was in the vicinity. It got more dangerous when El Coco began to fire some warning shots.

The chase continued through the streets of Laredo until they arrived somewhere near the downtown area. It was on Valerie Street where the vehicle being chased lost control and hit a bus bench. El Coco fired another shot—this time hitting the driver near the chest. Nearby Border Patrol, who heard the gunfire, responded, and El Coco disappeared into the night. A detailed description of El Coco's car—the sky-blue 92 Super Sport Impala—allowed the Laredo Police Department to arrest him later that night in North Laredo near Shiloh and San Dario Avenue. The stereotype that often plagues the good people of Laredo, Texas, had been fed for the night.

Luis was processed and held in a holding cell. He was scheduled to visit with the judge the next morning and was cuffed and sat in an office until they crossed the street to visit the judge. Coincidentally, he was placed in the same office where a Texas Ranger, an Ice agent, and U.I.S.D. police were going over the Elsa Cuellar case earlier in the week. Luis noticed the photo of the family that had been confiscated in the search warrant pinned against the wall. Luis stared at it with familiarity. When a Texas Ranger came in with his morning cup of coffee, he was caught by surprise at a man being held there temporarily. He noticed Luis staring at the photo and made a passing remark.

"One big happy family, huh?"

"Is that what you think it is, *ese?*" Luis said with a smirk.

"Well, if it's not, then what is it?"

"You're the cop and can't figure it out?"

"Why don't you tell me. Make me smarter. Enlighten me with your wisdom," the Texas Ranger said without being phased by Luis's aggressive nature. At that time, a group of Webb County deputies came in to escort the prisoner to the court across the street. As he was being escorted out, he looked toward the Texas Ranger.

"It's an advertisement *ese.*"

"Oh yeah, and exactly what are they supposed to be advertising?"

"The girls' man, don't you know anything?"

"And you know this because. . . ."

"Because I pay for one all the time."

"Oh yeah! Which one?"

"Look, I ain't saying no more. Just look for the girl called Imelda and let her know her boyfriend won't be around for a while, alright." It was the last thing he had time to say before being taken to see the judge.

For some time, it was these types of occurrences authorities had been depending on to get closer to Elsa Cuellar. The continuous problems the kids under Cuellar's roof were causing on their campus were allowing police to get closer. In this case, it was one of Cuellar's very own clients who had said too much under the influence of the drugs or alcohol he had used that night. As police expected, El Coco recanted his story when he was sober stating that he did not know anyone named Imelda and did not know what the police were talking about. Still, as far as the District Attorney's office was concerned, these incidents were not enough to depend on because there was the question of the reliability of the source.

It made sense to many of the different agencies involved that children were being advertised. They were aware of the many family photos being shown around, but this is exactly how Cuellar operated. She used tools that were not illegal to break the law. Simply stated, there is nothing against the law about taking a family photo.

This is one of the few group photos found with Elsa Cuellar in it. Some authorities believe family photos were used as an advertisement while others told me they did not think so because Elsa Cuellar is in the photo. However, I side with the theory that it is an advertisement. Elsa Cuellar would have to appear in the photo to show the offer is genuine and not a sting operation. This photo provokes the obvious question, who are these children and where did they come from?

The children were often made to look happy. If I was able to show you the expression of the girl in the center, her face would tell a completely different story. The question here is, are those who appear genuinely happy in this photo aware they are victims?

Photos like this were believed to be used as a way to advertise the girls to adult men. Under the disguise of a happy family picture, the girls could easily be victimized. There simply is no way to know which of these girls are victims. Some will not discuss it while others believe their relationships with older men were genuine.

15

The Pressure Mounts

ON MAY 24, 2022, AROUND THE SAME TIME I WAS SITTING DOWN TO lunch with two United Independent School officials, Salvador Ramos was entering Robb Elementary School in Uvalde, Texas with an AR Platform assault rifle. By the time we finished our lunch, nineteen children and two teachers had been killed. A grandmother was in critical conditon in the hospital and the questions surrounding school safety were being thrown in different directions at different people. This is usually the time when politicians decide to try and answer these questions rather than combat them before such horrible incidents take place. Very often, the actions of school employees serve as cries for help—cries that are often ignored.

The pressure on Elsa Cuellar was beginning to mount. While she was able to conduct herself in a way that kept her out of the reach of law enforcement, too many people associated with her were being less than model citizens allowing police to get closer to what was happening inside her home. Along with this, however, came possible threats to the U.I.S.D. campuses. It appeared that the closer the police came to Cuellar, the closer she got to the school. No one was able to understand the association between a young boy who was having behavioral issues in class and the man who claimed to be his father; however, the address listed for the child was Elsa Cuellar's Manor St. address. The existence of this man would never have been known by police if it had not been for his behavior on campus.

While two district police officers walked the campus, they noticed a car driving too fast for the school zone. The driver parked erratically and one of the officers approached him. He warned him about driving too fast on campus and the man became irate. He blamed the school for his driving because they are the ones who called him in. After all, they seemed eager to have his son picked up. The officer adamantly insisted the driver change his driving habits while driving on campus. The driver stopped listening and stormed into the campus to address the school's concerns. He signed his son out at that time. The second officer recognized the man as having also been the father who responded to a case at an elementary school where a nine-year-old boy was acting out sexual behavior, but the elementary fell under a different address zone than those who attended the middle school.

Later, the same man was called in because his son had not been in school, once again, and the father was very agitated with the police and the school. He was speaking in a loud voice, kicked the door open on his way out, and did not show signs of being interested in his son's well-being. The father did not take kindly to the consistent meetings.

Days later, an attendance clerk waited for the father again outside the campus because the son continued to be absent. This time, a second man got out of the car and approached to listen in on the conversation. Whether or not this was an intimidation tactic is not known, but the police knew that since there were no criminal records for the father, they could not keep him from driving onto campus. The connection to the address on Manor St. was never made and the issues with the six-year-old boy at the other school were not relevant to the attendance of the man's son, so there was little the officers could do. With a father who could potentially be a risk to the school with such a short temper, the officers thought it imprudent to push him on matters not related to the son's attendance. Shortly after, the son was withdrawn from the school, but even with the father having no business on the campus, the vulnerability of the students and staff became a topic worthy of discussion. It was much too easy for parents like this to come to campus in the wrong frame of mind.

From: ~~████████████ ████████@████████~~

Sent: Monday, May 20, 2013 5:07:15 PM CDT

To: ~~████████@████████~~

Cc: ~~████████@████████ ████████@████████~~

Subject: Police Action

Mr. ████████

On Thursday, May 16, 2013 I contacted your office in reference to the arrest of one of our student parents. I wanted to make sure that the safety of our students and staff was not at risk. I spoke to your dispatcher, which in turn had officer ████████ from ████████ Middle call me back. I explained to Officer ████████ that approximately 3 weeks ago Officer ████ from ████ Middle was called to our campus, because the son of this particular parent had not been picked up on time. When the parent arrived to our campus, he came in speeding in his vehicle, Officer ████ approached him advising the parent that he needed to control his speed and the parent began to get agitated with Office ████ after talking to him for awhile the parent settled down and came into the campus and signed his child out. Two weeks ago the same parent came to campus to speak to our attendance clerk, Mrs. ████████, the child of this parent had been out of school for a week, so my attendance clerk needed to discuss with the parent the absence policy. During the course of their conversation, the parent once again began to get aggressive and raised his voice, ignored what Mrs. ████████ was saying and left kicking the front door to the school. Then last week, I waited for the parent outside with his child, because once again the child had been out of school for several days, the parent walked towards us and again I explained to him that his child need to be at school on a daily basis. During the course of our conversation, I noticed a young man exit the parents car and approached us. This young man walked over to us and was listening to our conversation, keeping an eye on my actions. Once he saw that I was no threat to the parent, the young man began walking back to his car and I finished my conversation with the parent.

Office ████████ stated that since the parent has not been convicted of any crime that we are still obligated to let him onto our school premises. I am concerned because obliviously this parent is set off very easy and I want to avoid any situation that may arise. But as per Officer ████████, we will continue to work with this parent until further notice is given by your office.

Below is the article of the parent in question, thank you!

In this email, a staff member expresses concern for the school's safety. In a case like this involving so much confidentiality, staff members can run risks.

PATRICIA—LAREDO, TEXAS, 1996

Diego wasn't allowed to cross into Texas legally, so it was up to Patricia to go for both of them to get a job that paid well enough to get by. It was during one of her assignments as a cleaning lady that she first met Elsa Cuellar. She was a kind woman to her and always seemed to have helpful advice. She always looked after her baby Natalie because Diego did what he could at the meat market a block from their home in Mexico. Soon, Patricia was attending the church where Elsa preached. It was here she first heard her being referred to as *"La Pastora"* and gained an even more profound respect for her than she had before.

La Pastora was everything Patricia needed in a friend. Elsa had many children in her home that she believed were taken in because they were homeless. By the time Natalie was two years old, she had spent many of her days at Elsa's home and sometimes spent the night as she was growing close to some of the other children in the house. Having Elsa watch her daughter overnight when Patricia had to return the very next day for work was convenient. There was no reason for her to believe that she had misplaced her trust until things began to change with her second pregnancy.

"That is wonderful, Patricia. The Lord is blessing you with another little angel."

"Yes, I am very excited."

It was not out of character for Elsa to interfere in a person's life, so when she offered advice on managing the birth of her second child, it did not seem unusual to Patricia. The pastor often advised young women, especially if they were expecting a child. The counseling and advice continued well into the pregnancy, and by the time Patricia reached her ninth month, the advice began to sound redundant. One evening they spoke for hours until it was time for the young woman to go home. It was going to be a weekend; she planned to take Natalie with her, but *La Pastora's* husband Miguel approached her outside.

"Patricia, I heard the news. Congratulations."

"Thank you, Miguel."

"Listen, how about you allow us to take care of Natalie tonight?"

"Oh, thank you so much, but I would miss her too much over the weekend."

"Well, that's the thing. You see, I was hoping you'd come back tomorrow. I am throwing a surprise party for Elsa, and I could really use the help pulling it off. I am willing to pay, of course."

Patricia was delighted to take part in any celebration for Elsa. With a big smile, she agreed to do it for free. Miguel then took Natalie without asking and quickly vanished into the house. Patricia thought it was unusual behavior but dismissed it since it was not uncommon for them to watch over Natalie when she was expected the following day. When she got home, she conversed with her husband about a sudden change in heart about Elsa.

"Diego, I was thinking of maybe finding someone to watch Natalie here in Mexico while I go to work."

"Why would you do that? *La Pastora* watches her for free."

Money had always played a big factor in the household decisions Diego made. He had no choice. The economic situation he was assimilated into did not allow much room for sacrificing anything they could save. He was a hardworking man but did not have a lot of skills to attract the corporate world. His father was a merchant and was not home often. Diego did not have an education and did what he could with whatever capabilities he could offer. He hoped to learn more about becoming a butcher at the meat market and maybe have his store someday. Certainly, he did not lack ambition, but for the moment, he needed the financial resources to pay someone to watch Natalie. When the issue had nothing to do with finances, he was usually passive with Patricia.

"I know, but things feel different now. It's almost as if they want to keep Natalie, and it just feels funny."

"You know how people are with small children, Patricia. They get attached to them. She's just trying to be an aunt or something like that. Didn't you say that she adopts a bunch of children?"

"Yeah, but they don't have parents. Natalie does."

"Speaking of that, where is our daughter? You don't work tomorrow."

"I'm going back. Miguel is having a celebration for her, and he needs help with it."

"On a weekend?"

"He is willing to pay me something for my time."

"That would be okay then. Have fun."

Patricia did what she could to contribute to the home. Because of this, she did not reveal to Diego that she was already feeling close to having the baby. Physically, she was not up to assisting with the celebration; if she had brought Natalie home with her, she might have found a reason not to go. Now, she was compromised—more by having to get her daughter than helping with the party.

Before the actual celebration began, a special service was held in Elsa's honor. Her sermon captivated all in attendance as she delivered what she felt were sentiments from God himself. Some of those present cried at the very sound of her emotional tone, and others raised their arms towards the heavens from their knees. The room was filled with an overwhelming sense of devotion. It became too much for Patricia to manage in her condition.

"*Pastora!*" She cried out. She clenched her stomach and sat on the floor. Her contractions made it clear that she was going to go into labor. Elsa took great care to have Patricia sent to the hospital. "But *Pastora*, I cannot come to an American hospital. I do not have money!"

"Do not worry, my angel. I will take care of everything. You need to get to the hospital."

It was a kind gesture and a wonderful opportunity for Patricia. She was grateful for the opportunity to deliver her child in an American hospital. After a moment, they realized that it might have been a false alarm. The contractions stopped, and Patricia was not feeling ready to give birth. Suddenly, a man approached them from inside the church. He was dressed in old scrubs. They appeared to be more military scrubs than from a hospital, but he took the liberty of examining Patricia's eyes. Elsa looked concerned. "What is it? Why are you checking her?"

"Who is this?"

"This is Don Felipe. He is a midwife."

"A male midwife?"

Patricia's concern over a male midwife went ignored. Elsa continued to show concern. Felipe looked at the patient's pupils and made a recommendation. "I don't think you should take her to the hospital before she receives a vitamin shot."

"Vitamins? Won't the hospital give me what I need?"

"Oh, Patricia," Elsa intervened. "You must be careful here in America. If the doctors here have any reason to believe you have not taken care of yourself or your baby, they can take them away from you. You might even lose your right to cross back into Laredo, and you will never see your children!"

The thought of what Elsa was saying was very frightening for Patricia. She was not sure what was happening or why the process of having her child was becoming so complicated.

"Well, I don't feel like I need the hospital anymore."

"I should give you the shot anyway. You want to make sure you are good and strong for the American doctors." Felipe suggested.

Patricia reluctantly accepted the injection. She did not want to do anything that would jeopardize her having her baby in America if it was at all possible. She always had the option of having her child in Mexico but wanted something better for her children than what she had to go through. In minutes, Patricia fell asleep without having any recollection as to why she passed out so suddenly. When she woke, she had already given birth to a new baby girl. The weak mother was confused and disoriented. She could feel the change in her body and knew she was no longer carrying a child. "My baby? What happened to my baby?"

"We took her to the hospital to get checked."

"The hospital? Is my baby okay?"

"Yes, a beautiful little girl: Belinda."

"No, if I had a girl, I was naming her Valerie after my mother."

"You get your rest. We'll take care of those small details later."

Patricia was not feeling well physically, but she was also not very comfortable with the scenario. The events leading up to her daughter's birth did not feel right to her. Her abdomen was in a lot of pain, and she saw a bedspread on the floor by the corner soaked in her blood. She knew at that moment that labor was induced with the injection she received and that it was not vitamins that were put into her body. For the moment, she decided to play along as if she believed everything Elsa was doing was for her own good. She needed Elsa's help to get better. Once she felt her strength was back, she would take both Natalie and Valerie back home where they belonged.

Fortunately, she felt much better sooner than she had expected. A week had expired, and she had yet to meet her daughter. During breakfast, she casually inquired about her baby in a way that did not make her seem too concerned. "She is getting all the medical attention she needs, Patricia. You should be able to pick her up tomorrow," was Elsa's reply. Patricia had no intention of waiting for the next day. When evening came, she left Elsa's home and walked to the hospital. She was scared that her baby was sick and was not told, but when she inquired about her child, the hospital had no record of a mother with her name. Patricia was not an educated woman, but she knew Elsa Cuellar had her baby checked, having filled out the paperwork with her name. She tried to inquire, but the hospital would not release information on other patients. After all, how could they know the real mother was standing before them? Patricia's fear had transformed into anger. She walked almost three miles to get to the hospital, and her baby was probably already at home she had just left.

It was late when she made it back home. She woke Elsa up by pounding on the door. She knew it took the pastor time to roll out of bed and gave her a few minutes. She finally made her way to the door and answered it unalarmed: "Sister, it is very late. Is everything okay?"

"I am not your sister, and I want to know where my baby is right now!"

"You're tired, Patricia. You are also medicated. This is why you do not recall giving me the rights to her. Go to the hospital and check. Everything is in order."

"I did no such thing. If you are a woman of God, how can you expect the Lord to believe such a lie? I also went to the hospital, and when I tried to show my I.D., I saw everything I had inside my purse was missing. I know you took it with all my documents to cross back; I want them back!"

Elsa approached the scared woman and got face-to-face with her.

"I did no such thing, and if you start spreading those kinds of rumors, I will make sure you never see your daughters again. Do not forget I am also a lawyer. I have many political connections. I also have connections that are not so political. Go home! You are no longer welcome here. I will call the police, and without your papers, you will be deported. Do you know what happens when you get arrested? They will never allow you back in this country."

"There is no reason for me to get arrested."

"You are trespassing, and I asked you to leave."

Patricia was in complete shock, but she was also afraid that Elsa was not lying. She was not well versed in immigration law, but she knew getting arrested would not serve her well. She did leave as Elsa asked, but she did not return right away. She returned to the hospital and spoke to a nurse about what had happened. The nurse was kind and attentive, but she had never managed a case like this. She broke the rules for Patricia and checked on Elsa Cuellar's involvement with her daughter.

"*Señora*, I am so sorry, but there is only one Elsa Cuellar, and the baby she brought in for observation after being delivered in a home was named Belinda."

"That is my baby nurse. She renamed my own daughter."

"I don't know what to say. All the papers seem to be in order. We have a birth certificate and everything here for a Belinda Cuellar."

Patricia began to cry uncontrollably. The nurse was so touched by the emotional cry that she asked her to wait. A police officer who was taking a statement on an assault was leaving the hospital, and the nurse stopped him for advice.

"I've seen this many times before, lady. It doesn't surprise me."

"Babies are stolen all the time here?"

"Do you really believe that? You said all the paperwork is in place, right?"

"Well, yes."

"I must have had a million cases of mothers who give up their baby for adoption and then come to regret it. Tell her it's a civil case now—not criminal. She just has to get an attorney and go through the process like everyone else."

When Patricia got the news from the nurse, she was deflated. She almost fainted and dropped to her knees. The hospital treated her and gave her some food. She was released early that morning, and the defeated woman returned home to her husband without either of her daughters.

IS ELSA CUELLAR REPEATING HISTORY?

Patricia's case is not unique to how Cuellar operated. The creation of an illusion was her talent, and she did not allow it to go to waste. She took advantage of the classical American perspective of what slavery is and made sure that her treatment of people did not meet that definition even if what she was doing constituted slavery by contemporary standards. She knew well that when Americans thought of slavery, they instantly thought of chains, forced manual labor, and African Americans. Few in society have learned that modern-day slavery comes in a much different way, but this does not mean that it is not real. Kevin Bales and Ron Soodalter recognized this in their book *The Slave Next Door.* They write: "Where the law sanctioned slavery in the 1800s, today it's illegal. Where antebellum masters took pride in the ownership of slaves as a sign of status, today's human traffickers and slaveholders keep slaves hidden, making it all the more difficult to locate victims and punish offenders. Where the slaves in America were once primarily African and African American, today we have 'equal opportunity' slavery; modern-day slaves come in all races, all types, and all ethnicities" (6).

Patricia's case serves as an example of how some social problems can get lost by the impact that is created by other issues in society. For example, issues of teen pregnancy have increased the number of young girls who decide to give up their child only to regret it later. With this as an increasing problem, Patricia's case was classified as having fallen into that same category of women who regretted giving up their child. It was as if Cuellar knew that today's problems in society would allow her to carry out her operation undetected. If she did not know, she was one of the most fortunate criminals ever to commit an international crime. When the skill of creating false documentation is added to this mix, Cuellar's probability of being caught decreases.

One ICE agent I had the pleasure of interviewing says that Cuellar was not as smart as people thought and that she had implemented strategies that had never been done before, but this is not necessarily true. In the early 1900s, thousands of foreign-born women were being exploited to come to the United States and work. Many of these women were forced into prostitution. Specifically, the city of San Francisco had an influx of Asian women being brought into American soil illegally and forced into the sex labor society. Initially, these women were promised a good living in the United States and much like Cuellar, fake contracts and paperwork were created to finalize their new status in American society. Most of these contracts had stipulations that would allow them to purchase back their freedom, but these conditions made it impossible for them to do this. In most cases, and much like Cuellar's Mexican victims, the Asian women did not know English well enough to read or understand the contracts being presented to them. Another parallel to how Cuellar ran her underground business was how the social problems tend to feed off one another creating the illusion that one person's problems are the same as everyone else's. Early in the twentieth century, there was a significant rise in prostitution in the San Francisco area that camouflaged those women doing it for a living from those who were trafficked illegally from another country. In most cases, it would not be known if an Asian woman was trafficked until they died under conditions suggesting enslavement.

Historically, the law has failed to successfully identify victims of trafficking as much as they do today. It is not possible to legislate what one can see, for instance, you cannot pass a law making it illegal to not have the ability to identify a trafficked person. In 1910, James R. Mann passed the White Slave Traffic Act. Sadly, this law was mostly used by authorities to enforce racist sentiments and establishments were being raided throughout the country to deport new immigrants working as prostitutes (11). This was a problem for two reasons: First, while the workers were being deported, the perpetrators who brought them to America illegally never saw a day in court. Secondly, the American women who were enslaved did not have the benefit of being rescued through deportation and remained slave sex workers under brutal conditions. Even with the acknowledgment that human trafficking would not be tolerated and the passing of new laws, everything seemed to fall in place perfectly for traffickers just as it did for Cuellar over one hundred years later.

16

The House on Kearny

March 2013, Laredo, Texas

DISTRICT POLICE WERE SENT TO AN ELEMENTARY SCHOOL THE MORN-
ing of March 5, 2013. Juanita Mendez was sitting in the lounge at the
nurse's office, waiting to be tended to. It looked as if her hair had been
washed there in school. Investigator Alexander Rodriguez, who was
called, was not sure why they needed him initially until the school's
assistant principal emerged. Myra Santos had been the vice principal for
the district for quite some time, but the investigator had no occasion to
work with her until now.

"Officer?"

"Yes," he responded, looking over to the little girl. "Did she shower
here or something?"

Mrs. Santos motioned to him to follow her into her office. "Juanita
had a severe case of lice. We had to wash her hair repeatedly with medication. Her hair was also full of dry mayonnaise."

"Mayonnaise?"

"Yeah, supposedly her mother told her it kills lice, and it was being
used on her head."

"What do the lice do—overeat and die of obesity?" The nurse
laughed. "I don't know, but you know how these home remedies surface
every now and then."

"So, what am I doing here? I don't normally handle lice cases."

"Well, come here." Mrs. Santos had the investigator look at the child's student file. "This is what I came across when I tried to call the mother."

The investigator leaned over the file and saw the address as being on Kearny Street, which was new to him. However, he did notice the mother's name: Elsa Cuellar Alvarado. He had not seen Alvarado's name too often, but it was the photo of the same woman and the name of the same husband. Investigator Rodriguez became frustrated with the case and became more so after hearing the rest of what Mrs. Santos had to say. "That's not it."

"You mean there's more?"

"She says that her older brother hits her a lot. She was complaining about an injury to her backside."

"How old is the brother?"

"According to the information I have, he's 30."

"That's a pretty big age discrepancy."

"Yeah, and when I asked Juanita to let me look at her injury, it looked more like something else."

"Sexual abuse?"

"It looks like it, but there's more."

"Jesus, Mrs. Santos, how much of this can we take?"

"It is not so much an injury as it is a blister."

"My God! She has a sexually transmitted disease?"

"It looks like it."

"Well, call CPS, will you? I'll have an officer do the report and wait for them. I'll be back this afternoon."

"Okay."

The officer had reached a point in the Cuellar case where he simply could not tolerate one more child being hurt. The American justice system does what it can to remain faithful to the Constitution, but many of the U.I.S.D. officers involved found it relatively lenient, at times, when cases involving children are concerned. There is too much required for search warrants and arrest warrants. The District Attorney's office wants a certain amount of convincing evidence, and when they felt they found what was needed, it just was not convincing enough. Juanita was the last child he wanted to hear about without learning the truth. He went to the address on Kearny Street, which listed Elsa Cuellar as a relative and emergency contact information. He wanted to drop by unannounced to avoid her interacting with Elsa before he spoke to her. Contacting Elsa personally would have been a pointless approach. She was much too sinister to cooperate or speak a word of truth.

The house on Kearny Street was poorly kept. The yard was dirty without a single blade of grass to add color. A few chickens were loose in the yard, but nothing like what Elsa Cuellar housed in her home. He did not expect to get an answer, but Yolanda Esparza came to the door holding a baby. "Yes."

"Yolanda, I'm with the school district police. I'm here to talk to you about Elsa Cuellar. She has you down as an emergency contact and a relative, so we can save a lot of time by you skipping the part when you deny knowing her."

The woman seemed passive. She did not deny knowing Elsa Cuellar. She set the baby down on what appeared to be a homemade playpen and pulled out a cigarette.

"Are you really going to smoke that in front of the kids? They'll have cancer before they're in school."

Yolanda put the cigarette behind her ear and avoided eye contact as if she was embarrassed. The officer decided to speak to her nicely. She seemed more like a victim than she did a conspirator to him. "Look, Yolanda, I understand you might be close to Elsa, but I need something here. Children are being hurt in ways I can't discuss with you right now. If you know something and don't cooperate, you can be just as liable. I can help you if you help me."

"I don't know what to tell you. What do you want?"

"For starters, and this is just for me really, what in hell is the deal with all these chickens? Do you guys want to open a Popeye's or something?"

"They have many children to feed, so we do cook some of them, and get eggs from others."

"What about the fighting roosters? They don't lay eggs."

"Elsa fights them sometimes."

"At her house?"

"Yes."

"Gambling?"

"Yes."

"Are they violent with the kids?"

"Sometimes. The kids think that they are all chickens, and they can play with them the same. But the ones used for fighting bite them."

"Doesn't Elsa put them away for the kid's sake?"

"No, she actually thinks it's funny."

The officer got up and walked around the place. He could hear cartoons in the other room, so he was sure there were more children in the house. He wanted to be careful as to how he approached Yolanda. He did not want to lose her. "I like chickens. I've been wanting to buy some small chicks, but they've been hard to find. Maybe you can help me sometime."

"Yeah, sure."

Yolanda removed the cigarette from her ear and placed it in her mouth without lighting it. She was still trying to avoid eye contact but was beginning to look more comfortable. "I don't want to hurt you or your children, Yolanda. I just want to know what I'm dealing with. Elsa is far too old to have babies in her house, and unless she had her first child when she was twelve, she is too young to be the mother of those adults in her house. What's going on?" Yolanda started to cry.

"I don't know, officer, I really don't know. I never wanted anyone to get hurt. I just needed money and to become a citizen, and Elsa said she could help, that's all. She brings me, kids, to babysit, and that's it."

"Yolanda, if that was it, you wouldn't be crying."

"I thought she wanted to help kids and their mothers. I don't think she meant to break any laws. At least it started that way."

The officer was getting a glimpse of the power Elsa Cuellar had on the people whose lives she entered. Nothing in *La Pastora*'s history suggests she ever wanted to do anything according to the law. There was too much evidence to make the argument that anything happening to the children in her custody was intentional. "Why so many children, Yolanda? It is so difficult to feed them and to take care of them."

"The money, sir."

"Money? You mean she gets welfare for them?"

"Welfare is just part of it."

"Go on."

"She has kids in Mexico too. She trains them to work as prostitutes."

"I guess she knew to keep that business on the other side of the border, hu?"

"Officer, you didn't hear this from me, did you?"

"No, that's fine. I can't do much about what she does in Mexico."

The officer made his way to the door. He didn't think he was going to get much more but certainly got enough. He turned to the sound of small steps running out of the back room. He was surprised to see little Bobby Diaz there. "Hi, sir."

"Bobby, what are you doing here?"

"Elsa had some business in Mexico, so I'm watching him during his suspension," Yolanda answered. "You two know each other?"

"Yeah, I was there for the complaint they made against him when he threatened the teacher."

"The counselor will be here to see him later today."

"Well, that's good. I hope everything goes well."

"I know why you're here," Bobby continued. "You're here about the little boy, right?"

"What, little boy?"

"The one mommy stabbed and threw away in the trash."

"What? Bobby, come here. What are you talking about?"

"The boy who got mommy mad for not behaving. She stabbed him and threw him away."

"Where did this happen?"

"At Nena's ranch."

"Bobby, that's enough. Go to the other room and watch television," Yolanda said.

"Who is Nena?"

"A friend of Elsa's."

"She has a ranch?"

"Yeah, in Mexico."

Another story to add to Elsa's file, yet an additional case law enforcement in Laredo had no jurisdiction over. The rage within him was mounting with everything new he learned about Elsa Cuellar. Almost everyone she encountered became her victim.

"Yolanda, let me ask you something before I go?"

"Okay."

"Is Elsa your real aunt?"

Yolanda began to cry again. She may not have admitted it, but the officer could detect a sense of relief in her to be able to remove all this information from her chest. It was therapeutic, and now was a good time to express herself without any fears. "I don't know, officer. For a long time, she made me believe she was my mother, but then changed her story."

"Why would she do that?"

"I found out she could not be a natural mother to no one."

"Why is that?"

"Don't you know?"

"What?"

"She has no uterus. It was removed when she was a young girl."

Yolanda finally provided the officer with something concrete. There was no way that Elsa Cuellar could be a biological mother to any of the children that were living under her roof. In fact, she could not have been a biological mother to anyone in the world.

The Interrogation

HAVING WHAT AUTHORITIES NEEDED TO SECURE A SEARCH AND ARREST warrant did not necessarily mean they had enough for a conviction. Everyone involved in the case knew that extracting any kind of meaningful information from the woman known as *La Pastora* and her husband was not going to be an easy task. Elsa always appeared to be ahead of law enforcement in one way or another. Upon hearing that the school district was getting suspicious about Imelda's behavior, Elsa filed a formal complaint with the Laredo Police Department, stating that older men had possibly raped Imelda. To protect these men, she never gave a name claiming not to know who they were. It did not help that Imelda claimed to have consented to sex with more than one of these men. Whether Elsa coached her to say this was never known, and although a minor cannot consent to sexual conduct, it makes a rape case against assailants with no name very difficult. Her guard was already up from a conversation she had with administrators and Investigator Alexander Rodriguez the month before the search warrant. She now feared she had already said too much.

APRIL 2013—ONE MONTH BEFORE THE ARREST

The portly woman made her way through the double doors. She made it seem as if walking was difficult, but Investigator Rodriguez did not believe her. Elsa had a profound skill at making people believe something that was not real. For Rodriguez, all she was doing was making it appear as if having brought her in was an inconvenience to her health. Her face was stale and with a lack of emotion. She did not appear worried but did not seem happy. An expression of surprise would soon invade the lines on her face and change her pulse when she learned why she was there. Previously, she was told they needed to have a parent conference for Bobby Diaz, but they did not tell her for what. Elsa made it clear that she did not speak English, but most of the population in Laredo, Texas, speaks Spanish, so this would not be an obstacle to preventing the meeting. Most likely, she did speak English; Cuellar had too many contacts to deal with deeper into the United States.

The school principal, Investigator Rodriguez, and the Director of Student Admissions were all present. The principal began the meeting cordially in Elsa's preferred language. "Mrs. Cuellar, thank you for being here today, but it's important that we meet to clarify some issues with your son Bobby."

"I've always had behavior problems with Bobby."

"His behavior is not the cause for this meeting." The principal looked over to Rodriguez as if she did not care to pursue the interrogation's legal aspect. It was always difficult for school districts to get into litigations that could cause problems. The principal knew she had no choice but to continue.

"We had some questions about the documents used to register Bobby in school."

"What kind of questions?"

"We have two separate birth certificates for him and wondered which is the correct one."

"They are both correct, ma'am. My son has dual citizenship."

The principal looked over to Rodriguez, who quickly interjected. "Mrs. Cuellar, I am sorry, but a country does not issue you a birth certificate if you were not born there. The documentation to certify dual citizenship is something else."

"They must have made a mistake." she said softly. Alexander looked back at the principal. Everyone in the room knew this was not a possible mistake to make. "We had another concern as well, Mrs. Cuellar," the director added. "We looked into the paperwork for Bobby's twin brother. Their place of birth was listed as two different places."

"They made a mistake there too."

"Was the different years a mistake as well, Mrs. Cuellar?"

"Yes."

"So where were both boys born, here or in Mexico?" The principal rejoined.

"Here, they were both born here in Texas the Rio Grande City."

"Okay, Mrs. Cuellar," Alexander was losing patience. "We're going to need to verify the documents with vital statistics in Rio Grande City. Understand that this is for the children's safety."

Elsa appeared to be bothered by this last statement. She knew that vital statistics would have no record of these children being born in Rio Grande City. She felt the need to resort to extreme measures and burst out crying. No one in the group asked her why she was crying; everyone present knew the stress of keeping up with so many lies had overwhelmed her. The one thing they did not see coming was the next claim she would make in her defense.

"Okay, officer, okay. The documents are fake."

"I know," Alexander said.

"The truth is that I have raised these children as my own, but they are not mine."

"Whose are they, Elsa?" Alexander had grown tired of being formal with the woman. He hoped addressing her by her first name would provoke the truth out of her. Instead, she created her version of the truth.

"The children are a result of my husband's infidelity. I agreed to raise them as my own. I swore to take this secret to the grave with me. Only my attorney knows the truth." Those in attendance thought it was unusual for her to blurt out having an attorney like that. It was her passive-aggressive way of reminding the school that she had one. To the members at the interview, it did not mean much, but Investigator Rodriguez knew exactly where her threat was going.

He had learned through one of the Texas Rangers that Elsa's attorney was Cuate Talamantes. He was a notorious defense attorney whose reputation was earned mostly by defending criminal organizations. The extent he would go through to win a case was limitless, and Rodriguez knew he was the perfect attorney for Elsa to have.

"Do you mean to tell me," the principal continued, "that none of the women your husband has been unfaithful with have wanted their children for themselves?"

"Yes, he finds his women in Mexico. Most will agree to have their child raised in America."

"So, they just give up their child like that?"

"Yes, you have no idea. Someone recently gave me a baby because they did not want to take care of it. It is a sickly child, and they did not want to bother raising it."

"So, they just gave it to you?"

"Yes."

The investigator had no proof, but he felt Elsa was trying to explain away a baby in the house in case Imelda revealed too much about giving birth. She quickly accused the intellectually challenged girl of having a wild imagination. It did not work! No one gives up children so easily and in those numbers. The warrants for arrest and search would not be difficult to obtain.

Now, Elsa was being held while regretting what she had already divulged. There was no way to take back what she had already said at the conference, but she knew better than to make the same mistake. She was very quiet and did not answer anyone who spoke to her. She waited silently for her bail bond hearing. Once they were there, her attorney Talamantes was shocked to have learned that the prosecution was asking for a one-million-dollar bond. He was even more surprised by how much Investigator Alexander Rodriguez knew about the case at the bond hearing.

"Mr. Rodriguez, how long have you been with the district police?"

"Three years or so."

"And with that experience, do you feel qualified as an investigator?"

"My experience is not with the district, sir. It's with the twenty years I served with the Laredo Police Department. Most of those years were as an investigator."

Investigator Rodriguez could tell that by the look in Talamante's eyes, he had not done his research on the officer. If he had, he would not have taken his questioning in that direction. Still, he continued the attack.

"And with that experience Investigator Rodriguez, what makes you believe my client can afford a one-million-dollar bond?"

"Well, she has numerous bank accounts here in Texas, Tennessee, Peru, and Mexico. Oh, and she made millions selling babies!" he blurted out sarcastically. He expected an objection, but Talamantes held his ground.

"And how do you know that Mr. Rodriguez?"

"I believe the law stipulates that as an investigator, I don't have to reveal my source, Mr. Talamantes. I only have to reveal what I know."

The annoyed attorney looked back at the honorable Judge Joe Lopez.

"He's right about that," he said.

After a few more routine questions, the slick attorney found it more beneficial to get Rodriguez off the stand. In the end, the bail request stood, and Elsa Cuellar would have to dig very deep to get out of jail on bail. The team was very confident she would remain in jail until it was time for the trial. In the meantime, Investigator Rodriguez needed to collect more evidence. This would prove to be a difficult task. Even if he had found it, a twist in the case would derail everything law enforcement had worked for.

The job of any agency working toward preventing human trafficking can be a very difficult task. The reason for this is that there is a tendency for neither those suspected of trafficking nor the victims to avoid any cooperation with authorities. In the case of Cuellar's victims, they did not want to lose the home environment that had been so meticulously provided for them. While in America, those standards are not considered sanitary and abusive, the conditions in Mexico remain far worse. Because of this, law enforcement usually must rely on less reliable sources in their investigation. With increasing advancements, technology has allowed criminals to communicate with one another without being caught or without their lines being tapped. For now, the best strategy for the fight against trafficking is looking in the right place. So much of human trafficking–related strategies tend to focus only on the sex trade, but thousands of people are being trafficked for other reasons. For Cuellar, there was sex involved, but the true profit came in the babies the victims would bring into the world.

18

Revisiting a Murder Case

AFTER THE BAIL BOND HEARING, INVESTIGATOR RODRIGUEZ RETURNED to his office to learn that two women were waiting for him. He figured they were the same two women who had been calling him and leaving messages. It was not like him forcing people to go see him physically, but he had been so consumed by Elsa's case that he had not returned their call. In recent days, the last thing on his mind was parents complaining that their kids were being bullied. As it turned out, that is not what they were there for at all.

The woman appeared to look worried and tired. She carried herself in a manner that told Rodriguez she was a much more stress-free woman at one point. Something had taken a toll on her, and she somehow believed the officer could help with that. The other woman was quieter and just stood a step behind. It wasn't cold outside, but she wore a sweater. She looked down to the floor as the other woman spoke. It was as if she expected to get scolded.

"What can I do for you?"

"I read about the Elsa Cuellar case in the local paper."

"I'm sorry, ma'am, but I can't tell you anything more than what you read."

Investigator Rodriguez sat down to begin some paperwork, hoping to fend off all those curious about the case. It was not going to be as easy with the media, but what little they knew had made the local news.

"That's not why we're here."

"Filing a complaint?"

"No, sir, I want my son back."

"Your son?" Suddenly Rodriguez became very interested.

"I'm Jennifer Ortega. The boy you know as Bobby Diaz is my son. The girls you know as Natalie and Valerie are her daughters. She's Patricia Flores."

Rodriguez rose slowly from his chair. He instantly had two witnesses that could attest to the crimes Elsa Cuellar had committed. With testimony from them, much of what would have previously sounded like speculation could be proven. The investigator had a difficult time containing the joy and excitement that boiled within him. He started asking questions the defense attorney might ask them, just to see what their answers sounded like.

"Jennifer, why are you just now coming forward?"

"Neither of us could legally cross until recently." Patricia finally joined in the conversation. "Even if we could, there were always shady characters following us in Mexico. We never knew for sure, but we felt Elsa had sent them. It was intimidation, I guess, we don't know, but we just didn't have enough to fight for our kids. She has all the documentation saying the kids are hers."

"Well, her documentation isn't worth a shit anymore."

"How are our children, Mr. Rodriguez?"

"Look, I can't discuss the kids just yet. I know you're anxious, but I don't want to do anything that would jeopardize our case against this 'Pastora.' Let me take your statements for now and assure you that Child Protective Services is involved. Hopefully, you guys will be reunited soon."

It was a great feeling having the two women there. Still, Rodriguez was uneasy. He had been in law enforcement for a long time and was aware of the risks that her punishment could be minimal. At the time, the only thing that would stick was fraudulent documents. Depending on the judge and Talamante's underground pull, she could get off with simple deportation without having to spend one single night in prison. The prostitution case was even more challenging to prove. So many of these girls were brainwashed into thinking these older men were legitimate boyfriends. It was a case much too easy for Elsa to claim innocence for. Luis "El Coco" was very fortunate that his shooting victim did not die, but he was still sent to prison for aggravated assault with a deadly weapon. His testimony for a jury would be useless even if he was convinced to testify. First, Luis would never testify without getting a deal. His testimony would only be good if he was willing to acknowledge having sex with a child. Because this could incur additional charges and a longer sentence, this was not likely to happen. For an offense of that magnitude, the District Attorney is not likely to give him a deal. If he did, the defense would poke at the idea that he only testified against Elsa to get that deal. These are the kinds of things that sit in a juror's mind.

Rodriguez did not have enough for a child abuse case either. There was much abuse taking place; the problem was that it was being initiated so subtly that Child Protective Service had not been able to justify removing the children. It is always a sensitive area to remove children from their parents. No matter how many immoral acts had been committed against these minor victims, fact of the matter was that they had been raised to believe in loyalty to Elsa, and explaining the immoral nature of the acts would do little to convince the victims they had been wronged. To these innocent minds, she was not the monster that law enforcement officials said she was. She was their mother, and they would lie for her if they had to.

So, after pondering over the case for a while, Investigator Rodriguez felt a solid thing to pursue in hopes of sealing *La Pastora*'s fate was to revisit the murder case of the fourteen-year-old boy Juan Valentine Alonzo. Everyone in law enforcement knew that she conspired in some way in that child's death, but no one knew the extent of her involvement nor was there any strenuous effort to find out the nature of her involvement. Rodriguez's first step was to reach out to his friends with the Laredo Police Department. The one thing that could bring old friends together in Laredo, Texas, was a cookout. Fajitas, sausage, barbecued chicken quarters, ribs, and the coldest beers in South Texas made for a wonderful reunion at Rodriguez's ranch. Among those invited was Marcos Ayala, the lead investigator in Juan Valencia's case.

Marcos was a respected veteran of the Laredo Police Department. He and Rodriguez were close friends before having retired. Marcos was fully retired, now living out his days fishing and watching cases on the

Discovery Channel instead of investigating them himself. It was a great time they were having that night. So fun; in fact, Rodriguez almost forgot what he wanted to talk to him about in the first place. They had the additional entertainment of watching his dog Bo run around with the wildlife to deflect work-related talk. He wanted to make sure the dog was completely trained before taking him to the ranch. Bo's previous visit to the ranch found him in an altercation with Gus's horses. Rodriguez had to fire shots in the air to separate them. Now Bo sat loyally next to his owner, watching the horses on the other end. Occasionally, they would throw dirty looks at each other, but they had become more civilized over time, and the night was peaceful.

"So, Marcos, I wanted to ask you about Juan's murder. Do you remember that from some years ago?"

"Yeah, I believe so – 1998, wasn't it?"

"Sometime around there."

"Crazy case, what did ya want to know?"

"Everything. I want to know how Elsa Cuellar was tied into this."

"Oh, her? Yeah, well, it got a little complicated, but yeah, I'll tell you what I remember."

Marcos Ayala's Story: Laredo, Texas, June 18, 1998

The day had been long for Detective Ayala, and it was only noon. It was a Thursday, and he had it in mind to take the rest of the day off and the entire day Friday to play a few rounds of golf and put some steaks on the grill. Most detectives will agree that making plans during a missing child investigation is not a good idea. Fourteen-year-old Juan Valencia Ramirez was reported missing from his home on West Bustamante Street on June 1. Neighbors alleged he was taken at gunpoint by two other young men. It was always difficult for investigators to understand a motive for kidnapping a boy that age. It was for this matter that on his way out the door, Marcus got a call from Pedro Martinez Delgado—chief of police with the Nuevo Laredo Police Department in Mexico.

"Good afternoon, chief."

"Neighbor, how are things in the United States?"

"Ah, well, our president is getting into a lot of trouble. It seems he's quite the lady's man."

"I saw that. We're trying to keep our president from making deals with drug cartels, and you guys are worried about your president because he got a blow job."

"Maybe we're just jealous, chief. You got something for me?"

"Yeah, I have two men you might want to talk to here. They're the ones who put a gun to your kid and took him on a ride."

"You're kidding?"

"Not at all. They seem to have quite a bit of information and thought you might want to talk to them."

"You bet I do. Is the kid still alive?"

"From what I can tell, yes, but maybe you should come talk to them."

"Let me get clearance to cross into your pathetic country, and I'll be there," Ayala joked. The chief broke out laughing. "Okay, we'll be here."

Marcos Ayala, two other investigators, and an FBI agent all crossed International Bridge 1 to meet with the two boys. When they arrived, Chief Delgado took them to the office where they were being held. Mexico was a different country with a different set of rules, and Marcos wanted to take advantage of that. They did not have any more space for separate interrogations in the small office, so the pair had to be questioned together. The two men were Vicente Guerra and Rogelio Tobias. Both were in their early twenties, and neither appeared to have a friend in the world besides each other. Of the two, Vicente seemed to be the more loquacious, so Ayala started with him in Spanish.

"Where you guys from?"

"Matamoros, sir."

"How old are you guys?"

"Twenty-four."

"Are you guys okay? Can we get you some water or some food?"

Their eyes lit up as if they had not eaten in months. They jumped at the opportunity.

"Food? Really?"

"Sure," the FBI agent said. "Delgado, can we get something for these kids to eat?"

"Sure, let me send the secretary to bring them something. You, men, want anything?"

"We're good," Ayala answered for everyone. "I need to know something very important, Vicente, and I need to know the truth. We didn't come here to get jerked around, so just give it to me straight. Is the boy still alive?"

"Yeah, I mean yes, he's tied up at the ranch."

"Where? Here or on the American side in Laredo?"

"On your side."

"Tell us what happened."

Vicente looked over to Rogelio Tobias, who shrugged his shoulders at him as if to say: *it's up to you if you want to tell them.* Marcos thought he would place them at ease. "Look, I can't just take you back to the United States. It doesn't work that way. You're safe. I just want to know what happened and why you took Juan. We're just trying to understand so we can return him back to his family. His mother is awfully worried."

Vicente paused for a while and finally began to talk.

"Tobias and I were just hanging out back home in Matamoros. We like to keep the word out that we are free for jobs."

"What kind of jobs?"

"Sir, we live in Mexico—any kind of job. We just want to eat, you know? I tried getting normal jobs, but there's no money in them. I've tried finding something in America and crossed over a few times, but it's not that easy. So, when we were offered the job to go pick up Juan for $10,000 pesos, we thought it was a great opportunity."

"Who offered you the job?"

"I don't know his name. Everyone just calls him *Cuerno*."

"Why? Does he have horns or what?"

"Yeah," Vicente said softly. "Like the devil," he added.

"Alright, I get it. What happened next?"

"One of *Cuerno*'s drug runners, 'El Popo' in Laredo, kept $35,000 of his money. He hired us to go collect it. If he didn't have it, we were supposed to bring him to *Cuerno*. If he wasn't there, we were asked to bring one of his family members as ransom until he paid it."

"Who is this Elsa Cuellar lady? She's listed on the report, but I don't have anything on her."

"Elsa?" Vicente looked over to Rogelio. It was obvious they were very afraid of her. Marcos did not want to lose the momentum of the interrogation. Luckily, the food arrived, and this opened the door to a comforting suggestion. "Well, look, the food is here. Why don't you tell me all about that while you guys eat?" Vicente appeared to like that idea.

Cuerno was a broad-shouldered man. His chest stuck out like a bull, and his knuckles looked like hairy pool balls. He was intimidating in his appearance but also very convincing in his speech. This made him very useful on the streets. He had two cards in his deck. He could convince one to work for him by way of physical intimidation or by his persuasive manner. The opportunities he presented always painted a picture of great wealth and future promotion. Vicente and Rogelio were the perfect pair for him. They were vulnerable, not all that intelligent, and hungry.

For 10,000 pesos (under $500), the two agreed to kidnap "El Popo" or a family member until the debt was paid. He was given two kilos of cocaine to sell, but its profit was never seen. Instead, he used cocaine as payment on the streets and traded it for sex with addicted prostitutes, got a motorcycle, and of course, used some for himself. It was a dangerous gamble that would seal his fate. The two men were given the address on West Bustamante Street in Laredo, Texas, and were taken across to the American side by an experienced *Coyote*. They first had the dubious task of getting to Nuevo Laredo from Matamoros, which was about a three-hour drive. Once there, they would cross directly into Laredo. It would not take long to get directions to the street, but they first had to complete a different task. They were asked to contact Elsa Cuellar. They did not know at that time why they would be contacting her, but they knew better than to question Cuerno's instructions.

Two days before the abduction, the two men were picked up by Elsa at the bridge. Vicente had worked with Elsa before in Matamoros. He would do small jobs for her, such as delivering drugs as payments, picking up money, and escorting new clients through Matamoros. Of course, not all her clients were willing participants. Many were young girls from the United States being taken to the red-light district in Matamoros. Vicente knew much more than he wanted about Elsa Cuellar, but that was not his apprehension about seeing her again. His reluctance came from a different experience he had with the woman most called *La Pastora*.

He was twenty-one when Elsa first started making small advances. She eventually took him as what most would consider a sex slave. This is not something most men complained about, and "no" was certainly not something Elsa was used to hearing. Without warning, Vicente was having sex with Elsa under outlandish circumstances. To him, she was what would qualify as a "freak" in bed. She sometimes involved other men and other times women. This would not be an experience to complain about to the average twenty-one-year-old male, but the situation was not always appealing. When other women were involved, they were not always attractive and, at times, grotesque. A bigger problem was when she would involve other men. He was once one of three men she asked to have sex with her at the same time. She had them play a game to see if they could all fit their penises in her mouth at the same time. Of course, this action could not be accomplished without Vicente's own penis having to touch the other men's parts. This was his last experience with her, and although he was aware of her association with Cuerno, they never had to work together through his orders. He had no choice but to meet with her as he was told. If he wanted details, he would have to ask for them later.

The reason why Vicente and Rogelio were hired would be known very quickly. Elsa drove them to a ranch she had just outside Laredo. She never directly implicated herself in Cuerno's plan, but she began to explain certain features of the ranch, blind spots, possible Border Patrol crossings, and what area had the softest dirt to dig. Vicente had been to this ranch before, in fact, some of his sexual exploits with Elsa were at that same ranch. She had never been so descriptive of her property before this time. It became obvious to both men that this is where their kidnapped victim was going to be held. Once the tour was over, Elsa took both men into the ranch house to rest for the night and to have sex with both of them at the same time. Vicente had predicted that was how the night would end.

Two days later, on June 1, 1998, the two men borrowed a vehicle from Elsa and made their way to their destination. It was not difficult to find. The area was open, and the lot was easy to detect. It was a mobile home in need of repair. At first, they thought it was vacant, but they could see movement inside. The two men looked around to make sure no one was watching. It was 6:30 p.m., so it was not very dark yet. Rogelio knocked on the door. A young fourteen-year-old boy answered.

"Are you El Popo?"

"No, that's my *carnal*, but he ain't here right now."

"When is he coming back?"

"I don't know. He's been gone a couple of days."

That is all the men needed to hear. In keeping with Cuerno's orders, the two men took out the weapons given to them and placed the barrel on the boy's head.

"Hey man, what's going on? I told you I'm not Popo!"

"Shut the fuck up and get in the car!"

The frightened boy felt no other alternative but to comply. He was forced into the back seat. Rogelio sped off while Vicente rode in the back with the gun to the victim. He placed a black cover over the boy's head so he wouldn't know where they were going. They urged the victim to stay quiet, and he did. Sobs could be heard from the inside of the face covering. "Just calm down *ese*. You'll go home when your brother pays what he owes."

"You're gonna kill me, aren't you?"

"Not if your brother pays."

"He ain't got shit to pay you with. I'm fucked. I know I am!"

"Just shut up!"

They arrived at the ranch. The young boy was tied up, blindfolded, and placed in a secure room.

"Now what, Vicente?"

"We just wait for Elsa."

"What do we do with him if she doesn't come back?"

"She'll be back. This is her property, *pendejo*. Besides, Cuerno gave us some extra cash to buy the kid food and stuff. It'll be alright. We did our job."

"Fine. I'll just wait."

"Everything is cool, alright. Just chill. I need to get rid of this car we borrowed."

"You're leaving me here alone with the kid?"

"Are you afraid or what *ese*? He's a kid, you have a 9mm, and I can leave you my .38."

"Shut up *culo*! I ain't afraid. Just do what you have to do and bring back food."

Vicente arrived at Elsa's house on Monterrey Street. She had arranged for someone to meet him about exchanging their vehicles. Vicente never asked where the car he used came from, but he was more than happy to get rid of it. It was a 1987 four-door Ford Taurus. The man he would meet was going to take that car and leave him with a white Spirit. For the next ten days, Vicente and Rogelio supervised their captive. Elsa would show up frequently with instructions from Cuerno, and the last one they got was to leave and that someone else would relieve them. Little did the two hired men know that neither of the two brothers even knew Elsa Cuellar, nor were they involved in any criminal activity. They were about to change the lives of an innocent family forever.

After having listened attentively, Marcos Ayala had suspicions about what he just heard. He had been investigating too long to have been taken in by Vicente's account.

"Do you mean to tell me that when you left, Juan was still alive?"

"Yes, he was fine."

The interview was interrupted by Chief Delgado. "Elsa Cuellar is here to post bail for these men."

"That's up to you, chief. I have no jurisdiction here."

"Well, I can't deny the bail if she's got the money, but I thought you might want to talk to her."

The FBI agent quickly accepted the offer. "I'd like to talk to her." He went to the next room and saw an expressionless woman sitting comfortably in the chief's chair. She did not appear afraid of authority and was confident in her demeanor. The agent wanted to assure her that her psychological tactics were pointless to him. "Elsa Cuellar?"

"Yes, officer."

"I understand you own property in Las Lomas just outside Laredo."

"Yes."

"We'd like your consent to search the property. We have reason to believe a crime has been committed there."

"A crime? On my property? Why, that's impossible, officer, but yes, of course, please search all you want."

The agent was surprised by her cooperation. He fought off the urge to tell her he was not an officer to keep the gentle interaction going. The arrangement was made for the property to be searched while the interviewing team was still there. Elsa arranged for one of her older daughters to meet the men there to show them the property.

While the men waited, several agencies got to the ranch. When they first arrived, the area had the appearance of a place that had been cleared recently. For a ranch, it was much to clean. Things were organized and cleared out. Finally, an area with a faint odor of decomposition took the search team to the ranch house's rear. It was approximately four meters before they reached the fence and one and a half meters to the left of the footpath where they came across the shallow grave with branches thrown on top of it.

Marcos Ayala returned to where the suspects were being held. "Are you sure the boy was alive when you left him?"

"Yes," Vicente said.

"Then you might want a good attorney. He's not alive anymore." Neither of the men appeared surprised at this news. "Look, an expert excavation team from McAllen is going to be there in the morning. If you had anything to do with this, there's going to be some of you on that boy."

The men remained pensive and looked at each other. They did not stand much of a chance to escape the predicament they currently found themselves in.

"We killed him," Vicente finally said softly.

"How?"

"We shot him four times."

"With what?"

"A twenty-two."

Investigator Rodriguez leaned back on his chair and threw Bo what was left of the rib he was eating. He could not believe that having Elsa present at the very moment the search was conducted, she was allowed to leave. "Why didn't they hold Elsa and the men there?"

"Shit, I don't know really. Elsa could easily claim she had no idea. She was so cooperative, and the only two men who could place her there were those two men they had in custody, but they were found murdered just a few days after they posted their bail."

"Right. I wonder who ordered that?"

"Yeah, I wonder."

Investigator Alexander Rodriguez was very familiar with the rest of the case. The slugs at the scene and the .22 caliber weapon would go mysteriously missing from the evidence room. Marcos's experience had shed light on the murder of Juan Valentine Alonzo, but it was not enough to get the interest of authorities and secure a conviction along with the other crimes. With the only two people who could testify against her having conveniently been murdered, Elsa had once again sidestepped a legal land mine.

19

The Carnival

AS INTELLIGENT AS ELSA CUELLAR WAS ABOUT OPERATING UNDER THE law enforcement radar, she was not educated about the possible psychological outcomes that could come back to haunt her. She took for granted the emotional and psychological effects the children could announce in public through their behavior, and this proved to be her most critical mistake. This mistake is most apparent with behavioral issues in some of the younger children in the household because the younger they are, the more sensitive the case can be. Earlier in Cuellar's career she was able to dodge serious problems when in 2005, one of the six-year-old girls in her household was acting sexually in the classroom. The little girl was inviting a boy in her class to kiss her "between the legs." It was a statement the schoolteacher found to be a very premature thing to be familiar with at her age. The United Independent School District administration contacted Child Protective Services, but the little girl was removed from the campus by the guardian before they heard anything else regarding the case.

The screening process for children waiting to be adopted and the prospective parents is intensive, but the focus is usually on whether the parents are the right fit for a child and on the potential environment the child will be living in. There is no way to predict, measure, or test if an adopted child will adapt to their new surroundings in an emotionally sound manner.

Although I do not have actual numbers, I do recall my time at the Webb County Juvenile Justice Alternative Education Program. This

INVESTIGATION REPORT

C.P.S.
Copies

| Case Name: Cuellar,Elsa |
| Case #: 25654910 |

Intake Received:	10/3/2005	Caseworker:	
Investigation Initiated:	10/14/2005	Supervisor:	
Investigation Completed:	12/8/2005	County:	WEBB
Investigation Approved:	12/9/2005	Office:	, TX
Overall Disposition:	Unable to Determine		
Risk Finding:	Risk Indicated		
Recommended Action:	Family Pres		
Safety Decision:			
Safety Plan Completed:	No		
Sensitive Case:	No		
Priority:	2		
Multiple Referral:			

Intake Narrative

Intake Received:	10/3/2005	Reporter Name:	
Stage ID:	31465726	Rel/Int:	School Personnel
Stage Type:	SXAB2	Person ID:	

Person Notes: The caller works at in Laredo.
The OV attends this school.

Document worker safety issues, special or sensitive case handling information on the Special Handling Window.

GENERAL INFORMATION/DESCRIPTION:

25341022   CPS   OPN   Cuellar,Elsa   WEBB   CPS Fam Preservation

The OV (6 yo f) lives with SB (7 yo f), SB (7 yo f), SB (8 yo f), SB (9 yo f), SB (10th grade m), SB (7th grade f), MO and FA.

The OV has been making sexually explicit statements that are inappropriate for her age. On 09/30/05, The OV told a 1st grade classmate to "kiss me between my legs." The OV also kissed a fellow 1st grader on the lips at recess. It is believed that this is not age appropriate behavior. The OV has been saying "wee-wee" a lot lately. The OV was asked where she learned this term and said that her FA taught her about it. The caller did not know what "wee-wee" refers to or how the FA made the OV aware of this term.

The OV complained of having a rash today (10/03/05). The OV blamed the rash on the FA and said "my dad is hurting me." The caller did not know the details of how the FA hurt the OV.

The OV is generally unkempt and is often seen with dirt on her face and with uncombed hair. The OV appears well fed.

, SWIS I
Staffed with , SWI Supervisor

CONCLUSIONS:

CPS, SXAB(risk of), P2; A 6 yo child is exhibiting inappropriate sexually acting behavior. The AP is unknown and therefore may still have access.

25065757   UTC   CPS   CLD   WEBB   Investigation

This is the original communication regarding the 6-year-old girl's sexual behavior. Most educators who dealt with this child felt her knowledge of sex was extremely premature. How did she know so much and why?

was the school where juvenile offenders were sent so they would not fall behind in school while serving lengthy suspensions at their public school. I was stationed there as one of the probation officers and remember talking to so many youths who were either adopted or living with a relative that was not their natural parents. Research has found a strong correlation between misbehavior and those not living with their biological parents.

Behavioral issues were not the only thing haunting Cuellar. She could never have guessed that her history could come back to haunt her at some point. It is important to note that not all of Cuellar's attempts to manipulate potential victims went smoothly, but this was not something that could be predicted. The border region is an unusually large place, and one would not expect to encounter someone familiar with one area approximately three hours away. But Laredo is a place that can draw people from many places throughout the state if it is the right time of the year.

The fall months leading up to and after the Christmas break promote a very festive time in Laredo, Texas. In September, the Expo-Mex or *La Fiera* festival arrives across the river in Nuevo Laredo, Tamaulipas. It once attracted more people than it does today, but many still go. After Halloween and Thanksgiving, the city of Laredo enjoys its Christmas break off. Once the New Year celebrations end, the annual carnival comes to town highlighting the Washington celebration, a local parade, and of course the Jalapeño Festival. It is a joyous couple of months for the people of Laredo and many of its citizens, especially the children, who take great measures to enjoy every minute of them.

With so many people attending these festivities, conflict is inevitable. In this case, it came in the form of a threat made against some of Cuellar's children and even their homes. The details of the incident changed drastically from one account to another, but this is expected in dealing with anyone associated with the Cuellar household. When Laredo police responded to death threats being made to the Cuellar family and their children, no one expected to hear an accurate summary of what happened, but one story specifically stood out above all others; there was good reason for this. One of the boys being held for being threatening had some very interesting things to say to the police officer involved in the case.

WHY EDDIE THREATENED TO KILL NATALIE AND VALERIE
Palmview, Texas, November 2011

Even for November, it was an uncharacteristically cold day for that part of Texas. The sky was clear, and the birds sang as they did on a spring day, but the Canadian chills made their way down the entire country and overpowered the sun's rays all along the McAllen border. Here in Hidalgo County, Eddie and his parents, Angelica and Saul, crossed into the United States. The plan was to get to Minnesota, where they had several close relatives. Eddie's uncle had already spoken to his boss and agreed to give Saul some work on their turkey farm. It was late in the season, but with Thanksgiving still twenty days away and the Christmas celebrations to come after, there was much work to do.

Finding the right *coyote* to cross them was not easy. Many experiences have been reported of immigrants being charged a ridiculous amount of money only to be abandoned in almost impossible areas to survive. Saul was a man of good character, and his kind nature attracted the right people. He was friendly, hardworking, and very devoted to his family. He had never hurt a soul in his life but was vulnerable in the sense that he never expected anyone to hurt him either. Sadly, that is not how the world rotates.

His kind nature led him to a man who could cross him into Hidalgo County from Reynosa. The irony is that Reynosa was fast becoming one of the most dangerous border cities along the Mexican line. Extortion, murder, and cartel violence plagued the area in record numbers. On the alternate side, McAllen was recognized as one of the safer border cities to live in. It was a clean area populated by good people. The Flores family was looking forward to arriving there with eager anticipation. An older man known only as *El Conejo* showed them the way for a price that Saul felt was reasonable. It was still difficult for him to get, and it took him nearly two years to save for it. A man who worked for *El Conejo* on the McAllen side would pick them up and take them to a shelter in a secluded farmland. They were allowed to spend one night, but from there, those who were crossed were on their own.

It was a frightening thought to suddenly be in a foreign country with nowhere to stay after the first night, but the Flores family had something that few other immigrants had, that is, a specific destination and a job waiting for them. The dilemma to overcome was getting to Minnesota through the U.S. Border Patrol checkpoints. Saul was smart enough to know that even if the ranches weren't riddled with motion sensors, it would take extra money for a guide. There were only a few other immigrants in the shelter that night. Saul got into a conversation with a man who had been traveling for months. He was a middle-aged man but didn't seem to have a care in the world.

"Where are you guys going?"

"We have family in Minnesota. Any idea how we can get there?"

"Not without money or English."

"If I had as much money as I do English, I might be able to do it."

"You're lucky. Most people coming through here can't say a word in English."

"What good will that do me if I can't even move within the country?"

"Well, there is this one lady who can help."

"Oh, yeah?"

"She's an attorney. Her name is Elsa Cuellar. You ain't far from her. She is in Palmview just down the road. She is very good at speeding up the process to legalize illegal immigrants."

"How does she do that?"

"I don't know. She's an attorney. She must have her connections."

The man told Saul where he could find the woman. Angelica was skeptical at first, but it was an excellent option to explore. The difficulties of crossing the country without detection were real and provoked ideas of finding work there in McAllen and staying for a while. The reality of the family's situation was that there was no time for that kind of plan. They needed shelter, food, and jobs. These things take time and being on the street until it happens was unsafe.

By the morning, the family had found Elsa Cuellar's office in Palmview. They were surprised by the simplicity. There was no writing on the office door or pictures hanging on the wall. There were no workers or computers, and her assistants were her two daughters, whom she introduced as Natalie and Valerie. "I am preparing them for law school. Aren't they beautiful?"

Eddie didn't think so, but the parents agreed to be cordial with Elsa. She was a kind woman and spoke with a tenderness in her voice that comforted the family. She explained away the look of her office as having recently relocated and is in the middle of a transition. She spoke at some length about the process to expedite their paperwork. Neither Angelica nor Saul fully understood the process she was speaking about, but she related the steps with such conviction that they were assured she knew what she was talking about. Everything was in motion for the family to be legal. It was so easy; they couldn't understand why more immigrants did not come to her. Elsa explained that it was the cost.

"Unfortunately, it does take personal favors to get this done, so it can be costly."

"How much?"

"$20,000."

"My God! That is a lot of money."

"Do you have anyone who can maybe help? A personal loan you can pay back or a fundraiser?"

The family exchanged looks. They hated to ask the family who had already done so much to get them a place to live and work in Minnesota. It was the only route to take. They were all they had in America.

"Well, I do have some people in Minnesota, but I don't know that they have that kind of money."

"See what they can do, and we will see what we can figure out from what you are able to collect. Would you like to set something up for next week to see where you are with the collection?"

"Yeah, we'll be here at the same time next week."

Surviving for a week was going to be difficult. Luckily, there was no one to enforce the rules about staying only one night in the farmhouse outside McAllen. The family was able to stay there, solving their problem with shelter. Saul did not have much money, but he had enough to afford to eat at least modest portions. They strategically ate things that had a filling effect on the stomach. Bread, flour tortillas, and oatmeal were good choices. The more difficult thing was finding telephones to call their family in Minnesota. Sometimes, Saul would knock on random doors to borrow someone's cell phone. The people in the area were usually nice. They did not feel threatened by the sight of a family needing the phone. It might have been more difficult for Saul if he were alone to gain that kind of trust.

When he finally contacted his family, he explained the situation. He had a brother and cousins who were very excited to hear of this opportunity. As expected, they did not have $20,000, but they reached out to the community at the turkey farm and had a fundraiser. In all, they collected and raised $11,000 by the end of the week. For the remaining amount, Saul's brother sold a truck that meant a lot to him. His brother meant more. The truck sold for $5,000, and the Turkey farm owner agreed to put in the rest if he agreed to work it off with interest. It was an impressive collaborative effort that put Saul in debt to a lot of people. In the end, he would be good for it. He was an honorable man, and people trusted him.

A week later, the money would be sent via Western Union directly to Elsa. She confirmed receipt of the money and asked the family where she would deliver the papers. The family would be at the farmhouse until they were able to prove citizenship. First, they would have to go to the immigration office and submit the application. "Immigration office?" The thought frightened Angelica.

"Oh, don't worry. Once they see my signature and that I am an attorney, they won't deport you. That would be illegal," Elsa explained. This put the family's mind at ease. They completed the documents, and Elsa offered them a ride to the immigration office while she took care of the rest. The family was overwhelmed with the excitement only freedom can induce. It was a joyous moment that merited a celebration.

"After we leave the immigration office, we will go for a nice lunch. I don't mind using what I have. We just cut the time it will take us to get to Minnesota by months."

Elsa drove them to the immigration office and set a time to meet them back at the farmhouse. Eddie waited outside the building while his parents went inside. He did not feel like waiting in long lines. He wondered what it would be like to go to high school in America and make friends in a new country. He thought about the prom and maybe playing for his school's soccer team. While in this reflective state, Eddie noticed a commotion somewhere at the front door; he kept his eyes on the situation as it escalated and noticed that his parents were among those involved in the commotion. The young boy froze in fear, not knowing what was transpiring.

Several ICE agents arrived and handcuffed Eddie's parents. The young boy did not know it at the time, but his parents were being deported. The application they submitted for legalization was a false document. There was no Elsa Cuellar registered as an immigration attorney in the entire state. The family had been deceived at the cost of $20,000. The young boy contemplated running toward the agents so he could get deported as well, but he remembered a conversation he once had with his father about this very situation.

"If ever you find yourself in a position to have to choose Eddie, always decide on staying in the United States. Once you work towards becoming a citizen, you can always return to see us." Of course, Eddie never thought that advice would ever have to be taken in a real-life scenario. At the time, the fourteen-year-old boy did not know if his father would want him to take that advice at such a young age. The incident happened very quickly, and as he contemplated these uncertainties, the time to consider these matters with a more definitive answer had expired. Before he could think any further, his parents were gone and would, without a doubt, be in Mexico by that evening.

The steps to take for the young boy without his parents were uncertain. He was scared, alone, and without any money. He thought about returning to Mexico. The international bridge was not far, but the home he previously knew in Mexico was no longer at the family's disposal. He had no idea what his parents would do. He thought about making it to Minnesota on his own to work on the turkey farm, but two factors derailed this track of mind: he did not have the money for a guide or food to get there, and he did not know how those who helped his father with $20,000 would feel about him now that those expecting repayments were taking a loss. It was a very difficult predicament for a boy that age; he knew he would have to think cunningly to survive.

Eddie spent some time crying and asking strangers for money. Few had no money to give, while others were simply unwilling. The second night was the most difficult when several storms hit the South Texas region. Tornadoes, hail, and strong winds made it difficult for Eddie to find shelter. He finally decided that looking for his parents in Mexico would probably be safer than looking for a way to live in the United States. He was on his way to the bridge when divine intervention in the form of a stranger pulled alongside him.

"Excuse me, young man, do you need some help?"

Her name was Yolanda Linares. She worked for a social service program called HEART, part of a larger statewide system designed to help children between the ages of seven and seventeen. Eddie was frightened at first. His English was better than many boys his age who were born in America, but he was still not very confident.

"I am a little hungry. Do you have a dollar or two?"

"I have something better than that. Get in."

The HEART program had a shelter for runaway kids in place. Yolanda was a caseworker and set Eddie up with bed, food, and dry clothes donated during the holiday seasons. After Eddie ate and took a shower, he was taken into Yolanda's office for paperwork. The caseworker was extraordinarily nice and comforting. She insisted on being called "Yoli" and shared some of her childhood experiences with Eddie. The young boy remained cautiously optimistic. He could not help but think back to the last person who seemed to be nice to him. For now, he had no choice but to trust her. He was being fed, sheltered, and making friends who also faced hardships. After a week, he had grown fond of Yoli and mildly regretted having lied to her.

He did not feel comfortable not knowing his fate if he told her the truth. Eddie invented a story about his mother having left him on the side of the road because she chose a new boyfriend over being his parent. When asked where he was born, he said he was born in Austin, Texas. He claimed he didn't have any of his documents and did not expect to see his mother anymore. Yoli listened with as much empathy and vowed to help Eddie. After a month, she was able to find a suitable foster family in Laredo willing to take Eddie in and work with him. The Resendez family treated him well and provided for him in a way he would never have experienced in Mexico. He missed his parents very much and, at times, cried himself to sleep under the blankets.

His foster parents were both attorneys, so Eddie had plenty of time to himself. The new guardians were excellent providers, but their profession also kept them busy. The boy wondered why a couple would take on such a task with their demanding jobs and future political careers. Could they not have children of their own? Perhaps the funding they received from the state? To Eddie, it did not matter. He was happy to have a room and food. He was enrolled in the Laredo Independent School District and made a lot of friends. By the time he was sixteen, he was in a new home. The Resendez couple decided to give up on foster parenting when they both quit on each other. The divorce was too much for any of them to take on single parenting. This did not phase Eddie. He was older, had developed thick skin in the past two years, and had made many friends. He met his first girlfriend, Gabby less than a year after being taken in.

It was February, the week of Valentine's Day. Miguel, Gabby, and Gabby's sister Gloria decided to go to the carnival. It was an annual event in Laredo and part of the Washington celebration. Eddie did not fully understand why they celebrated Washington's birthday. He died shortly after Laredo was founded and long before Texas was even part of the United States. He did not care much for the historical aspects; he enjoyed the parades, festivals, and, of course, the carnival. It was here that Eddie would exhibit an anger he had never felt before. Both Gabby and her sister were known in their school as rebels and had been in a few fights at school. That did not match the profile of people Eddie usually associated with, but a teenage crush is a powerful emotion. So, when Eddie explained to the two sisters why he was so upset, they too aided him in the confrontation.

In the line to get on the Zipper, Eddie saw the very distinct faces of Natalie and Valerie—Elsa's daughters. Being that Eddie had already related his experience to the two sisters, all he had to do was say, "That's them!" for the girls to know who they were. Eddie's heart pounded inside his chest like a jackhammer. At first, he did not know how to react or what to say. He did not know what to do or who to call. Many questions came to his mind. *Who do I call? What could they even do at this point? What proof do I have? Would my citizenship be revoked because I lied about where I was born? How could I prove anything? Did Elsa Cuellar use her real name?* With such a common name along the border, Elsa would not have to use an alias and simply deny knowing the family. With every question that had no answer, Eddie became angrier and angrier. Before he was consciously aware of what he was doing, he found himself yelling profanities at them and calling them names. He was assisted by the two sisters, who started threatening to kill the girls.

Neither of the two girls appeared to remember Eddie—an indication they had run the scheme many times before. They stared blankly at him. It made Eddie consider they did not even know their mother was a crook. The disgruntled boy made sure they knew of his displeasure calling their mom a "Whore!" and a "Fuckin liar." The yelling got so loud that carnival security threw them out. Gabby was a year older than Eddie and already drove. They used her car to wait at the main exit. There were so many people, they never counted on finding the girls again—but they did. The very distinct faces of the two girls jumped out at Eddie. His fury began to spill from within his body. Images of his parents being taken away by immigration agents were suddenly stamped on his mind. The nights he spent crying for his parents, and the fear he endured in a new country. The overall emotional pain the mother of these girls caused Eddie began to carry him to an emotional state he had never experienced.

They followed the girls driving erratically and coming close to crashing into them. The scared girls foolishly led Eddie and the sisters to their home. It was the only place they could think of seeing. The sisters parked outside the house, and they began throwing rocks from the street against the front door. Eddie continued to yell profanities and threatened to kill the family. He did not have a way of knowing that Elsa Cuellar was not a good person to threaten. He was very fortunate that Elsa's husband took a different route and called the Laredo Police Department. They arrived within minutes, and the three outraged teenagers were taken to juvenile detention.

"So that's what happened?"

"Yeah, that's what happened, sir. Once I got to the house, I wasn't even yelling at the daughters. I was yelling at their bitch mother."

"Did you ever share this with anyone?"

"A few people, but no one seems to care."

"They care, Eddie. It's just hard to go after something we can't prove."

"Yeah, I get it."

"Why are you in here now?"

"My girlfriend and her sister shoplifted from Walmart, and I was with them."

"Based on your history, you might want to find a new girlfriend."

Eddie acknowledged the advice with a smile.

CASE SUPPLEMENTAL REPORT   Printed: 05/08/2013 11:21

aredo Police Department   OCA: *13005924*

THE INFORMATION BELOW IS CONFIDENTIAL - FOR USE BY AUTHORIZED PERSONNEL ONLY

Case Status: *EXCEPTIONALLY CLEARED*   **Case Mng Status:** *EXCEPTIONALLY CLEARED*   **Occured:** *02/22/2013*

Offense: *TERRORISTIC THREAT*

Investigator: ▓▓▓▓ (6618)   **Date / Time:** *02/22/2013 01:35:24, Friday*

Supervisor: ▓▓▓▓ (2522)   **Supervisor Review Date / Time:** *02/22/2013 23:25:48, Friday*

Contact: *Alvarado, Miguel* ▓▓ *Manor Rd, Laredo* ▓▓   **Reference:** *Incident Supplement*

ON FRIDAY, FEBRUARY 22, 2013, AT APPROXIMATELY 23:22 HOURS, I, OFFICER ▓▓▓▓▓▓
RESPONDED TO ▓▓ MANOR RD. FOR A REPORTED FIGHT IN PROGRESS.
UPON DISBURSING EVERYONE AND OFFICER ▓▓▓▓▓▓ FILING CASE REPORT #: 13-▓▓▓▓, I
MADE CONTACT WITH COMPLAINANT #1, MIGUEL ALVARADO (DOB 09/29/49) OF ▓▓ MANOR DR.,
WHO STATED SUSPECTS ▓▓▓▓▓▓A (DOB 12/12▓▓), ▓▓▓▓▓▓ (DOB 03/02▓▓), AND
▓▓▓▓▓▓ (DOB 03/19▓▓) THREATENED HIS DAUGHTERS, ▓▓▓▓ AND ▓▓
▓▓▓▓, BY GOING OVER TO THEIR RESIDENCE, AFTER HAVING AN ALTERCATION AT THE
CARNIVAL, AND STATING THEY WERE ALL GOING TO SEND PEOPLE OVER TO KILL THEM.
SAID REPORT WAS FILED AND THERE IS NO FURTHER INFORMATION AT THIS TIME.

This is the original case supplement of the incident at the carnival.

20

Where the Children's Loyalty Is

AUTHORITIES WERE RUNNING OUT OF TIME TO PRESENT SOMETHING new. Elsa would be in front of a judge soon, and the police did not have anything concrete to add to the case. There was no doubt that she had something to do with the murder, but they had nothing on her for that. The only two witnesses were dead. Marcos Ayala later told Investigator Rodriguez that Vicente said to him that they only killed Juan and had nothing to do with the bodies in the drums on the side of the ranch house. It was a peculiar statement, but nothing could be done about this. The rings on the dirt confirmed there had been barrels or drums there for some time, but no drums or barrels were ever found. The US Marshalls were also convinced of illegal organ selling, prostitution, and selling babies, but there was nothing concrete that would hold up in court. Investigator Rodriguez was a supporter of the legal system, but he understood the imbalance of what it takes to prove one is guilty versus the complexity of having to let them go. Unless the older children testified, Elsa would only face twenty-two counts of falsifying government documents. He feared they might just deport her.

He thought a visit with some of the kids might do some good. He found it difficult to believe that in rooms with writing all over the wall showing signs of wanting to die, there would not be at least one child willing to open with the truth. *Isn't anyone in the house tired of this woman? Don't they want to escape?* Rodriguez asked himself these questions, and with this in mind, he decided he would begin with Imelda's most recent case. He thought of her because she was one of the victims who were

157

most willing to talk to law enforcement. Time was not only against authorities for how soon Elsa would be appearing in court; it was also a factor because of the victim's age. So many of the other victims were already at an age that placed them a year or two away from being adults, which brings them more freedom to make their own choices. They would soon be leaving the house to be on their own without having to testify against Elsa. They would much rather go on their own without feeling there would be a target on their back.

Investigator Rodriguez had the luxury of knowing many people within the law enforcement and social service community in Laredo. He found the best approach to meeting with Imelda. She had been temporarily placed in a foster home. With her mental limitations, he was unsure she would be an effective witness against Elsa and her husband, but he was trying everything he could. He asked the current legal guardian, Sylvia Muñoz, to stay with them as a witness. Already, he noticed how different Imelda looked under the proper care. Her complexion was glowing; her hair was clean. The self-applied nail polish had been removed—the one that covered the dirty nails. The dirt under the nails was also removed. She had on clean clothes, and the "chickenpox" on her arms had healed. She may have received treatment for her skin. The "hickies" on her neck had faded, and the officer could see a different person in the color of her eyes.

"Hi, Imelda, do you remember me?"

"Yes."

"This is a nice house. Do you like it here?"

"Yes, they're nice, but I sometimes miss my mom."

Investigator Rodriguez tried not to show he could not understand how this innocent child could miss her previous environment after being placed in the current one. He reminded himself that she was a slow little girl and did not see the world through the same scope he did. For Imelda, she had not been the victim of any crime. In her mind, she had been removed from the house because she had lice. She was taken from the only mother she ever knew and the only place she called "home." That was Elsa's way, and the investigator knew this. She would strip children of their identity. The only thing her victims knew about themselves is what she allowed them to know. Sadly, everything she gave them the freedom to understand was a lie.

"Imelda, can you tell me a little more about what happened in your home?"

"It was okay."

"Were you always happy?"

"Not all the time, but it was okay."

"When was the first time you did not feel happy at the house? Can you remember?"

"Yes, I remember really good."

IMELDA'S CHILDHOOD—SEPTEMBER 2005

The school day had just begun. It was a typical day for most students, but it had been a difficult start for Imelda. She was a difficult little girl for teachers to work with. Aside from not having the capacity to retain much of what was taught, she had been behaving most unusually. After some time, the principal advised the teacher, Teresa Ramirez, not to contact her for disciplinary issues unless there was a risk to the child or her classmates. Patience had been wearing thin among the administration. With cases like Imelda's, it is easy for society to lose track of what schools are there for, that is, to educate. Many do not realize school systems are too often burdened with incidents that are outside the scope of academics. It is a reality of the field that must be dealt with, and Mrs. Teresa Ramirez learned of this early in her career the day Imelda walked into her classroom.

Before the September 2005 incident, she had heard reports from the boys in the class that Imelda had been making sexually explicit suggestions. She thought she had heard Imelda herself one morning tell another first-grade boy to "kiss me between my legs." She thought she had imagined it. A five-year-old girl would not know anything about that. Or would she? Now that she was being told of her classmates' similar experiences, she decided to keep a closer eye on her. The difficulty for first-grade teachers is in the credibility of children. Even if she believed them, adults at home could always explain away the behavior. Imelda showed no signs of physical abuse, so she thought the better idea was to catch her saying something explicit herself.

Over the next two weeks, Mrs. Ramirez noticed a gradual change in Imelda. She looked dirty and neglected. Her fingernails appeared to be black, but at times, the black looked more like dry blood. In the morning when she arrived at school with dry dirt on her face, she decided she would not wait to hear another inappropriate comment. Mrs. Ramirez would bring this to the administration's attention immediately. After discussing the situation with the principal, they brought Imelda to the waiting room in the lobby. While there, a staff member noticed the child touching her privates. Mrs. Ramirez was discussing the case with the principal in the office.

"Mrs. Ramirez, the little girl in the lobby, is touching herself."

"She's what?"

"I don't know what she's doing but has her hand deep down in her panties touching herself."

"Bring the little girl in here now," said the principal while picking up the phone. They had seen enough and felt they had sufficient cause for CPS involvement. It was learned that Imelda had been scratching herself because she had a severe rash on her vagina. When CPS asked her how she got the rash, she responded by saying: "My daddy is hurting me." No matter what angle the case worker used to question her, they could never get Imelda to be more specific. Whether or not she was reluctant to share details because she was ashamed, was loyal to her father, or did not have the vocabulary level to express herself was never known. Still, the case needed more convincing testimony than a simple: "My daddy is hurting me." In the outside world, the obvious nature of what the little girl was saying was very clear. Inside the courtroom, the expression was simply much too vague.

Imelda's case was not in vain. When CPS learned of Imelda's experience, they learned of fourteen kids in the household. This number contradicted the district's records that eleven children were attending the district. Investigations by CPS officers revealed that one of Imelda's sisters was caught masturbating inside the classroom at her school. They were only two years apart and could not understand why they were attending different schools. The young girl had been leaving class suddenly without any explanation, wearing the same clothes daily, and appearing excessively withdrawn. She would not tell her teachers anything when asked, and her mother would never answer the phone.

Another young sister in the household was questioned at a different elementary school. She reported to CPS that her only meals were the ones she got at school. She also witnessed her brother and sister "doing things" that sounded very much to the CPS officer as if they were having sex. When asked why she smelled that way, the little girl reported sleeping outside with her puppy named Lazy and that he would often "poop" or pee on her. The young girl was said to have an infected wart on her rectum, but whether it was transmitted sexually or through infection from the dog's urine could not be ascertained at the time.

When one of the young males in the household was questioned, he confirmed much of what his sisters were saying. He discussed the lack of food at home and said Elsa would lift the girls by their hair when they misbehaved and that their father would use a red hanger to hit them in their "private" area. The investigation was slowly becoming a horror story. The case against Elsa Cuellar and her husband was mounting, and the CPS officers were getting confident, that is until they interviewed the older siblings in the household.

Investigators with the state were disappointed to have had all the testimony from the children refuted by the older siblings living with them. They denied everything the younger children stated and said there was always food in the home and the environment was loving and nurturing. The following day, a home visit was made. The house was exceptionally clean, the refrigerator was filled with food, and all the bedrooms were made up. Elsa showed the caseworker that the males and females had separate rooms in different parts of the house. The caseworker took some time to interview Elsa separately.

"Mrs. Cuellar, when will your husband be home?"

"My husband, he left me a long time ago."

"So, when was the last time he met Imelda?"

"He's never met her. He left me for our maid a long time ago."

"What happened then? Did he leave you while you were pregnant?"

The caseworker was having a difficult time believing anything Elsa was saying. She thought that by pressing her a little, she might cave in with some information. With every question, the frustrated woman got deeper into her lies. Elsa lowered her voice and whispered to the caseworker as if trying to conceal what she was about to say to the rest of the kids in the house. "I had the birth certificate reflect I am her mother. In Mexico, I can do that legally because I am an attorney there. I did this because I got custody from her mother. She was a schizophrenic lady and was always high on drugs. Thank God he put Imelda in my path."

"I don't see anything in the paperwork about you being an attorney."

"I am," was all she answered with a stoned face. The caseworker was aware of Elsa and her husband's connection to Mexico. He could have left the minute the girls were interviewed, and no one would have known the difference between a man who did not play a recognizable role in society. He was at home most of the time, but he never connected emotionally with any of the children. He is not someone they would miss during his absence.

"I'm just curious, Mrs. Cuellar, why do you suppose so many of the younger children gave us the same story?"

"It's Imelda. She brainwashes the other kids. She has a wild imagination. What do you expect? She's a kid. She tells them to go along with all kinds of things. She has an imaginary friend who wears a white nightgown and kills children and uses her to intimidate the other kids."

"They say you pull their hair."

"Only when I'm braiding it. I never harm these girls. I am a good parent."

"I hope you understand why I have to ask these questions, Mrs. Cuellar."

"I understand, but you also have to understand children. I will do what I can. I will take them to the doctor about the rash."

"More investigation will take place, Mrs. Cuellar, to determine if this is a suitable environment for the children."

This statement was not well received by Elsa, and her face indicated that very well. Her demeanor changed from a cooperative religious woman to a vindictive perpetrator.

"That is fine, ma'am, but keep in mind that I can be gone to Mexico by the morning. I will not let anyone take my kids from me. Something bad could happen to you before that happens."

"Are you threatening me, Mrs. Cuellar?"

"Have a good day, ma'am."

On her way out, Imelda ran toward the caseworker and hugged her. Elsa pulled the child from her. "Goodbye, ma'am."

"Goodbye, Imelda. I will see you soon, and please stop thinking about the lady in the white gown, okay? She's scaring your brothers and sisters." This, of course, was said intentionally. When Imelda asked her, "What lady?" The caseworker gave Elsa a stare as if to let her know she knew she was lying. At this point, it would be difficult for Elsa Cuellar to find anyone outside the children she harbored who would believe anything she had to say.

It was a stressful meeting but one that had to be done. The caseworker heard rumors about Elsa intimidating other caseworkers with threats. They eventually closed the case and left their job. She had to demonstrate to Elsa that not everyone she threatens will walk away from the well-being of children.

Some of the information Investigator Rodriguez received was from Imelda. Sylvia gave him the rest. It was a sad story for him to hear. Whenever children are involved, there is no limit to how much sorrow that can bring to a person.

"So, the last time you remember being happy was before people started asking you questions?"

"Yes. I think so."

Rodriguez did not get any new information he could use. The older kids had been coached well, and he now knew where their loyalties lay. It would be next to impossible for police to have Elsa Cuellar convicted on anything else other than falsifying documentation. The lack of cooperation was going to be very problematic in this case.

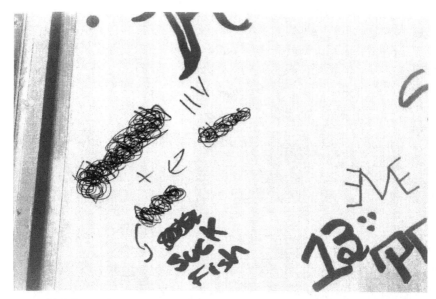

Photo 20.1 This is one example of the kind of writing that was on the wall at Elsa Cullar's house. Other original writing indicating suicide cannot be shown because it was not possible to exclude the child's name. The names in this example were scribbled off. Local authorities believe some of these signs are gang-related, but ascertaining if they were drawn by one of the children or one of the adults could never be established.

ESTADOS UNIDOS MEXICANOS

REGISTRO CIVIL

No. DE CONTROL

4314182

EN NOMBRE DEL ESTADO LIBRE Y SOBERANO DE ___ NUEVO LEON

Y COMO OFICIAL ___ UNICO ___ DEL REGISTRO CIVIL DE ESTE MUNICIPIO O DELEGACION,

CERTIFICO: QUE EN EL LIBRO No. ___ UNO ___ DEL REGISTRO CIVIL QUE ES A MI CARGO,

EN LA FOJA No. ___ 213638 ___ SE ENCUENTRA ASENTADA EL ACTA No. ___ 92 ___ DE FECHA

19 DE NOVIEMBRE DE 1999 ___ LEVANTADA POR EL C. OFICIAL ___ UNICO

DEL REGISTRO CIVIL ▬▬▬▬▬▬

EN LA CUAL SE CONTIENEN LOS SIGUIENTES DATOS:

ACTA DE NACIMIENTO

NOMBRE ▬▬▬▬▬▬▬▬▬

FECHA DE NACIMIENTO ___ 06 DE ABRIL DE 1997 ___ HORA ___ 1:50 A.M.

PRESENTADO: VIVO ☒ MUERTO ☐ SEXO: MASCULINO ☐ FEMENINO ☒

LUGAR DE NACIMIENTO ___ AGUALEGUAS, NUEVO LEON

COMPARECIO: EL PADRE ☐ LA MADRE ☒ AMBOS ☐ PERSONA DISTINTA ☐ REGISTRADO ☐

PADRES

NOMBRE MIGUEL ALVARADO RIVERA NACIONALIDAD MEXICANA EDAD 50 AÑOS

NOMBRE ELSA MARIA ESTHER CUELLAR ARMENTA NACIONALIDAD NORTEAMERICANA EDAD 37 AÑOS

ABUELOS

ABUELO PATERNO ▬▬▬▬▬▬ "FINADO" NACIONALIDAD MEXICANA

ABUELA PATERNA ▬▬▬▬▬▬ NACIONALIDAD MEXICANA

ABUELO MATERNO ▬▬▬▬▬▬ NACIONALIDAD NORTEAMERICAN

ABUELA MATERNA ▬▬▬▬▬▬ NACIONALIDAD NORTEAMERICAN

TESTIGOS

NOMBRE ▬▬▬▬▬▬ NACIONALIDAD MEXICANA EDAD 19 AÑOS

NOMBRE ▬▬▬▬▬▬ NACIONALIDAD MEXICANA EDAD 25 AÑOS

No. DE CERTIFICADO DE NACIMIENTO ___ 1046716 ___ C.U.R.P. 19 002 01 99 00092 8

PERSONA DISTINTA DE LOS PADRES QUE PRESENTA AL REGISTRADO

NOMBRE • • • • • • • • • • • • PARENTESCO • • • • • • • • • EDAD • AÑOS

SE EXTIENDE ESTA CERTIFICACION, EN CUMPLIMIENTO DEL ARTICULO ___ 46 ___ DEL

CODIGO CIVIL VIGENTE EN EL ESTADO, EN ___ AGUALEGUAS, NUEVO LEON

A LOS ___ 19 ___ DIAS DEL MES DE ___ NOVIEMBRE ___ DE 1999

EL C. OFICIAL UNICO DEL REGISTRO CIVIL, DOY FE

NOMBRE   FIRMA

GOBIERNO DEL ESTADO
DE NUEVO LEON
DIRECCION DEL REGISTRO CIVIL
OFICIALIA PRIMERA
AGUALEGUAS, N. L.

Photo 20.2 This Mexican birth certificate is fake. It is one of many versions U.S Marshals found.

21

Joaquin

Mexico City, August 1994

JOAQUIN MENDOZA HAD NOT BEEN FEELING HIMSELF THE PAST FEW weeks. At first, he believed he might have been overworked. His hours at the textile *maquiladora* were long. They had to be if the check was to be significant enough to make a difference. His wife Flor urged him to see a doctor, but he did not think the issue was severe enough to spend money he did not have. It is often the case in Mexico that people who are trying to keep their heads above water will sacrifice things that are seen as of great importance to many for the sake of their own families. Joaquin and Flor had a little girl they named America after their hope of someday becoming citizens. They never thought of risking their daughter's life from cross the border illegally, so both Joaquin and Flor worked hard to save enough money to go through the legal process, no matter how long it would take.

Joaquin endured the pain for as long as he could before feeling forced to go to the doctor. It took some weeks before getting the news of his cancer. The detection was early, and the expectation of recovery was positive, except for the fact Joaquin had no way of actually paying for the treatment. Flor pleaded with him to do what he could, but financially, there was no solution for fighting cancer. Together, they decided to turn their faith toward God and agreed to join their friends and listen to a guest speaker that was scheduled at their church. Joaquin and Flor had never been devoted Catholics, but they had been feeling the need to get closer to God with everything they had been going through.

The religious assembly was taking place in a remote neighborhood. The Catholics in the area may not have appreciated a lecture from another denomination so close to the *Basilica de Guadalupe*. The gathering was larger than the couple had expected, but this made them feel better about the speaker. Her name was Elsa Alvarado, and she had been known by many as *La Pastora*, who could perform miracles. She helped everyone who needed it and had no limits to how she was willing to assist others. The rumor was that her preaching often sounded like she was singing, even if she was merely talking because she spoke the Holy Bible's words with such eloquence and passion. It was exactly what Joaquin and Flor needed: inspiration.

No one could ever hold a person accountable for wrongdoing when they turn to Christ for emotional support. In fact, it is often encouraged. Still, one must always be careful when the common folk preach the words of God. Usually, the passion with which the words are being sung to followers comes from a serpent's forked tongue. The vulnerable couple was impressed with the woman's demeanor and the energy with which she related God's will. It was poetic to hear her speak, and the command she took of the room was profound and soothing. The feeling of hope and inspiration the couple was seeking had at last been found.

After the service, the couple got in line to meet Elsa Alvarado. Many wished to shake her hand and request a special prayer for a specific problem they may have. After waiting an hour, they were finally able to converse with the godly woman and explained their current situation.

"I am so sorry to hear that. Let us pray together for your health and to ensure you have a long life with this beautiful little girl. What is your name, sweetheart?"

"America."

"What a beautiful name, America. How old are you?"

"I am almost this many," she said, holding up six fingers.

"Wonderful, let us pray."

Something about the prayer had a profound impact on the couple. They believed God himself heard Elsa's words and that he would deliver on her request for health. They were already a block away from the service when a man at the sermon caught up to them. "Excuse me, I am sorry to bother you."

"No, that's okay," Flor said. "Weren't you at the service?"

"Yes, I am Reverend Gomez, and *La Pastora* Alvarado was so moved by your situation, she would like to speak to you more about it. She believes she can help."

Joaquin was very interested in what he was hearing. He was now beginning to feel that he was drawn to the spiritual lecture by divine intervention. In the most vulnerable times in a person's life, the malicious resort to using God for comfort, knowing well they do not qualify for such a task. It is not owed to fatuity that those like Joaquin fall under the enchantment of religious tones; rather, it is the faith brought to them by a wolf in sheep's clothing. It was clear that Flor and Joaquin were in a mental state to look for signs of something more sinister in those offering to help. For this reason, when Elsa offered them an exceptional doctor to examine the ill man, for no cost, it was a gift from the Lord himself.

The family was so grateful that they had Elsa go to their home for a homemade supper the following week. The family was already stretching their grocery budget as far as it could go, but they felt it was the least they could offer the woman who had given Joaquin such hope for longevity. Three days after the supper, the appointment was scheduled in Taxco, which was a little over one hundred miles from Mexico City. The doctor who received them was a short stalky man with a long beard and a pleasant smile. He was very sincere in his welcoming and began to ask questions about Joaquin's health. His immediate concern for her husband's health was comforting to Flor, who held her daughter tightly by the hand.

"Hello? I am Dr. San Miguel. Who are you?"

"America?"

"Very nice. Tell me, America, how would you like for me to make your father feel all better?"

"I would like that."

The doctor invited Joaquin in. He took him to the back of the building, and Flor was asked to wait in the front. She was surprised they took her husband to the rear of the building. She had been under the impression they were at Dr. San Miguel's home. Their current location looked nothing like a hospital or a medical facility. Elsa was very reassuring, and Flor felt better after discussing the location with her. She blamed away the manner that the building was kept on budgetary factors and that Dr. San Miguel liked to help many people for free as he was helping Joaquin. Flor was made to understand and waited for nearly four hours before Dr. San Miguel emerged. "What is it, doctor? Is my husband okay?"

"Oh yes, he is fine. The procedure went very well, and he will recover just fine."

"Procedure?"

"Yes, he does not have cancer, *señora*, and I am so sorry you had to go through such stress with false news."

"He doesn't?"

"No, he had an infection in his kidney, and I went in to treat the infection. He will be fine."

The sense of relief relaxed Flor's entire body. She had not realized how much stress she had been harboring inside her until she released it. The family would not be able to survive without his work, no matter how meager his wage was. Elsa was very kind to the family and got them a hotel for the night. It was a small town, but she accommodated them at the best place she knew. Joaquin was still weak, but they helped him to his room. Dr. San Miguel suggested that he would rest much better there than at the old building he used as a hospital. Joaquin agreed after having seen the conditions in which he was treated. He was concerned with cleanliness but quickly observed the strict sanitary measures Dr. San Miguel was taking and did not question it any further. The table where he was treated did not appear to be the typical operating table. The walls were old, with chipped paint and cracks on the floor. Later, when his wife told him what Elsa had explained to her, the scenario made more sense. They were both very happy and hoped to repay Elsa when they returned to Mexico City before returning home. They prepared a nice place to sleep for America on the sofa, and the couple accepted a lovely meal from Elsa and fell into a sound sleep for the night.

The morning brought a new set of challenges for Joaquin and Elsa. Both woke up with very big headaches. At first, Joaquin believed it might have had to do with the procedure. He did not ask what was put in his body to sedate him. He felt very weak and had a lot of pain in his back. He explained the reasons for how he felt, but he had no way of understanding why Flor felt so bad. When they woke, they were surprised to see that they had not eaten half of their dinner. The food was a better meal than they were used to, and they were both very hungry. Neither could remember falling asleep. They discussed their dazed state for a while before realizing it was nearly four o'clock in the evening. Joaquin was more confused than he had ever been. *How could we have slept so long?* he thought to himself.

The bigger question came at a higher cost to their emotional balance: *Where was America?* Flor checked the bathroom in complete panic. The little girl was not there. She ran through the halls screaming for her, but there was no answer. Joaquin called out to Flor since he was too weak to follow, but his pleas fell on deaf ears. She was hysterical, running through the hotel and screaming her daughter's name. Some people dismissed her cries as excitement for having become a citizen, but it was her daughter she cried for. Momentarily, she arrived at a feeling of peace, having convinced herself that her daughter may have been taken by Elsa and was caring for her since she had slept so long. With this idea in mind, Flor ran to the reception desk and asked for Elsa Alvarado's room. She was told that no one by that name was staying at that hotel. The frantic mother reasoned that she could be a guest at Dr. San Miguel's home. Taxco was a small place, so residents would know a man who was providing free medical service. This idea would also provide no hope.

"I am sorry, *señora*, I have never heard of that doctor. Most of us here go to Mexico City for healthcare."

Flor rushed to the medical building two blocks away only to find a group of men mining for silver under the building's base. She ran through the halls calling for her daughter. One of the men stopped her before she went too far, warning her of the danger. "*Señora*, please, you cannot be in here. It is very dangerous. There are unmarked holes in some of these rooms."

"I am looking for Dr. San Miguel."

"I am sorry, but no one by that name works with us."

"He doesn't work with you?" she cried. "He practices medicine here."

"You must be confused. This building has been abandoned for many years. Perhaps it was a different building."

Flor knew better. She was standing in the building where her husband was treated the previous day. She was sure of it. She could barely see the path back to the hotel room because the tears in her eyes clouded her vision. Flor had no recollection of her walk and found herself back in the room silent as a mute. Joaquin laid back in the bed, covered in sweat. He had developed a fever, and the scar left by the surgical procedure was becoming infected. Tears began to flow slowly down his face when he saw his wife return with their daughter. He knew that something was very wrong.

The following year was very difficult for the couple. Authorities in Mexico were uncooperative, stating that there was little they could do with the information they had. No one had ever heard of Elsa Alvarado, and the facility where her religious assembly had taken place denied having leased the building to anyone by that name. Their records for that night had a different name for a different event. No one had ever heard of Dr. San Miguel. There was no record of a practicing physician in all of Mexico with that name. In *Cuerna Vaca*, there was a doctor by that name who was a dentist, but when Flor investigated him, it was a different man.

Problems for Flor were not limited to her daughter's disappearance. During the past year, Joaquin's health had become worse. They finally decided to go to a local loan shark to get the money they needed for medical attention. It was then Joaquin learned that he did have cancer, and the lack of attention had given time for it to spread. He further learned that the procedure done to him was not to treat an infection of his kidney. Instead, it was surgery to remove it. Dr. San Miguel had stolen Joaquin's kidney. Six months later, Joaquin died. Feeling alone without her daughter and husband, with the added burden of waiting for the loan shark's men to come after her, Flor visited the most beautiful and largest hotel in Mexico City, went to the parking lot at the top of the building, and jumped.

There is no definitive way to ascertain whether this incident had anything to do with Elsa Cuellar. With both Cuellar and Alvarado being such common names and with the rise of incidents of organ theft in Latin America, it would be extremely difficult to say for sure the subject of this project was the same Elsa. However, knowing with precise accuracy that the subject of this research has been known as Elsa Alvarado Cuellar at some points in her life leaves that bitter feeling that she may have something else in her history that is just as sinister as anything she had ever done that would never be known, never be on the record, and would never face justice for.

22

Operation Cabbage Patch

May 20, 2013

THE SCHOOL DISTRICT POLICE REACHED OUT TO HOMELAND SECURITY on April 24, 2013. They had finally collected enough information to get attention from outside agencies. Currently, Investigator Alexander Rodriguez knew of eleven different children that Elsa had claimed as her own. After what he learned about her not having a uterus, he knew this was not possible. He was certain there were more children, perhaps under the names of other mothers who worked with Elsa. The keen woman had various driver's licenses with different names and had listed different husbands at different schools. The most damning piece of information was the use of social security numbers belonging to deceased individuals and birth certificates that made no sense. Now, officials had secured a search and arrest warrant for both Elsa Cuellar and her alleged husband, Miguel. The focus now was on how to execute them successfully.

The design was for the school district police to stop Elsa and Miguel as a regular traffic stop. It was made clear their cell phones needed to be secured. From there, Elsa would be transported back to her home, where the search warrant would be executed. Different agencies would be involved in what came to be known as "Operation Cabbage Patch," named after the similarities between Elsa Cuellar and the classic Cabbage Patch Kids. School district police would provide outside security to avoid any outside interference or contamination of the scene. Elsa knew many people, and her age and appearance could not cloud judgment. It was more than a routine search. ICE agents would secure the property and, along with the Texas Rangers, would collect any documents or evidence that could confirm the suspicions of any wrongdoing. The Laredo Police Department also participated. They were also responsible for securing the evidence at ICE facilities.

Thousands of dollars were seized in "Operation Cabbage Patch." Weapons, false blank documents, photos, and children were all found in the home. The children were transported to the Webb County Child Advocacy Center. In all, authorities found $14,000 in cash, $30,000 in money orders, and boxes of Texas driver's licenses. Investigator Rodriguez looked around the house and was repelled by the living conditions the children were being housed in. The furniture was placed randomly throughout the house without any sense of décor. Trash, dirty laundry, and food covered the floor. Live chickens ran throughout the house and the yard. Some areas of the home smelled like human excrement and urine. Still, the most disturbing thing for Rodriguez was the writing on the walls.

The rooms where some of the girls slept had been tagged with black markers. Statements expressing how tired they were of living were written clearly on the walls. Artwork of stick figures stabbing themselves was drawn above their beds. Many forms of concerning expressions covered the walls. It saddened the investigator to see the children in such pain. He realized that this was more than just a legal crime. Elsa had stolen their life, their memory, and their childhood. She had embraced an act of immorality that had ruined these children for life. These internal injuries will carry on into adulthood, yet there was nothing in the state's penal code that allowed a specific additional criminal charge for this. Suddenly, Rodriguez's reflections were disturbed by a man ICE was escorting outside the house in handcuffs. He did not look familiar to the investigator. He reached out to one of the Texas Rangers who was taking photos of the area.

One of the things that bothered the investigator is that he thought he knew everyone that was involved in Cuellar's home. The Texas Ranger knew very well the suspect they were taking out of the house was Tony Mata. He was a fugitive from Mexico and was wanted in connection with an explosion that took place at a nightclub called *La Sombrilla* just outside Monterrey, Nuevo Leon in Mexico. He was the same man that had gotten Investigator Rodriguez's attention in his earlier visit to the house and who provided a false name. His real name was Antonio Manrique Escobedo Mata, but he went by *El Grillo* (the Cricket) on the street.

A search was also conducted on Bustamante St., where Elsa held her religious lectures. Children were found there as well, and they were handed over to Child Protective Services. Many boxes of documents were seized, and the information they had was very telling of what Elsa had been doing for as long as twenty years. It appeared as if she kept a file system that showed she had helped well over five hundred women obtain false documentation to enter the United States. There was no way for authorities to know whether this means there were also over five hundred children that she had taken. The only children they were aware of were the ones currently registered within the school district; any ideas about children in Elsa's history would be speculation.

The Texas Ranger was getting ready to leave the scene when he stopped to look around the house. He could not believe the conditions where the children were being kept. A crime scene technician showed a small jar to the Texas Ranger. There was something unrecognizable inside it floating in an unidentified fluid. Something was floating inside a jar in a jelly-like substance. Upon closer look, authorities agreed they could be looking at a human fetus.

"Jesus Christ!" The Texas Ranger reacted. "What the hell kind of childhood did this woman have that she could do something like this?" It was sickening for authorities to know Cuellar and those around her could keep a fetus in a jar. It was also disturbing that when Mexican fugitives thought of a haven, they would think of her. *El Grillo*'s story is frightening, and he had no business being around children.

23

The Fugitive

Monterrey, Nuevo Leon, July 2000

IT WAS NOT UNCOMMON FOR *LA SOMBRILLA* TO BE FULL AT MIDDAY. Drinking, laughing, and celebrating are part of Mexican culture. One may argue it is the most festive culture on Earth. Never mind the reason to drink, just celebrate. Reasons to enjoy life are for those who do not understand living. At least, this is the way Polo Marez and Efrain Contreras felt about their time. They were young and relatively new to life and how to manage it. Indeed, they had not been acquainted with logic, nor had they made the connection between rational thinking and how things work. So, when *La Bala* Espinoza petitioned them to make a small delivery, they were honored to have a man of such stature involve them in his enterprise. The doltish nature of the young men created a smokescreen over the reasons why they were chosen. It was not because they were strong candidates to complete a mission; instead, they were insignificant to the world and dispensable if something went wrong.

No one knew *La Bala*'s real name. Most people engaged in his line of work live by aliases to make it more difficult to be tracked by law enforcement. Those who lived by an alias were respected, admired, and feared. It is an interesting combination of emotions elicited by society, but what should one feel when the organization that is killing enemies in mass numbers is the same group of people who provide housing for the poor, schools for the children, and food for the hungry? Still, the most life-changing thing that can be offered is employment. Efrain and Polo felt blessed with such an offer while sitting in the park doing nothing more than talking and drinking *Tecate*.

"Ay Polo, when I get to America, I'm going to find me the most beautiful American wife."

"*Cabron*, what makes you think you can take care of an American woman?"

"*Pendejo*, I want one to take care of me!"

They laughed as they drank and enjoyed their modest life and shared their goals for the unforeseen future. They were relaxed in their efforts to make any progress, but they were not with a complete lack of ambition. In Mexico, the number of people who needed money far outnumbered those who did not. It was not difficult for Tony Mata to find the two impractical young men. He was known on the streets as *El Grillo* because he often used a cricket sound to communicate with his associates at night when they could not see each other. Others say he was a hitman who only killed at night when the victims were asleep. Like crickets, he would not let people sleep. Of course, this was not something Efrain or Polo knew about Tony Mata. They saw him only as what he represented himself to be: a messenger for *La Bala*.

El Grillo stood close to the two men and lit a cigarette before introducing himself. Both young men looked at him curiously and began to laugh. "Check this guy out. He has the entire park, but he wants to stand next to us. I think he likes you, Polo."

"No *idiota*, he's here to tell you he had your mother and is your real father!"

"You guys tell me the truth," Efrain continued. "Did you guys have a blind date? I can leave you two alone. Did Polo ask you here?"

"No, *La Bala* sent me," was his response. He casually flicked his cigarette to the feet of the two young men who had changed their demeanor and stopped their joking. Polo was not sure the man was being truthful. "You know, if you use *La Bala*'s name and you don't really work for him, he'll have you hung in a place for the entire town to see."

"I know that fool. I'm the one who does the killing for him."

"Do you have any proof?" Efrain also wondered. The man appeared to be getting frustrated. "You mother fuckers, do you know any other

Mexican on this side of Monterrey with full quill ostrich leather boots? Now, do you guys want to afford a pair of your own or not?" The two men looked at each other and noticed that *El Grillo* was holding a briefcase.

"Yeah, sure, what's in the briefcase?" Polo wondered. The man took out a roll of money and handed it to Efrain.

"You men complete this task, and I'm sure the *patron* will have more for you."

"What do we do?"

"Go to Monterrey. Be there by tomorrow night when *La Sombrilla* is in nightclub mode. Go to the bar and ask for Sevedres De Luna. When they ask you who you are, you tell them *El Grillo* sent you. They will let you in because they will be interested in what is in this briefcase. Do not open it until you get to De Luna, or you're both dead. He will pay you extra on top of what I just gave you. Monterrey is an hour away, so get moving. I know you pieces of shit don't have a car, but you have money now, so figure it out."

Tony *El Grillo* Mata gave his instruction and vanished as mysteriously as he had appeared. The two men were left alone to discuss freely, but they were not given much of an option to accept or decline the responsibility of the task. "What do we do, Polo?"

"What do you mean? We can't say no. He left the briefcase with us. We don't even know where to find him to give it back."

"If we hurry, we can catch up to him."

"Do you think he's walking like us, you idiot? He's gone! Besides, look, he already paid us."

"So just like that, we're in?"

"Efrain, why are you so paranoid? This is the opportunity of a lifetime. Come on, let's have some fun on the way. We've got money."

"Are you sure about this?"

"What can go wrong? He didn't even ask our names. Do you really think he can even find us? Do you know what is probably in this briefcase? *Plata culero* . . . lots of *plata* that we can borrow."

It took some convincing. While Efrain did not possess any more cognitive ability than Polo, he was more logical in his suspicions of a briefcase filled with money being given to two strangers to deliver without asking their names. After discussing the matter for a while, Efrain convinced Polo that they should open the briefcase to make sure they were not being used as mules to deliver drugs. "Look, if the briefcase has money, we will take it. But if it has cocaine, we get rid of it and use the money the guy gave us and vanish." This was Efrain's paranoid idea, and Polo agreed to it.

They found a private area near a statue at the park where they could work the briefcase over. It took some time, but they were finally able to get it open. As predicted by Polo, the suitcase was filled with money. They both looked at each other in amazement, never believing they would see that amount of money in their lifetime. Efrain was still very suspicious about why that kind of money would be entrusted to two strangers whose names they did not know. Polo's enthusiasm for the mission relieved Efrain of any further concern, and the two were on their way to Monterrey.

Along the way, they stopped at the red-light district. They entered a bar called *El Gallo Prieto* and they spent their evening with girls who were more than happy to spend time with men who could afford it. They drank and spoiled themselves until late that evening. Efrain began to get nervous about the time they had to get to Monterrey. They still needed to find a car. "Relax, Efrain. *Chingow*, I'm not married to not have to deal with all that shit, and here you are acting like an old lady."

"I just didn't like the look of that guy. I don't want to piss them off. Let's just get to Monterrey, and whatever extra time we have before going to *La Sombrilla*, we can use it for fun there."

Polo displayed a huge grin on his face. "Ah, *mi amigo*, you do think things through, don't you? Of course, Monterrey has women too, no?"

"And tequila."

The two friends went directly to the bus station. Polo used money from the briefcase to pay for two tickets. Efrain did not take a liking to this action. "What are you doing, Polo? Are you trying to get us killed?"

"What? This is a business expense, isn't it? What good is it for him to give us money if we have to use our own to do the job?"

Polo's reasoning did little for Efrain's comfort level, but it did enough to get him to go along with it. When the two friends arrived in Monterrey,

Nuevo Leon, the evening was festive with people covering the streets at different bars. The annual carnival had arrived the night before, which attracted many tourists from different places. It was a great place to enjoy Mexico's happier side, but like in most festive scenes, money is always a constituent part of enjoying oneself. The number of tequila shots thrown down by the two men was enough to render a horse unconscious. It was a modern medical miracle that they could even walk, but what could be said for the maintaining of their physical faculties could not be said for their mental capacity. Their judgment was distorted beyond measure, and although they were able to save some of the money that was provided for them in the briefcase, they had spent a dollar too much.

Neither of the men realized how much lighter the suitcase had gotten since they had received it. They never considered how casually they have been carrying the case as they drank. Few thought anything of it. Perhaps they felt it was nothing of significance if they had it so loosely among so many strangers. But now the time had come to deliver the suitcase to *La Sombrilla*, which they made their way to sometime in the early morning hours. People were still walking the streets, and the carnival showed no signs of slowing down. Business in Mexico is important; earning potential is never unnecessarily brought to a halt. The two men entered the bar with complete disregard for the possible danger they exposed themselves to with a suitcase containing less than it should have.

Perhaps, it would have made little difference to the outcome of the young men's fate in the end. Without their knowledge, a more sinister plot had been designed at the expense of the foolish boys. With every hour that passed between being given the assignment and their journey to Monterrey, Tony *El Grillo* Mata was lurking nearby within viewing distance. He had been witnessing every dollar Polo and Efrain spent. He was around the corner of every bar they entered and within touching distance of every whore they petitioned. Had *El Grillo* cared anything about the money, the two men would be dead. His interest was more in what he prepared to deliver to the contact person in the secret compartment the suitcase had. It was hidden so cleverly; there was no way for either of the obtuse friends to discover it. It was their inarticulate nature that qualified them to carry such an important delivery to the contact person in *La Sombrilla*.

They both arrived at the bar area as previously instructed. They were too intoxicated to realize they were not nearly as courageous as they were behaving.

"*El Grillo* sent us," Polo announced to the bartender with conviction. The bartender continued to dry the shot glasses he was cleaning. He waited for further confirmation that Tony Mata was the one who had sent the two men. He never said a word or even acknowledged that he heard what they said. Polo and Efrain looked at each other with confusion before the latter decided to pursue the role of the tougher of the two. "Well, since you're not going to answer us, let me have a shot of *Patron*." To this, the bartender did react, and he placed two shot glasses in front of the two men and filled them with *Patron* tequila.

"But let me tell you, something *amigo*." Efrain continued. "If after I throw down this shot, you don't send us to whoever we're supposed to speak to, we're leaving and taking this money with us. And we're going to finish what's been a hell of a night with every dollar that's in here."

The bartender threw the rag he was using to dry the glasses on the bar and disappeared into the back. "*Orale* Efrain, you sounded like a real tough guy. I almost forgot what a pussy you are."

"Shut the hell up, Polo. We represent some tough men, so let's act like it, alright?"

The bartender never emerged, and the two men decided to abort the mission and explain to *El Grillo* that the contact was uncooperative—that is how these two innocent men believed it worked in the world of organized crime. It did not get to that, however. They were met by two very large men at the door who blocked their path and motioned to look behind them. There at a long booth sat a man whose mere appearance suggested he was the man they came to see. Polo and Efrain walked slowly toward the booth. The intimidating sight of the men brought back a sense of sobriety in both friends. It was then they began to experience a sense of concern for the missing money. It was a legitimate concern that came to their minds much too late. They were now sitting in front of a man they called Sevedres *El Toro* De Luna. He must have earned that name for a much more sinister reason than his broad chest and the tattoo of a bull on the side of his neck. He never addressed the two men and immediately unsnapped the briefcase.

"This was supposed to arrive locked!" He yelled as he slammed his fist on the table. There was nothing Polo or Efrain could do but take deep swallows. When they did, it felt as if they were trying to pass a brick through their throat. Their emotional constitution had found a new cure for being drunk. They had never been soberer in their lives. De Luna opened the briefcase and erupted in laughter. "This is a joke—right *muchachos*? It is either a joke or intentional suicide—So which is it?"

Before the men could answer, a phone rang within the briefcase. This seemed to have surprised De Luna—a look his men would not often see in him. He searched around the briefcase and followed the sound to the secret compartment. He found the cell phone and answered it without saying anything.

"Toro?"

"Grillo?"

"Yes, are my men there?"

"Yes, but if this isn't some fuckin' joke, you won't be getting them back. Where's the rest of my money? I want it right now, Grillo, or there's going to be a problem!"

"Don't worry. When we hang up, press #9 for instructions on where to get it."

"*Orale* and I might just kill your men anyway for making this complicated."

"Go ahead."

Tony Mata hung up. De Luna was impressed with his lack of concern for the two men. He looked at them: "Your boss must not think much of you two dickheads." He pressed #9, and in simultaneous form, a large explosion shook the entire earth for over a ten-block radius. Car alarms went wild, and *La Sombrilla* became an inferno. The massive ball of fire shot to the sky like the devil shooting from the earth into the heavens with fiery wings. All within perished, whether they were targets of the design or not. The few who survived ran to the streets as incomplete beings. Some were without their arms—others with dangling eyes.

The fireworks from the carnival disappeared behind the orange night sky that made it seem like daytime. It was a spectacular display of unnecessary violence. Whatever De Luna owed *La Bala*—he paid for it all with others' lives in addition to his target.

A few miles down the road, Tony *El Grillo* Mata pulled over and called his boss.

"It's done, boss."

"You sure?"

"Positive."

"Make sure those two idiots you hired don't talk."

"They won't."

The story about *El Grillo* is related as told to me by the previously mentioned *El Viejon*, who readers will learn more about in a future publication. While this figure was not found to be associated with child trafficking, questions surrounding his sexual involvement with some of the young girls in the house came to life. *El Grillo* was returned to Mexico and sent to a Mexican prison without any collection of his DNA. He had been a fugitive for thirteen years, but whether he was at the Cuellar residence the entire time could not be ascertained. His criminal status at the time of the research for this project is unknown.

It has been previously said, but not enough, that Elsa Cuellar was a smart woman. She knew exactly how to stay away from the clutches of law enforcement. For many years, there had been rumors of her having women working for her in *La Zona*, which is the red-light district in Nuevo Laredo, Mexico, across the bridge from Laredo, Texas. There were several problems with this information. First, it came from sources that might not be considered by a court of law. Much of the information obtained about Cuellar had this problem. What law enforcement had learned came from sources on the street. Secondly, there was no way to prove this. If Cuellar did have victims working for her in *La Zona*, her workers would easily blend in with the other prostitutes who are not associated with her. Perhaps the most significant problem and the most obvious is that even if it could be proved Cuellar was a madam for prostitution, *La Zona* is in Mexico outside the jurisdiction of American authorities.

This red-light district existed before it was called *La Zona*. It is said to have been visited by Pancho Villa and his soldiers where they would pay for sexual services. Later, it was given the name *La Zona*, to indicate that it was an area of social and legal tolerance where prostitutes could work legally. During the prohibition between 1920 and 933, the banning of alcohol led many visiting Americans across the border into Mexico. The prostitution business boomed and the idea of *La Zona* as a legitimate moneymaking business caught the attention of many businessmen both Mexican and American. Earlier in my writing career, I had taken a tour of this red-light district, but things did not go well. I did not know I was not supposed to take pictures and they took my camera, my belt, and whatever money I had in my wallet. This time, I found a different strategy, that is, have *La Zona* come to me. I asked others for months before I found a local doctor who of course asked not to have his real name mentioned. My intention is not to ruin anyone's medical career, so I decided not to assign even a fictitious name for fear someone may be misled into thinking it is a different doctor with no knowledge of the red-light district in Mexico. I met with this doctor at North Central Park in north Laredo, where we looked like two good old friends trying to keep our belly fat down. He told me that although he did not call on women from Mexico as often as he used to, he still used the service at least once a month. When asked if these girls were from *La Zona* or from somewhere else, he said: "Both man, my contact will get me, girls, from wherever she can. Sometimes they are from *La Zona* and other times from somewhere else. There are even times during the summer when business is booming that she has to borrow girls from Reynosa or places deeper in Mexico."

This information was very interesting to me. I could not help but ask how these girls came to the United States side. "I honestly don't know," the doctor explained. "I know they're illegal because they are always very careful not to get caught by border patrol. But how they get across so easily and just return, I don't know." The manner these women were crossing so easily seemed familiar and wanted to learn more about that part of the doctor's experience. I asked him if he had ever heard of Elsa Cuellar and he said no, but he did relate a story told to him by an older lady named Alicia in the days when he would go to *La Zona* before he became a doctor.

NUEVO LAREDO, TAMAULIPAS, MEXICO, SUMMER OF 1998

She had no choice. Twelve-year-old Lucy Ventura had to go to work with her mother. It was not uncommon for children in Mexico to go to work with their single-parent mothers. Sometimes, the children were put to work as well: usually without being paid. This was a much less acceptable scenario by most human moral standards. Lucy's mother, Ana, was a prostitute in one of the many establishments found in *La Zona*—the red-light district in Nuevo Laredo. She was asked to do numerous things during her shift. She would sometimes be assigned to dance topless at one bar, have sex with men at others, or do a donkey show at any of the establishments. Normal men did not care much for the donkey show. It was the most brutal thing that could ever be done to either the woman or the animal.

One could always tell which of the men did not have an appreciation for such things. They were the ones outside the bar throwing up. Most could stomach the woman dancing on the donkey; their intestines began to make a sound when they would see the woman perform oral sex on the innocent animal. They would often penetrate the poor mule with a banana and present one of the drunk men in the audience with the challenge of eating the fruit from between her legs. Still, it was those in position for closer observation that usually lost their lunch. One would have to be close to see the fleas and ticks from the mule that had been transferred to the dancer's pubic area. It was a disturbing sight and only one of many fantasies a man could achieve.

Almost every fantasy a man cared to experience could be fulfilled at *La Zona*. Desires ranged from experiences with underaged girls, boys, transgender, older, or groups. It did not matter much. There were no standards there. There was no code of ethics or moral regulations that were required to be followed. It was the playground for the devil, and men suitable to be his children enjoyed every second of it. The sexual environment along with the organized crime and violence that at times erupted there did not make it an atmosphere anyone with even a mild sense of moral standards would feel is a place for a child. But Ana did have some help. When she arrived at work, a lady looking to earn extra money would take care of Lucy until Ana completed her shift. Her name was Alicia Ramos, and she had become too old for prostitution. Even when she found the occasional male willing to pay her, they never gave her that much. She found herself earning more by taking care of the children of single mothers who worked there.

The more reassuring thing was her daughter's safety. A common practice for abducted girls is to use them as mules to cross drugs into the United States. They would spend weeks training girls to swallow large grapes without biting them. This would give them the skill to swallow balloons full of heroin. The girls were then told to swallow the heroin, and if they made it into the United States, they would go to a designated hotel where they were given food. The idea was for the drug runners to wait for them to defecate the balloons out of their system. Sometimes, the runners would get impatient waiting, and the poor girl's bodies were found opened from the stomach in the hotel room. They were cut open like animals.

It was a convenient arrangement for Ana. Before meeting Alicia, the best she could do was to keep Lucy in the room with her where she had sex with men. She would place Lucy in the closet with her toy doll and tell her to play and not come out until she was told. The curiosity was too much to resist for a child. This is especially true of a child who is in a closet where the door is nothing more than a shower curtain. Upon hearing all of the sexual sounds that tend to get released during sex, it was a natural inclination for the young girl to move the shower curtain to the side a little to see what her mother was doing. It was a bad scenario from the very beginning. Any time a child is introduced to sex in such a graphic way, it completely distorts their perception of it for the rest of their life.

Before long, Lucy wanted to dress like her mother to work. She wanted to be like her mother and get paid like her. The exchange of money was something she often saw, and in a country where earning potential is often limited, it was an attractive discovery for the young girl. Ana was doing her best to survive. Her daughter's well-being was important to her, but so was having enough money to eat. Ana was very confused as to what route she should take or what changes she should make in her life to ensure her daughter's safety. She was very happy to have met Alicia. The old woman was walking the paths of *La Zona* trying to sell her handmade quilts when she came across the little girl sitting outside a room her mother was in with a client. Ana never liked leaving Lucy outside; the room she was assigned for the night did not have a closet.

Alicia saw that Lucy was playing with her dolls. She was making them do sexual acts on each other and being violent in their treatment of one another. She had been living in *La Zona* for so many years; Alicia had lost count of how many times she had witnessed these young girls transpiring into what their mothers had become. She waited outside with the little girl until her mother came out. It was then she spoke to her mother about what she saw and how she could help. Since then, Alicia would take care of Lucy for a percentage of what Ana made for the night. Although it would cost Ana money to have her taken care of, it also allowed her to work more. It all worked out well for the struggling mother, and Alicia's assistance could not have come at a better time.

Within days of having been approached by Alicia, members of the Colombian cartel had arrived in Mexico to work out dealing with cartels in Mexico. One night they were taken to *La Zona* for a night of sport and entertainment. After some time, they began to take certain liberties with the women without feeling like they had to pay for the service. It was not in the girl's best interest to complain or refuse service without being paid first. It never ended well for the women who chose to take this route. The Columbian's visit to Mexico was extensive and at a high cost to the area. For the initial visit, Ana was able to avoid having to interact with any of them, but once their arrangement with the Mexican cartels had been established, their visitors from Medellin and Bogota came more frequently. It was during one of these visits that Ana's success in avoiding the men had run out.

His name was Diamantes Ojeda. He was a tall, well-built man. Ana rarely got clients as handsome and well sculpted as he was. She was appealing to him as well. Ana had always been a beautiful woman and took great care of her body. Under any other circumstances, she may have made a good living for herself. She often thought of having been a model or an actress. Instead, she sat on her unmade bed with her knees to her chest and her hair undone. This is not what Diamantes was looking at. He first noticed the shape of her legs and the natural curve of her hips. He was instantly aroused by the firm cleavage that lumped over the tiny shirt she was wearing.

Diamante's frame took up most of the front door. His thin shadow of a beard was neatly trimmed, and he smelled as if he just got out of the shower. His jaw was firm and shoulders high. He did not smile. Ana was afraid much more than she was attracted to him. His left ear was adorned with a diamond, and he wore a watch that could probably buy her a house if she sold it. He closed the door behind him and used a chair to secure it. He was with the cartel, so his reasons for doing that could be many. Was he going to rape her? Was it for his own safety? She had no way of knowing until he finally spoke.

"Take a shower."

He said this in the manliest tone she had ever heard from any man. She wondered what would have happened if she had been assigned a room without a shower. Not all the rooms had showers. Would he have just left and let her off the hook? Would he have killed her in a fit of disappointment? He remained poker-faced with his black pants, black shirt, and black coat. For anyone else, she would assume they were attending a funeral. For Diamante, it seemed befitting that the only part of the wardrobe that was not black was the shiny silver tips of his Dillon Western boots. Ana once worked at a shoe store and knew how much they were worth. They had a caiman belly vamp and calfskin shaft, bovine lining, and leather heels. It would be a shame if a man with his financial resources would take advantage of her without paying.

She had no time to think of these matters. She was given an order by a very dangerous man and had to comply. She came out of the shower completely nude. There were no towels in the shower, and she did not want to get her only clothes wet. Diamante was already on the bed with his clothes off. His bulging chest and sculpted abdomen made his tattoo work pop into three-dimensional figures. At first, she was scared that he would hurt her with violence. Now seeing how well endowed he was, she feared being hurt in another fashion. He still had not said a word to her other than asking her to shower. With such limited conversation and no directive to follow, she did not know how to act. She could think of nothing else but to sit next to him on the bed. She leaned back, not knowing his preferred position, but he seemed very comfortable taking command of the experience.

He had her one way and then another. Diamante took her body as if he had been familiar with it his entire life. She had orgasms she had never had before with anyone else. So many men had been with her, and none could boast of having done to her what Diamante had accomplished. He took her to a place of sheer ecstasy. The difference between him and any other client is that she wanted it. She did not care if she got paid or not at that moment. Not getting paid would make her feel as if someone wanted her for how pretty she was and not because she was a whore. Diamante was firm but not brutally hard on her. In the middle of the evening, she felt it—that feeling every woman wants to feel at one point in her life. She was not just being fucked; she was being made love to. It was not what she expected from Diamante Ojeda.

When done, he spoke again. "Wait outside by the door." Ana had never been asked to do this before. She waited outside the door and heard Diamante placing the chair back where it was to secure it. He showered, got dressed, and left. He did not say anything about the payment, but there was an envelope on the bed when Ana returned to the room. She opened it, and inside was one thousand American dollars. She burst into a mixture of crying and laughter. For her, it was a lottery that she never would have won. She would be able to do so much with the money and did not feel the need to be with other men for the night.

Diamante's fortune could not have come at a better time for Ana. Throughout the following week, men were not approaching her. She tried to look appealing, but men were not stopping at her assigned room. No interest had been indicated at all. She was confused and requested a different room from the man in charge of them. He declined her request without explanation. It was not common for a worker to get the same room night after night. This had been the case for Ana. She was given a corner room away from the central action. Still, she was disappointed in the men that did go through that area. They did not look her way. She began to consider that she was getting older and perhaps less appealing. She thought maybe she was pungent and did not realize it. She considered this after recalling Diamante had asked her to shower. She was becoming worried. She had good money for the moment but knew it would not last forever.

The first few days of the following week were just as slow. It was not until the end of the shift that a man walked up to her. He appeared to be intoxicated and unappealing to Ana. She had to take the clients that came to her. Adding to her fortune was necessary to ensure savings. He went into her room and pushed her to the bed. He smelled like a combination of sweat and cheap musk. She was not expecting anything as she had experienced with Diamante but braced herself for whatever came next. As she got ready, the door was kicked open. Two men went into the room without warning and took the man by the shoulders.

"Hey, what is this? I was here first!"

The men did not answer and dragged him outside. Ana heard a loud gunshot. Security often shot rounds to scare off drunks. The men who barged in, however, were not known to Ana. Perhaps they were new security. If they were, why would they drag off a client? She did not understand her recent luck. It quickly changed with the appearance of Diamante's figure at the door. Ana's heart raced with the excitement of being saved by a knight. Lonely women are not usually in favor of being alone with a cartel member. This one paid well; it was an opportunity she could not pass up. The night played out very much as it had the first time. He asked her to shower, and all else evolved in almost the same sequence it had in their first meeting. For Ana, the sex was even more passionate and pleasurable. On top of another thousand dollars, Diamante left her a pair of gold diamond earrings.

He spoke very minimally, yet there was something agreeable about his character. He was rough yet gentle. He was frightened and, at the same time, comforting. He was aggression with a luxurious representation. When he left, she could see the man who had been taken away earlier. He was in the middle of the street with a gunshot to his forehead.

It was then Ana understood the scenario. There would no longer be men coming to see her. Diamante had spread the word that no one was to petition Ana for sexual services unless they were willing to exchange their life for her. It was brutal, yet there was something romantic about it. She felt like a child. Diamante's actions gave her more confidence in him. As he left, she blurted out: "What is your name?"

"Diamante."

"Can we get a nicer room, Diamante?"

He did not answer her, but that same evening, however, she was placed in the most luxurious room in the entire establishment. It was rarely used for prostitution. Instead, it was a living quarter for the head pimp. He had recently remodeled a different part of the building for himself, and his old quarters remained vacant. It was more of an apartment equipped with everything Ana always dreamed of having in a home of her own. Diamante visited her more frequently, never forgetting the generous compensation and always remembering to bring her a gift. They became more emotionally connected over the weeks. Diamante became more talkative and shared some of his exploits and how he got into business with the Colombians. He was a gentler soul than he cared to admit.

"Why did you use to ask me to shower? Did I smell?"

"So, you wouldn't see where I hid my gun."

"So, when I was in the shower, you would hide your things? That was smart!"

The summer quickly ended, and by the time the Christmas season arrived, Diamante's relationship had reached a much different level. He began to take her out to nice places. Slowly, she detached herself from having to work in *La Zona* with Diamante as his only client. Relieving oneself from their duties within this establishment was not something women could usually escape unless they considered death an escape. Diamante had a presence there. Ana had yet to understand his role, but he was someone people did not say "no" to. If he wanted Ana out of the red-light district, then it would be so. Their evenings were now in fine hotels, the gifts more extravagant, the life more luxurious. It was the classic fairy tale for Ana. It was the life she always dreamed of, but never one she imagined would happen. Only one flaw in her current state shattered the night images in her head of the life she now had; Diamante knew nothing about Ana's daughter. There was a reason for this.

As the two were getting to know each other, Diamante had expressed never wanting to have children. Some reasons were selfish, such as not wanting the responsibility, wanting the freedom to do what he wanted, and preferring to use his money for something better. Other motives were more noble. He did not want to bring a child into his world; if he ever died, he did not want to leave an orphaned child or a single mother behind to shield off the inherited threats from enemies. Whatever the most important reasons were, Ana had no way of knowing. The one thing she knew with certainty was that he did not want children. She thought it risky to inquire about what children were to him. She did not dare ask if that meant he would not accept one if his girlfriend or wife already had it. If the answer was still "no," she would instantly burn the bridge to the life she had been living and the income she had been earning from one man who had grown obsessed with her.

Ana did not feel the need to tell Diamante anything about Lucy until she had a reason to. She was, however, growing concerned with Alicia's demeanor for having been watching her so much. There was no doubt Ana was in a better position to compensate Alicia for her services nicely, but there was also a matter of time. Alicia had personal affairs to manage and, at her age, declining health. The more serious concern came on Christmas Eve 1998. She never thought she would be any more impressed than she already was with her new prince. Like in previous times, Diamante proved he could go to the next level. He gave Ana a ring indicating he wanted to marry her.

"My business is done here, Ana. My laboratory is set up. I leave for Medellin in the morning. Will you come with me?"

"And if I do not?"

"Then all I will have is the memory of you. I will not be back."

Ana stayed quiet. Diamante expected her to quickly accept, not knowing she had a motive for remaining where she was.

"Look, I will not pressure you. If you are still here in the morning, I know the answer is yes. If you are gone, I will take my heavy heart to Mexico."

It was the longest night of Ana's life. She stayed in the room alone that night. Diamante had some last loose ends to tie up in Monterrey before they left in the morning. She spent most of the night crying. She was expected at Alicia's to get Lucy by 10:00 p.m. It was already 1:00 a.m. She did not know whether to tell Diamante about Lucy. The thought of losing the life she had was torturing her inside. The worms of greed had attached to her stomach and were eating away at it. What good would she be to her daughter if she returned to her impoverished state? She also considered the alternative. If Diamante was accepting of Lucy, what good would her life be among the Colombian cartels? It was a complicated dilemma she did not know how to manage.

In the morning, Alicia made Lucy breakfast. She had never stayed the night before. Alicia did not know if something terrible had happened to Ana or if she was enjoying a new carefree lifestyle. Whatever her reasons were, Alicia figured that after two full weeks expired without any signs of Ana, it was a safe assumption she would not be returning for her daughter. It is a disheartening situation that happens too often in Mexico. Alicia did not want any part of that. In her youth, Alicia was taught only one thing in her life: to survive. She was a prostitute by the time she was fourteen, and did everything she could to put meals in her stomach. She taught her own daughters the same skills she had and felt no need to be any different with Lucy. The little girl was not her responsibility. The child had to eat, she needed to go to school, and she wanted her mother. It was too much for Alicia to handle. As a result, she became bitter and aggressive. What was once discipline soon manifested into abuse. She could not afford to raise a child. The poor little girl would have to raise herself. By the time Lucy was twelve, Alicia was pimping her out to adult males.

The things these men made Lucy do are much too horrible for anyone to imagine. She was too young to owe her life to the devil, but that is exactly who she was working for. Everything that represented childhood in her life had come to a premature end. The loss of her innocence came in more ways than just losing her virginity. Lucy had lost everything in her life that made life worth living. In a world of fiction, she would find a way out, rise to power, avenge herself against her mother, and die a wealthy woman. Her life was in the real world, where fairy tales don't exist. Things would only get worse.

In February 1999, a man entered *La Zona* and specifically asked for Lucy. He looked around for some time and finally found her. He appeared to be familiar with the red-light district system, but Alicia had never seen him before. He went to the little house at the edge of the *La Zona* district where Alicia had lived for most of her life. Her mother would take clients to that same house many years before. Lucy hid under the table. She did not feel much like being with men. She wanted to play with her dolls. To her, it seemed as if the man was arguing with Alicia. The little girl had no way of knowing he was negotiating for her. According to this man, who refused to give his name, he knew of a woman in Laredo, Texas, who was interested in purchasing the little girl.

"What would she want with a little illegal girl in the United States? You can't get away with things like that over there."

"Don't worry about that. Just tell me if you are interested. What are you going to do, raise her yourself? It looks like you barely walk."

"She doesn't have papers. I don't even know her birthday."

"I told you already, *señora*, the papers are none of your concern. Do you want to get paid or not?"

A month later, Lucy was enrolled at an elementary school in Laredo, Texas. Her birth certificate said "Brianna Maldonado Ruiz." They called her that so often, she had forgotten her name was Lucy. She had a birth certificate, a social security number, and baby pictures in a family album that she had no way of knowing was not her. Lucy, as she was previously known, did not exist anymore. She had evaporated into thin air along with the South Texas dust. The dust had more of an identity than she did. People knew the dust was there and where it came from.

At the end of her first school year at a South Laredo elementary school, "Brianna" left the campus. An attendance officer saw her leave through the playground, and she got lost in a property lined with mobile homes. The school called the parents, but no one answered. They had no choice but to involve local authorities, and the Laredo Police Department was notified. A city police officer was the responder. He took the attendance officer's statement and used his testimony to follow the tiny sneaker prints that led to a mobile home less than a block from the school. The officer knocked on the door, and a male in his mid-twenties answered. He was shirtless and appeared drunk. The house was extremely messy, and the inside had a foul odor.

"Sir, Laredo Police Department, we are looking for a little girl named Brianna."

The male had every intention of denying having seen her, but before he could, the little girl called out. "Here I am." To the officer's shock, the child was completely nude when she came out of the room. The officer instantly drew his weapon and ordered the male to get on the floor. He was arrested immediately, and a female officer was called to get the girl dressed.

"Brianna, can you tell me what you're doing here?"

"Well, my mom and dad told me to come here every Wednesday during recess."

"Why?"

"I guess to help the man feel better. That's what my mom said."

"How are you supposed to do that?"

What the little girl described to the officer was a clear case of sexual abuse of a minor. He went to his unit and opened the back door where the suspect was being held.

"You know what they do to child abusers in prison, don't you?"

"Yeah, I do."

"I hope they do it to you every day, you fuckin prick." He slammed the door and went back to Brianna and asked about her home environment. "Where are your parents?"

"I don't know. Home maybe."

That is where the officer expected to find the couple, but it would not be that easy. The address listed in the school records was an empty lot. It was a piece of land that was owned by a deceased person. No one claiming to be the little girl's parents ever appeared; nothing in the little girl's file was a legal document. Brianna was a walking lie. She was taken to the youth shelter, where she was given a bed, food, and counseling. In the mornings, she would have a ride to school, but Brianna had become a problem for those around her. There were numerous complaints at the shelter and school about the confused child. She would get on the male students and model the sexual behavior that was natural to her. This was a serious proposition she was making at the shelter because some of the males were registered sex offenders on probation. After many meetings with the state, it was determined that Brianna would be better off receiving services in a facility for girls in Houston, Texas. Continuous suicide attempts had her transferred less than a year later to a hospital in Nashville, Tennessee. Two years later, Brianna died of kidney failure.

I was very interested in Alicia. I wanted to talk to her because I had some problems with the story. Certainly, details could have been lost in the translation of it, but Alicia knew far too much about this little girl's fate for her not to have known people on the American side who still communicated with her. Someone had to have been keeping her informed and this means it could have been a business and not so much the way she told the story. I wanted to meet her, but the doctor was certain she had already passed away. "She was already fairly old in 1998. I would be shocked if she was still alive. She'd be over 100." The doctor went on to mention that he did not even recall why she told him that story, but he met her outside a donkey show where women perform sexual acts on mules. "She was a friendly and sweet woman, but I honestly don't know what her role was there or if she lived there. There was something mysterious about her." Today, this doctor has married and no longer does business with anyone who could potentially ruin his career.

24

A Bad Day

It was going to be a bad day. Investigator Alexander Rodriguez knew this from the very beginning, considering the way things were slowly unfolding. He prepared his black coffee and took the morning paper to his truck. That's where he liked to have his coffee whether he was at the ranch or not. Investigator Rodriguez did not have to unfold the paper; it was on the front page. Elsa Cuellar's day in court had arrived.

Rodriguez's focus was now on the court date ahead of him. He showered, took out the Otter Wax for his boots, and made sure he played the right motivational music to keep him focused—Billy Squire would do just fine. He tried his best to keep his mind off the possibility Elsa could simply be deported. Twenty counts of falsifying government records should be more than enough for her to see a prison cell. He did what he could to find proof of the other charges, but there was always an existing factor that would not solidify the case. It would not have weighed so heavily on him if he thought there was reasonable doubt, but that was not the case. He knew exactly what this couple was capable of and what they had already done. If only he could tell the future. He regretted not having documented every detail of every single case involving a child when he was with the police department. Maybe he would have found a connection to this woman who has plagued his life, taken his sleep, and molested his mind. It was a fit of anger beyond control that would soon erupt into massive proportions.

He arrived at the courthouse early. For the past weeks, Alexander had been working closely with the District Attorney's office to make the strongest case possible. Prosecuting attorney Julia Cardenas had been a great help to Rodriguez. She took a very strong position on why Elsa should be imprisoned and found clever and legal ways to mention some of the other incidents that she was not on trial for. She worked tirelessly every day to secure a conviction. Black coffee, late-night snacks, and consecutive hours without sleep had all come together for this moment. One of the things that Investigator Rodriguez had always had a difficult time doing as a law enforcement officer was knowing who he could trust enough to know they would give it their all. He always worked with people that he hoped would go the extra distance when trying a case. He had cultivated a strong relationship with Julia and had no doubt she would come through.

He went directly to her office that morning. He was surprised she was not there yet. It was still a few hours before they had to be in court, but she had been so eager and excited about the case, he thought she would be there with a smile that could swallow her face. After waiting for fifteen minutes, he decided to call her.

"Good morning, counselor, where are you at?"

"I wasn't feeling well. I thought I'd take the day off." She sounded as if she had been crying.

"That's a joke, right? You do remember that today you butcher Elsa Cuellar?"

"I'm sorry, Alex. I thought you knew already; that's why I didn't call you."

"Knew what?"

"They took me off the case. They gave it to someone else."

"What? That can't happen, Julia. No one is going to know the details like you do."

"I'm sorry. That's why I'm not feeling well. I couldn't stomach being taken off the case last minute like that, but it's not my call."

Rodriguez already had concerns about the case. Now, his fears were slowly becoming a reality that was kicking him in the chest like a mule with rabies. He did not want to start the day like this. The news about Julia being taken off the case was enough for the rest of the week. He made his way down to the lobby at the courthouse and saw Texas Ranger

James Dugan, who had shown interest in the case since the search warrant was served on her property fifteen years before. He was still solid in stature but now had silver hair and extra lines on his face. He may have been close to retirement but had a look on his face as if he wanted to work forever.

Investigator Rodriguez approached him and asked if he was there for the Elsa Cuellar case. "What case partner? The bitch is walking!"

"What? Oh my God, when does this day end? What the hell happened?"

The Texas Ranger explained that on her first night in jail, Elsa Cuellar claimed to be feeling ill. The report is that she had been feeling so sick, they had to rush her to Doctor's Hospital in North Laredo. They had Cuellar examined and learned she had stage 4 terminal cancer. Doctors had given her two months to live, and the United States did not want the financial responsibility of Cuellar's health care. Investigator Rodriguez expressed his discontent with Cuellar only facing deportation for twenty-two counts of tampering with government records and Dugan dropped yet another bomb on the frustrated investigator. Elsa Cuellar's charges had been reduced to only one count of tampering with government records!

Perhaps his experience had given him that deep-down gut feeling something was not going to end well with this case. He was tired of it and did not want anything more to do with Elsa Cuellar. How one Mexican citizen can manipulate the entire American legal system on both sides of the border for so many serious crimes was beyond his understanding. Murder, organ theft, baby dealing, child abuse, sexual abuse, and prostitution individually are enough to put someone away for life. A person who had engaged in all of them was free today. Rodriguez sat in his truck and leaned back for extra breath and spoke to himself. *If she only had months to live, how much would that medical bill have been? If she was going to die, wouldn't the legal system have preferred to show justice working to the public and kept her behind bars?* Suddenly, Rodriguez stopped talking to himself. He stopped thinking. He stopped trying to answer the impossible. He picked up his phone and called human resources.

"Hi Rosa, this is Investigator Rodriguez. Can you check how much time I have?" he asked.

"You have 43 days, sir."

"Great! Put me down for all of them!"

He drove by his home, picked up his rifles, fishing reels, frozen hog meat, Bo, and drove off to the only place he could be himself. He got there at a quarter past noon, loaded his weapons, and went on a hunt.

On May 10, 2022, I received a message from a family member who wished to remain anonymous. I was told Elsa agreed to speak to me if I first allowed her to read the manuscript before it was published. There was no agreement to have her play a role in whether the work would be submitted or not, so there was no harm in honoring the request. I left my home for the long drive to Laredo very early on May 16, 2022. I made several stops along the way, speaking to various law enforcement agencies about child trafficking in the area. I did not know at that moment, but by the time I stopped for my first meal in Cotulla, Texas, Elsa Cuellar had passed away. Her death was a serious setback to my investigation, but I was much too close to Laredo to turn back. There were still some unanswered questions that only the District Attorney's office could help me with.

I was very fortunate to have had District Attorney Isidro "Chilo" Alaniz meet with me. Men in his position do not usually have time to spare for people's personal projects. His father had recently passed away; I thought maybe he was not up for interviews. As it turned out, he was more than happy to see me. "My father read your first book," he shared with me. "He was a big fan of seeing Hispanics succeed in the world." I felt honored that his father read my book *The Long Way to Mexico*. Chilo led me through a maze of different hallways sporting his customary jeans and cowboy boots. His tall frame towered over the numerous people needing a question answered until we got to his office. We chatted for a few minutes about Laredo and old friends when I finally let him know why I was there. Chilo was a unique commodity to interview, not only because he was the district attorney overseeing the case, but also because he was Elsa Cuellar's neighbor!

"I always saw some strange things at her house. There were always animals and a lot of people. But as strange as it seemed, there was nothing illegal that could be seen by the naked eye."

"Once you saw her go through your legal doors, did you know anything about her child trafficking, and if so, why was she never charged?"

"We had our suspicions Roger, and people are quick to judge the legal system, but in this business, there is what you know and what you can prove."

Chilo's answer was not something I could argue with. Elsa Cuellar was a master at disguising her activity. As many hours as law enforcement had spent on Elsa Cuellar, no "smoking gun" could ever be produced. The documents were doctored masterfully, and as for the victims, there was little to no evidence that they even existed.

WAS RELIGION THE PROBLEM?

While religion is intended to provide society with a sense of order and expectations, it has also served as some of the worst examples of human conduct. Arguably, no institution in our world's history has been at the root of so much of the hate, war, and crime our nation has faced more than religion. Still, we trust those who mask their evil intent through the glorious words of scripture and the service to God. Elsa Cuellar was no exception. She found a smokescreen for her actions through a religious path. Whether Elsa Cuellar was truly chronically ill during the time of her being set free or not has never been ascertained with any degree of satisfaction. In 2013, it was reported that she only had months to live; however, she was seen in Laredo, Texas, six years later at a local church preaching in December 2019. The name of the physician who declared Elsa chronically ill has never been released, and which members of law enforcement or the court system certified and verified her condition is not known.

On December 27, 2019, En Frecuencia, a blog covering news in the Mexican broadcasting industry, published a report titled "Felon in America, Station Owner in Mexico." The article highlights Elsa's efforts to establish a new non-commercial social FM radio station (XHCSAF-FM 91.3) in Tampico, in southern Tamaulipas, and her application for a social television station in Nuevo Laredo. It also notes that Elsa's daughter, Arlene Jasmine Elsie Alvarado Cuéllar, owns XHCSAC-FM 94.3 "Radio Mapastepec" in Mapastepec, Chiapas, and had applied for authority to build a TV station in Matamoros and that another of Elsa's children, Michael Jonathan Alvarado Cuéllar, held a concession for a cable television system in Nuevo Laredo and had filed for a radio station in Morelia, Michoacán. The purpose of Cuellar's efforts was to use her stations as religious outlets for her preaching.

It would be impossible to determine the actual number of children or adults impacted by Elsa Cuellar's actions. Sadly, the number of children who are now adults who do not know their mother and father are not their biological parents can never be ascertained. Also, the number of mothers currently in Mexico who never saw their children again after meeting Elsa will never be known, even with the most profound investigation. It would be impossible to determine how many babies were born to the female victims inside the Cuellar home without any official documentation to prove they even existed. Mexico continues to be among the world's countries with the highest rate of children who go missing daily. The inaccuracy of record-keeping makes it impossible to know the exact number, but the problem of child trafficking is evident when ICE agents uncover the operations on the United States side of the border. One out of every four people trafficked into the United States are children, while women and children make up 55 percent of humans trafficked and 98 percent are trafficked for sex-based business.

These unanswered questions, in this case, continue to plague Investigator Alexander Rodriguez today. Who declared Elsa Cuellar terminally ill? Where did the evidence connecting her to the 1998 murders go? Who paid that high bond for her to get out? Who reduced the charges from twenty-two counts of tampering with government documents down to almost nothing, and why? Too much time has elapsed, and these questions will, in all likelihood, never be answered, but the more important question remains: How many people out there are unaware they are victims?

Many believed Elsa Cuellar had passed away by the time this project was initiated. This proved to be false as her death was not verified until years after the research in this case began. Recently, I spoke to Investigator Alexander Rodriguez to tell him of the reports that Elsa Cuellar had been seen preaching in a Laredo church. He contacted the ICE agent assigned to her file and was informed that the docket for deportation hearings was so backed up they had not gotten to Elsa's case. Because of this, she could still move freely from Mexico into Laredo. This raised another question of concern: "Considering the nature of her actions, why wouldn't they expedite her deportation?"

It was enough that Elsa Cuellar was able to simply walk out of the courtroom a free woman. It was an unimaginable miscarriage of justice that some of the children were allowed to remain with her. It was said that Elsa was the only mother these children had ever known, and in the interest of their emotional well-being, they should remain with her. Some of these children are already adults and continue to stand firmly against any suggestion Elsa Cuellar is not their mother.

The mysteries surrounding this case may never be understood. It is the kind of case the devil applauds, and God-fearing people get frustrated with. Something ridiculously unjust is taking place, and the children victimized by this are still without a voice. At the time this project was completed, Elsa's status had only recently been known. Before her death, she remained a ghost to law enforcement. She was hiding in plain sight while under the guise of a servant of the Lord. As for whatever she was willing to tell me had I arrived in Laredo sooner, I would never know. The information she was willing to share was taken with her to the grave.

Me with D. A. Isidro "Chilo" Alaniz. Source: Author.

25

The Psychological Impact on the Victims

ONE OF THE MOST OVERLOOKED ASPECTS OF THE ELSA CUELLAR CASE is the number of people who suffered emotionally and psychologically from her actions. Many of those professionals involved in the case see it as one of the most disturbing things they had ever been a part of. While investigating and trying to dissect every aspect of this history, I could see the emotional impact many went through when dealing with Elsa Cuellar. I saw anger, tears, and genuine concern for the children involved. One school counselor told me, "I almost threw up when I heard some of the details of this case. It was something I only thought I would ever see in a movie." Even seasoned professionals with exceptional credentials such as attorney Al Greene says: "This is the worst case I have had to work in sixty-three years." I am no exception to the psychological burdens of this case. While doing research, I was plagued by various nightmares waking me in the middle of the night. I would dream my children were being taken from me; in one dream, I found one of my sons hanging by his umbilical cord in Elsa's closet. This is a dream I do not wish on anyone about their child.

It leaves one to wonder about the psychological impact left on the children. Many of the minors involved in this case are unaware they are victims. To this day, they accept Elsa Cuellar as their mother, even if they acknowledge she is not their biological parent. Toward the end of this project, I found and spoke to one of Cuellar's daughters who is now an adult and has children of her own. "Elsa was a great mother to me," she told me. "Every time I needed something; she would get it for me. I felt provided for." This statement was powerful to me. If this person had so much love for Elsa, how much would she have had for her biological mother? Perhaps Elsa had her favorites, or the daughter may have been raised to feel a specific way. After all, Elsa was intelligent enough to be kind to some of the children to refute what others may have had to say. In the interview, the young woman also recalls her siblings. "I remember there were at least sixteen of us."

"And do you know who they were or where they came from?" I asked boldly.

"No, I don't know." She responded in a soft voice. I was not sure if I wanted to push her too much, but I had been working on this case for so long, I wanted to make sure this young girl knew she was still a victim. I asked her if she was aware that she had a mother somewhere who was her biological parent. I was very surprised at how quickly she said "Yes, I know." After a brief pause, she answered, "Can you help me find her?" This was a heartbreaking question. Not only did I not know how to begin looking for her mother since the documents were fake, but it also revealed her inherent desire to have her real mother. I thought to myself, *If after coming to love Elsa Cuellar so much, this young woman still wants to find her mother, how many others feel the same way?* Research tells us that whether this young girl was comfortable with Elsa Cuellar or not is irrelevant.

In her research, Katerina Wegar found that the genetic factor in families plays a much more critical role than most believe. While the environment is an important aspect of human development, genetics continues to be an undermined factor that can have serious repercussions once those genetic bonds are severed: "The thriving western fascination with genes and genetics explanations in matters of human bonding and development over the past decade has allowed the genetic or 'molecular' family ideal to gain unheralded strength" (363). Elsa Cuellar went far beyond exposing children to families that were not of blood relation; she snapped the link to many of these children's cultures. The combination of losing genetic ties and their culture placed many of these victims in a position to have to manage the stress of assimilating into a foreign country. The risk factors for a child who is adopted have been attributed to the psychological impact of not sharing any physical similarities with the families they live with; psychological burdens are said to be higher than those living with their natural parents. This is especially true of adoptions that take place at an international scale because not only are the children detached from their genetic family, but also, from their culture (Modell and Terrell 155).

Research in adopted children has revealed clear incidents of socio-emotional issues in children who go through the adoption process. Furthermore, cognitive development may also be affected by the "pre-adoption adversities" that a child may have been exposed to during their time in an unsuitable environment before being adopted. It is argued in *Development of Adopted Children With History of Early Adversities* that placement into a suitable home does not remove the child's lack of understanding of why they were abandoned in the first place (31). As I read through this research, I realized that the psychological impact on the children of a case of this magnitude can never fully be understood because the existing literature is dominated by research on children who went through the system legally. In a case like Elsa Cuellar's, how can the trauma of having been adopted through illegal means be measured?

I felt very fortunate to have found one of the victims so late in my research for this project. Although she agreed to allow me to use her name, I decided it was unethical seeing that she may not have the level of understanding to make that decision for herself. I have also decided not to reveal anything about how she is currently living for her privacy, but I was able to see the impact that her childhood has had on the rest of her life. She told me a little about a "sister" that she still speaks with and there are strong parallels in the direction their lives have taken. This is no surprise since their experiences are virtually the same.

The stress and emotional ride the victims of Elsa Cuellar have taken were not only experienced through their time in the household. The stress of going through the legal system once Cuellar lost custody had its share of emotional trauma. The complexity of the process to place children promotes a stress level that is often not understood by victims of that age. The reason for this may have to do with the legal process itself. The stages for placing a child in foster care may at times be so tedious that children do not understand it; the confusion may create an emotional burden that is difficult to manage. One of the possible reasons for this has to do with how many adults these children must work with. Of course, these adults are strangers to these children. Attorney Al Greene represented some of the victims in the Elsa Cuellar case and explained to me how complicated the stages for placement can be: "A child is entitled to a guardian ad litem and an attorney ad litem," he said.

So, it came to me that instantly, children are exposed to two different adults in their lives they had never met. A guardian ad litem serves as a spokesperson for the child. As Al Greene states, "A guardian's ad litem role is to look out for the best interest of the children. An attorney's ad litem role is to serve as an advocate for the children as they would any other client." These positions are there to provide justice for the victims. It is difficult to achieve justice for children who cannot speak for themselves if they do not have someone speaking on their behalf. I wondered whether there was a way to decrease the number of people children had to be exposed to and as it turned out, Al Greene shared many of the same sentiments. "I prefer the dual role myself," he said. "I would rather serve as the person who can look out for the best interest of the child and also be able to ask questions in the hearing." He explained that a guardian ad litem is not allowed to ask questions; however, they can give a recommendation to the court based on the facts of the case.

In my conversation with Greene, I also came to learn that when the immigration issue comes into play, the process can become more complicated and require many more hearings. The problem with Elsa Cuellar's case was that it carried some immigration complexities with it because the true nationality of some of the children could not always be ascertained. The facts, in this case, provoked questions that were concerns of both ethics and justice: *If a child's documents are fabricated, then is the child a true citizen? If not, what role can the American legal system play outside deportation?* Additionally, the issue of time was a critical component of how much could be done for the victims here in the United States. Many of these cases took time to go through that process and if at that time a victim had aged out of the Child Protective Service system, those victims would now be adults left to fend for themselves. Once a victim is out of the care of Child Protective Service, the immigration status of the victim changes along with their status in society as a minor.

This was another problem posed by the family dynamics cultivated by Elsa Cuellar's domestic setting. Although research on the psychological burdens placed on children in households consisting of family members with mixed status is in its infancy, sociologists are beginning to understand the powerful impact it can have. Children can easily understand what it means to have their immigration status policed by the American legal system and the fears of deportation of a family member or themselves linger in their everyday lives. Through research, it is clearer now that delays in cognitive ability, mental health, and school performance can all be seriously impacted by exposure to these conditions (Gulbas and Zayas 54).

Elsa Cuellar's case poses many questions and unveils many holes in the legal system. These holes are extremely difficult to plug in because there is no way to predict what new scenario will be introduced in our society. This case shows the difficulties in legislating new immigration laws that will cover every possible situation. Elsa Cuellar knew this; it is because of this knowledge that she was so successful in her operations.

26

Reflections

As I was researching this project, my hope was that Elsa Cuellar was not enough to tarnish the reputation of Laredo, Texas. The good people in this wonderful city deserve better than to be part of a place recognized for one person's actions. However, citizens must understand that like all communities along the Rio Grande, Laredo harbors a vulnerability that can easily allow organized crime to penetrate the beautiful culture that brings to life this corner of the state. In working to learn more about this case, my hindsight became clear, and I began to question many personal experiences that made me wonder if they were in any way related to Elsa Cuellar.

In the mid-90s, I joined the Laredo Police Department. I was assigned a field training officer who would very often stop at a house in central Laredo. It was the night shift, so on quiet nights I knew the routine stop would be made. I always knew when we were going there because my training officer would always stop for snacks and a drink before going. He knew it would be a while, and I would need something to do as I waited. At that time, there was no explanation other than he was possibly having an affair. I would roll down the unit windows, listen for any calls we might get, and rest my head as I heard the distant train sound its horn at a close distance. Staying awake was very difficult, but I was in training and knew I could not fall asleep no matter how bored I became.

Some nights at the house were shorter than others. There were, however, those nights when by the time my field training officer emerged from the house, I could see a thin pink line on the horizon as the South Texas sun began to pierce the sky with a warning of a new day. It was a great feeling knowing I could go home after sitting in the police unit for so long. If any good came out of this experience was that my training officer would always give me good marks on the nightly report. Perhaps it was to keep me quiet. I did not know what he did in that house because I did not ask him; part of me did not want to know, but a few months later I wished I had. My field training officer was featured in the local news as having been arrested for child pornography and other charges related to harm against children. My heart began to race as guilt overwhelmed me: *Is that what he was doing in that house?* I never learned if that is what he was doing there or if that was an adult relationship outside his marriage, but the thought of being a certified officer outside the house where children were possibly being hurt consumed me emotionally for a very long time. I shared these feelings with a senior officer who made me feel much better: "Partner, you are a new rookie. You were doing what your F.T.O. asked. If anything, we are all responsible for not seeing this and not questioning what he was doing. You are only one part of a department that failed those kids." Of course, I still do not know to this day if that is what he was doing in that house, but I remember needing to hear those words.

After realizing law enforcement was not the best environment for me, I went into counseling at-risk youths. By this time, I had received my degree in psychology and would do home visits for families having problems with their children ages seven to seventeen. One specific case today reminds me of the work Elsa Cuellar was doing. It was in a housing project in South Laredo where I met the young man who I will call Freddy. He was a young child who did not understand what he was doing in that home. It was confusing to me because I thought the referral came from her mother. I spoke to his guardian who was very evasive saying she was taking care of the young boy for a friend who was having some personal problems. According to the seven-year-old boy, however, he had been there since he was a baby. I learned that the referral was made by the school and not this woman claiming to be the boy's guardian.

After pressing the woman for a little more information, she tried to blame her older high school son for Freddy's conduct. It appeared more as if she was disappointed in Freddy for being referred than she was in the older son for making him misbehave. She explained Freddy would become very irate and violent around her son. With her consent, I opened a case for her son as well. We asked Freddy to wait in the bedroom so I could speak freely about the woman's son. She agreed to let me go to the son's high school which was only a few blocks away. When I arrived at the campus, the school told me the student was absent on that day. Since the house was so close, I returned to inquire with the mother whether she was aware her son was not on campus. When I returned, deputy sheriffs and constables were at the residence after a neighbor called reporting someone going into the house through a bedroom window. I learned the boy missing from school had cut class to go back home and enter the house through Freddy's bedroom window to sodomize him.

I wondered how long this practice had been going on. The young man was arrested and taken to the Webb County Juvenile Detention Center. In speaking with the Child Protective Services officer involved, I was told that since the offender was removed from the home, they could not remove the child. Even after hearing about the conflicting stories between what the woman said and Freddy's account, there was no justifiable reason to have the boy removed. After being treated at the hospital, the boy was released. Because he had become an active case under the Child Protective Services system, I was not allowed to keep his case open by policy. I closed the case without ever having met the boy's biological mother or looking into the different accounts about how long Freddy had been at the house.

Later, in the fall semester of 2006, I was already teaching at the college level. I became good friends with a co-worker because we shared a common interest in chess. He was a much older man than me, but we seemed to get along very well as we spoke about life while playing chess and drinking coffee. He liked his black with sugar and no cream; I can only drink iced coffee, which he never understood. Still, we got past that one difference and cultivated a great chess relationship. This went on for some time before I noticed his absence from campus. He was not a professor, so there was no specific class I could go to and check his well-being. Because he was older, I thought maybe he had fallen ill. Instead, I learned he had been arrested for having been living romantically with a fifteen-year-old girl that could have been his granddaughter. It was ascertained through investigation he had a sexual relationship with the girl and was facing serious charges. Chess would have to wait.

Seven years later, a young man came into my classroom. He took one of my sociology classes and liked it so much he took another. Once he had taken all the courses, he was required to take with me, we kept in touch. He invited me to his dojo where he taught Brazilian jiu-jitsu. At first, I attended his class to be polite. Quickly, I fell in love with the sport and was there because my heart was in it. Soon, it got a little expensive for me; I told him I might have to stop and recover for a couple of months. "What? You can't afford $5 a month?" I froze at what he was suggesting. "What do you mean $5?"

"That's what I'm going to charge you to keep coming."

"You're kidding right?"

"Not at all," he told me.

I was very grateful and as luck would have it, one of my closest cousins Tony was also an instructor at that same academy. My student had made me an offer I could not refuse. He was a genuinely nice guy and enjoyed his company so much that a friendship blossomed. We spent days at Buffalo Wild Wings, shooting pool, and of course, watching MMA events. I figured I owed him for his generosity and hosted one of those MMA nights at my house. I provided all the food and paid for the event myself. He arrived with a girlfriend I did not know he had. She appeared to be very young. He was thirty-nine at the time and she seemed as if she was in high school, but I recognized her from campus and knew she was at least old enough to be in college. There was no concern on my end. My student played with my infant and toddler son as if they were his nephews.

With time, my goals took me to a different city, and because $5 jiu-jitsu courses were nonexistent in any other part of the planet, I had to let that go as well. Different cities did not interfere with our friendship. We kept in touch and would get together for dinner on my visits to Laredo. It was always great to see him until suddenly he was nowhere to be found. I called my cousin Tony to inquire about his well-being. He brought me up to date with news that I could not possibly have heard where I lived. My student had been arrested for the sexual assault of a woman and three children. Additionally, he had recorded himself having sex with a one-year-old girl. I had never in my life been in such disbelief that I got light-headed, but that is exactly what happened. My cousin had to repeat what he had just told me, and if it had not been coming from him, I would not have believed it.

I tried to communicate with several friends from the jiu-jitsu academy. I wanted to ascertain whether he would accept a visit from me. I wanted to ask him one simple question: *Why? Why did you do this?* This man had played with my children in my own home. Finally, I got the green light. My student had agreed to speak to me. I promised myself not to attack him and to try to understand as an alternative. Sadly, I never got the opportunity to do this. By the time I arrived in Laredo in December 2016, my student had hung himself in his jail cell.

Most recently, research into a new project led me to a woman who was forced to marry into a family from another country who came to the United States to establish their criminal organization here. She was only fourteen, and for the next fifteen years would be subjected to many of the family's dealings. She recalls seeing a chamber where children were kept. Unlike the typical stereotype, not all the children were Mexican, and this organization was not from Mexico. There were children from different parts of the world. She could not give me exact details but recalls houses in neighborhoods near businesses with underground tunnels connecting them. This, she says, is taking place in many US cities. Some of the things this victim witnessed are not only inhumane but evil. From cannibalism to sexual abuse, this person's story is one that can never come from a human's imagination. Life is stranger than fiction, as some say, and we will learn more about this victim in a future project.

After completing my investigation into the Elsa Cuellar case, I was left to consider how long she had been in operation and whether any of these experiences I had were in one way or other linked to her. Anything I could come up with, of course, is speculation, and have nothing concrete to tie her to the children in these cases. However, I could not help but wonder whether my experiences are coincidental or if my environment at the time was so plagued by people with an agenda to bring harm to children that it was impossible not to be around it. If that is the case, how many others like me are there? How many Laredo citizens may be around crimes against children happening directly under their chin but have not recognized the signs? We must recall Jose Almazan's observation that the signs of an abused or trafficked child mimic so many other circumstances that are common in low-income families along the border.

Now, I am left feeling helpless as I have grown closer to one particular victim. She is an adult now, but I see that sweet little girl who was stripped of her identity and of a chance to have a relationship with her biological mother. After our first conversation, I was not sure if she understood how much I wish I could help her. As mentioned before, these victims go through so many people; I felt like I was just another person she had to deal with. My hope was renewed when after our third conversation we hung up, and she called me back right away. "Hi, did you forget to tell me something?" The line stayed quiet for a minute before her childlike voice came through: "Can you help me find my mother?" she asked softly.

This request came with mixed emotions. On one hand, I was very pleased to hear some form of acknowledgment from the victim that she is aware that her real mother is out there somewhere. For so many years, Elsa Cuellar had manipulated many of her victims into believing she was their biological parent. I was overjoyed to hear that this victim had an interest in learning the truth about her history. On the other hand, I knew how very difficult it was going to be to find her mother. First, the victim had been under Elsa Cuellar's guardianship since she was a baby. Now as an adult, the victim and mother would most definitely not recognize one another. Secondly, the information on the victim's birth certificate cannot be trusted. Elsa Cuellar was a master at doctoring government documents, and I would be obtuse to believe that the listed parents were the only false data in the document. Last, the likelihood the mother lives in Mexico is very high. While it is possible the mother may be living in Laredo, this can be surmised with some degree of accuracy because selecting victims from Mexico with limited to no access to the United States was Cuellar's modus operandi.

As fate would have it, something miraculous occurred. It is such a miracle that I almost did not include it in this project because I was not certain how believable it would be. Divine intervention is not only a term people use; it is a real thing. When my niece married an attorney from New York City, there was no way for me to predict that a friend from the groom's side once worked for the secret service. Robert Kasdon is now retired and assists missing and exploited children: "We don't call them cold cases anymore," he explained to me, but they do look for children who have been missing for a long time. He was a kindhearted man who did not hesitate to offer his services. After talking for a while about life in New York he pointed out something very significant: "Now Roger, I'm going to do what I can, but remember that we generally look for missing children. In this case, we're looking for a missing mother."

I was well aware the odds of finding this victim's mother are minimal but I believe it was worth the effort. We cannot undo the damage Elsa Cuellar has caused, but if we can return just one victim to their biological mother, the nightmares I endured throughout this process would have been worth it.

27

Problems with Strategies to Combat
Human Trafficking

SIMPLY STATED, HUMAN TRAFFICKING WILL NEVER END! THE BUSINESS is much too profitable for organized crime to stop doing it. In addition, it is a very elusive practice easily concealed under a blanket of problems with immigration law. While border agencies can easily look at a package and make an assertion as to how suspicious or illegal it looks, the same cannot be said about humans. How can one stop human trafficking when not even the victims themselves are aware that they are being trafficked? Elsa Cuellar's case has inspired me to call this a "ghost crime" because nothing is real.

A friend of mine from Texas A&M International University asked me, "Is it frustrating not being able to use any of the real names?" I said, "No not really because we don't know what their real names are." Everything about trafficking minors becomes an illusion. Names, dates of birth, parents, place of birth, social security numbers, and immigration status become fabricated. Solanos, who are not even on law enforcement's radar, is willing to help in harboring trafficked children for the right price. Another common question I was asked by a different colleague is whether I was afraid to speak about Solanos even if I was allowed to interview some of them. I thought about it for a moment and responded as truthfully as I could. "Well, no because even after visiting with some in Mexico, I have no idea who those on the American side are. I can't even tell you who the ones in Mexico are. I don't pose any more threat to them than law enforcement."

To say the American legal system does not care about human trafficking would be a harsh and inaccurate statement. The problem rests on the strategies for combating human trafficking more so than the lack of concern for it. In the many interviews I have conducted with various agencies, I could see there is a genuine concern for the exploitation of humans, sexual enterprises, and especially the treatment of children. However, some of the measures put into practice to challenge this fall short of any truly aggressive approach toward minimizing this branch of the criminal world. If the approaches that have been taken in the fight against human trafficking are closely examined, it is easy to see how these initiatives are not only passive but also help those in this market succeed in their criminal venture.

RELIGION

The way religion was used by Elsa Cuellar to gain the trust of her victims is apparent. The word of God is a powerful influence in every society around the world. Minimal attention is placed on the many different interpretations of the same scripture. Various religions challenge one another to claim the right to the more accurate interpretation, and when they find themselves ineffective in arguing their points of view, words like "mystery," "faith," and "miracle" are used to explain away their lack of knowledge. People are afraid to "not know." The uncertainty of the afterlife is embedded deep in our souls and our love for God does not allow many of us to admit that we simply do not know.

From a religious standpoint, these views can survive. It is important to have faith and to have a belief in something greater than us, but when these ideologies are applied to combating evil in the secular world, it can be counterproductive. This is something the Bush administration is all too familiar with in their efforts to use Biblical points of view as a blueprint for policies designed to fight human trafficking. The Bush administration's use of theological language to promote such an atrocity in our society proved to be inimical rather than an expression of anti–human trafficking. In the First National Conference of Human Trafficking,

Bush announced: "the lives of tens of thousands of innocent women and children depend on . . . your daily efforts to rescue them from misery and servitude. You are in a fight against evil . . . Human life is a gift from our creator—and it should never be for sale" (Zimmerman 84). While his words powered across the podium encouraging thunderous applause, the oversight comes with the lack of consideration for the variations of inter-pretations of the Holy scripture. Furthermore, variations in how terms like "evil," "creator," and "misery" are accompanied by different religious attitudes about politics and politicians in general. Few have been known to abandon their spiritual belief system for awarding a politician any credibility in social matters. In *Religion and Politics*, Yvonne Zimmerman acknowledges that Bush's speech writer David Frum confirmed the use of the word "evil" as "self-consciously theological language." How then, can we expect to fight such an act as human trafficking while implementing a tool that has created so much division on a global scale? Is it prudent to use language that is universally interpreted so differently by millions of people? Zimmerman goes on to explain, "Evil does not simply com-municate that something is immoral; rather, evil characterizes a particular mode in which something is immoral. Though diverse religious traditions conceive of evil differently, in Christian thought, this term typically denotes that which separates humans from God. Therefore, evil can name a force or agent that affects separation from God or humanity and evil can describe a condition of separation from the divine. In either case, the metaphysical dimensions that evil implies signal a foray into theological terrain" (84). The Clinton and Obama administrations are not exempt from using religious ideology in policies regarding human trafficking either. While we will never arrive at a worldwide consensus on spiritual matters, it is critical that we at least come close to understanding the best way to express anti-trafficking policy.

THE CELEBRITY
There has been a trend of celebrity activists speaking out against human trafficking. No one can argue that having a figure the public identifies with and respects can have a potential impact on the public view. And as Dina Haynes observes in her article *The Celebritization of Human*

Trafficking, celebrities can more easily gain access to politicians than most common people can to better discuss these issues. However, Haynes also contends that the disadvantages of celebrity outcries against human trafficking come with disadvantages that contaminate the prevention process rather than assisting it. She attributes this to two principles: (1) the superficial or uninformed trafficking narratives that celebrities often present and (2) the celebrity's lack of accountability for the solutions they propose to ameliorate trafficking policies that may have adverse unintended consequences if implemented (26). This is especially true when celebrities establish some level of acceptance and credibility from famous public figures who detach themselves as mere advocates and become more active in their suggestions for new policies.

In matters of social issues, it is imperative to identify the credibility of those who are active in participating in the passing, amending, or creating policies. We have a responsibility to distinguish between those whose role is to bring awareness of a social problem from those figures who are playing an active role in the fight against it. The use of celebrities can cause someone to fall victim to this confusion and surrender to the illusion that something is being done about human trafficking while not understanding that what they are witnessing is someone making them aware of the problem.

THE ILLUSION THAT SOMETHING IS BEING DONE

Many of the social issues that have fallen under the public scope have provoked unmerited debate. The legalization of marijuana, prostitution, and the right to be pro-choice are only some examples of topics that have elicited heated debate over the years. The problem with these issues is very much like the conflicts presented with human trafficking, that is, most are happy with seeing specific legislation on paper. However, in matters of law, I have come to understand that there is a decisive difference between the passing of a law and the actual implementation of it. Very often, the latent effects of a policy are not felt until it has actually been passed. It is then we see debates and the pointing of fingers emerge in the political realm. These debates tend to have a hidden agenda tied to them. They create the illusion that something is being done about an issue rather than having the public realize these discussions are a sign that the policies that have already been passed are not working.

In no way is this approach intended to suggest people do not care about social issues if there is something written down to confirm action has been taken. What it does mean is there tends to be a lack of understanding between what happens at the state level versus the international level. The responsibilities and interests of each of these levels of government should not be confused or merged. Our tendency to do this as a society also creates an illusion, that is, when something is written down, governments at both the state and international levels are following that script together to combat a certain issue. In reality, law implementation ad law writing can be very different things. Carol S. Vance argued, "In text, intent often appears unambiguous and seamless, but through studying the state in actions, one sees that the implementation of law and policy can present a different reality altogether" (934).

It is for this reason that actions taken against human trafficking need to extend their legal hands far beyond what we can see in text. Vance acknowledges that this approach can take up more time and resources; however, this should be a non-factor when trying to put an end to such a horrible crime.

Another contributing factor to the creation of illusions (and probably the one that benefited Elsa Cuellar the most) is social media and the film industry. How our society has come to understand trafficking through the media lens presents various problems. First, as a society, we tend to individualize some of these social issues. For example, the National Center on Sexual Exploitation, Shared Hope International, and Exodus Cry are only three of many initiatives to stop trafficking. However, their emphasis is on females being trafficked for sex. This narrows the scope of where the interests of law enforcement will direct its attention. Further, it motivates other foundations such as Rights4Girls which focuses only on females. Many of these impressions about trafficking are cultivated in the film industry.

The film industry has profited nicely from airing themes dealing with organized crime. There seems to be a public obsession with the underground world because most people will never come to know it unless they experience it through Hollywood's interpretation of it. This was very important for Elsa because nothing she was doing in real life had ever been done in film. Coupled with the fact that there is a strong emphasis on sex trafficking, Elsa Cuellar was able to maneuver her operation safely because her victims were so young, babies, or given birth to on the American side. She also capitalized on the stereotype that all victims are female. This is far from the truth as many men are targeted for sex or their organs. This is why the crimes being committed because of human trafficking should not be treated as separate issues. Many crimes taking place in our country are a product of human trafficking. Treating prostitution as a separate issue from child trafficking is not only a mistake but also contributes to the trafficker's ability to go undetected. Elsa Cuellar is proof of this.

Still, one of the biggest impacts social media has on human trafficking was the one that surprised me the most. I was shocked to learn the psychological impact media had on survivors of human enslavement. While researching for this project, I reached out to several victims who had survived being trafficked. My goal was to try and find parallels between their experiences and those of Elsa Cuellar's victims. The case was so unique I wondered if others had ever been as articulate as Cuellar, or if they relied more on force. My efforts failed to establish such a correlation because the victims wanted money in exchange for assisting other victims. I did not have one compassionate response even after sharing a similar experience. I did get one response from a victim wanting to learn more about the case, but I never heard back after that. In looking into some of these victims, I understood why they wanted to be paid. The media had already made them out to be celebrities. Many of these victims I investigated had Facebook pages that looked more like a profile for a modeling agency. They were being disseminated all over Twitter, Snapchat, and TikTok. A few had already had a film made about their experience. I could see photos of them with other celebrities and some had agents. At the risk of sounding shallow, I could not help but wonder: *Had the media successfully made these victims grateful for what they went through?* For the sake of other future victims, I certainly hope they did not.

I could see the once-victims now had smiles on their faces, were living a seemingly wonderful life, and had used their experiences to profit. I have no reservations about this. It is a hundred times preferred over them still being enslaved or having psychological issues to such an extent that they would not even go out in public. I hope their success and journey to spread the word about trafficking continue. I am also not suggesting they are no longer having difficulties in their lives after such traumatic experiences. However, I was very surprised at the amount of money some of these victims asked for, the no responses to requests, and the lack of interest shown in learning more about Elsa Cuellar and what she did. I thought to myself, *If victims of the same crime don't have an interest or compassion, what am I up against as I move forward with this investigation?*

Thankfully, I found some very caring people along the way, mostly those in the school district and law enforcement, but the impact that the media had on these victims and glorifying their experience to be showcased as something they need to be paid for was baffling to me. I am doing my best to steer the victims I am currently communicating with in a different direction. I wish to encourage them to never forget what they have been through and to hold on to those sets of emotions in a healthy manner that could benefit others that may have gone through something similar. It is acceptable to be paid for your assistance, there is nothing wrong with achieving well-earned celebrity status, and it is certainly approved to move on with your life and be happy. It is not acceptable to forget those still being exploited!

28

What is Next?

THE LACK OF RESPONSE I RECEIVED FROM OTHER VICTIMS WAS NOT A complete disappointment. It gave me the idea to seek an alternative avenue—reach out to those in prison for enslaving humans. As it turned out, I was shown more regret and compassion by the perpetrators. However, one case got my attention more than the others for a few reasons. First, like Elsa Cuellar, the inmate who wrote back to me was a female. Secondly, the incident occurred in Webb County as did the events involving Cuellar. But one of the things that stood out to me the most was that the offender in this case appeared to be quite young herself at the time of the offense. It made me question the how and why of the case. Just as I suspected, I found Sandra Bearden to come off as a sweet, gentle person who fears God and regrets her actions. So then, why did this young girl do this? What social and historical factors led her to commit such a crime?

Sandra Bearden was a Mexican immigrant who brought a twelve-year-old girl with her from the state of Veracruz in Mexico. She brought her to clean her house and to help her care for her four-year-old son. In exchange, the young girl would receive the American education every Mexican parent wants for their child. Because Sandra was from Mexico as well, the family trusted her to take care of their daughter. Aside from missing their little girl, they had no reservations about giving their daughter the American Dream. At the time, Sandra was doing well for herself and had a luxury SUV and the appearance of someone who had done well for themselves as a Mexican immigrant in the United

States. With the approval of the little girl's parents, Sandra smuggled the child across the Rio Grande River into Laredo, Texas.

This would prove to be the worst decision the parents had ever made in their lives. Almost immediately after arriving, the little girl was exposed to some of the worst abuse that could happen to a child. Immediately, the girl was put to work. When she did not work at Sandra's desired pace, she would swing the broomstick over the little girl's back. One reported incident describes the broomstick breaking in two pieces over the child's spine. The little girl worked ruthlessly for continuous hours and if she fell asleep during these work hours, she would be awakened by pepper spray in her face. When I read this, I remembered going through pepper spray training in the police academy. We were sprayed unsuspectingly in a dark room in case we were ever put in a position to have to fight for our lives should we ever accidentally spray ourselves in the heat of a confrontation. We were all grown men in the academy crying like children at the extreme discomfort the spray brought. I could only imagine what the tiny pupils of this girl must have felt. And it got worse. One day after falling asleep when she was supposed to be working, Sandra penetrated the girl's vagina with a garden tool and broke a bottle over the girl's head. According to reports, this occurred on the girl's workdays. On her days off, things got more unimaginable.

When the young girl was not working, she spent her time chained to a pole in Sandra's backyard. She was not given any food or water. For those unfamiliar with Laredo, it can get very hot at any time of the year. Even during winter months, temperatures in the high 90s are not uncommon. The little girl did what she could to get help from neighbors, but the over eight-foot fence made of concrete obstructed any chance of being seen. The situation seemed hopeless. After four days of not eating, Sandra decided it would be a good idea to feed her. She provided the young girl with dog feces to eat. What choice did the little girl have? She could not stomach the stench of her meal, so as an alternative, she began to eat dirt from the yard.

It soon got to the point when the girl would spend her days going in and out of consciousness. The shackles on her wrists and ankles began to cut into her skin. These same shackles would get so hot with Laredo's blazing South Texas sun that they began to burn her skin. Finally, the little girl's body was nothing more than a shell of a person. She was no longer that robust little girl looking for an opportunity to have a good life. Now, she just wanted to live. Had Sandra just fed her enough to keep the girl from moaning, she may have gotten away with it. The abuse was too harsh for the little girl to endure without making sounds that helped her endure the pains she felt throughout her body. It was these sounds that were heard by a neighbor who had gotten up on his house to work on the roof. The moaning and whimpering got his attention and as he looked out into the neighbor's yard, he saw the little girl chained to the pole. He immediately called the Laredo Police Department and the seven-month ordeal had finally come to an end.

At the trial, the responding officer could not help but cry when he explained to the court what he saw. The little girl was so weak, she could not speak or walk. She had to be carried out on a stretcher. Sandra Bearden was taken into custody and in October 2001, she was sentenced to ninety-nine years in prison. Even while incarcerated, Sandra Bearden currently lives under much better circumstances than the ones she provided that little girl. This case is unique in the sense that the young girl is one of the lucky ones. It is a difficult thing to say about someone who endured so much, but most victims in these types of scenarios are never found. It is also different in that Sandra Bearden was caught and convicted; this too is a rare occurrence as child trafficking is very difficult to prove. The little girl has since returned to Veracruz, Mexico, and is safe with her family. Sandra Bearden is currently serving her sentence at the Hobby Unit in Merlin, Texas.

One of the problems we often face in society is to arrive at a point of feeling a sense of satisfaction when the offender of such a crime is sent to prison. However, this only guarantees society is safe for the moment from this particular offender and not from child trafficking altogether. This is why it is critical to ask questions and examine the social and psychological factors that may have led Sandra to commit such a crime. Unlike Elsa Cuellar, why did Sandra Bearden only resort to having one victim? Why did she use physical abuse so abruptly with no apparent signs of provocation? And, of course, why target a child from so deep in Mexico?

Most people might argue the obvious claim that an illegal child from Mexico is less likely to get her caught. Sandra, however, lived in Laredo, Texas. There are plenty of illegal minor girls on the United States side of the Rio Grande with their biological parents in Mexico.

I looked deeper into Sandra's case and found that she had described herself to be insane, but her attorney never filed that motion and was not considered a plea option in her case. I also learned that Sandra had refuted the claim that the evidence collected was sufficient to prove the allegations against her were true. With all the physical evidence in place, there was no way Sandra Bearden was going to win that argument. One might even ask: *Roger, are you seriously saying Sandra Bearden was treated unfairly?* My answer is absolutely not, but I did find it interesting Sandra was willing to attach the word "insane" to what she had done. If as a perpetrator of such a heinous offense, one is willing to declare the action as one that can only be committed by an insane person, then what led them to do it?

I reached out to Sandra just before Thanksgiving 2022 not expecting a response. She wrote back to me, and we began a "pen-pal" exchange that has allowed me to get to know her better. Like many prisoners, she has developed a strong devotion to religion and her reading habits are mostly Christian. She has had considerable difficulties discussing her actions, but I learn a little more about her with every exchange. She is pleasant, kind, and nothing at all like a person that would even get a parking citation. Unlike Elsa Cuellar, there was no criminal history, suspicions of murder, or any kind of legal radar being directed toward her. Sandra was a happy mother of a four-year-old living in a good neighborhood and enjoying married life. In one exchange Sandra sent me a greeting card and wrote:

Roger,

For me, to dare greatly means the courage to be vulnerable. It means to show up and be seen, to ask for what you need, to talk about how you're feeling, to have that hard conversation. Most people think vulnerability is weakness, but vulnerability is sort of the cornerstone of confidence because unless you can allow yourself to take the risk to be open, to live as a wholehearted person, when you can do that, you recognize that you're really like everybody else and that gives you the confidence to be yourself, which is all you really need in life, is to be more of yourself. You can get to the courage without walking through vulnerability period. I don't know the circumstances under which your aunt passed away. I don't know what to say but I am here.

Sandra,

January 28, 2023

When I first came across her opening line—"For me, to dare greatly means the courage to be vulnerable"—I could not help but wonder what in her life had made her feel she had to carry a sense of vulnerability. Her letter was immediately followed by the importance of a person being seen to ask for what they need and to "talk about how you're feeling." Although we have not gotten that personal at this point, I could detect a sense of regret for not having done these things herself. But what was she feeling? What is it that she wanted to talk about? Who did she need to have this "hard conversation" with? God or someone in her life?

I aim to answer these very difficult questions in a future project as I continue my research on the sociological factors that may have led to this disturbing crime. It is easy to judge others for their actions, but it is extremely difficult to explain them. It is, for this reason, I include this case though it is not related to Elsa Cuellar, to encourage this conversation about human trafficking, to ask those difficult questions that may inadvertently bring some form of discomfort, and to challenge ourselves to come up with a possible solution.

THERE SHOULD BE

curbside | delivery

FOR THINGS LIKE

PEACE,

HEALING

&

HUGS.

This is the front of the greeting card sent to me by Sandra Bearden. Can someone believe this sentiment after the type of crime they have committed? Or should we consider that this person existed before the crime and something beyond our current understanding drove her to her actions? Source: Author.

Roger, ~~for me,~~

To dare greatly means the courage to be vulnerable. It means to show up and be seen, to ask for what you need, to talk about how you're feeling, to have that hard conversation.
Most people think vulnerability is weakness, but vulnerability is sort of the cornerstone of confidence, because unless you can allow yourself to take the risk, to be open, to live as a whole-hearted person, when you can do that, you recognize that you're really like everybody else and that gives you the confidence to be yourself, which is all you really need in life, is to be more of yourself.
You can't get to courage without walking through vulnerability period.

I don't know the circumstances under which your aunt passed away.
I don't know what to say. but I AM here.

January 28, 2023

As I continue my research, can Sandra Bearden give us valuable information into what drives a person to human trafficking? Source: Author.

29

My Return Home

In May 2013, I became aware of Elsa Cuellar and the blanket of suspicion she had waving over her head by numerous law enforcement agencies. Almost exactly ten years later, on February 19, 2023, I conducted my last interview regarding her case. It took place in the small town of Zapata, Texas not even an hour from Laredo. From that interview, I would be making that nearly six-hour drive home and bringing what had turned into exhausting research to an end. Still, I will not be able to completely keep her off my mind as I strive to do what I can about locating the biological mother for some of the victims I am still in touch with. With numerous agencies involved, I am cautiously optimistic that our search will bring forth positive results.

There are several types of victims I hold dear to my heart. There are those who to this day deny any wrongdoing on Elsa Cuellar's part. In their experience, she was an excellent provider and a loving "mother." She was a woman of God who delivered her sermons with the enthusiasm of a person who had met the Lord personally. She was a woman of hope for those in desperate need and was there to assist mothers and their children. She did them the great justice of forgoing the American immigration process and magically appearing with their approval to walk freely into the United States. She was a hero. I feel a strong sense of compassion for these victims for obvious reasons and hope they can continue to live their lives peacefully as though everything in their past was normal.

Others are aware something was terribly wrong. Most of the victims who fall into this category have an extremely difficult time discussing their past. I did not push them to. Who am I to infringe on their efforts to restart their life? I was happy to know them, speak to them, and learn at least some of what they had been through and what they heard. One victim told me there are still times when she wakes up in the morning and looks out towards the ocean in her new home near Corpus Christie and asks herself: "Who am I?" It is a very difficult question to ask and an even more complicated one to answer. I wish with every fiber of my being I could be of more assistance to them. Their life-altering history can never be erased and since they are still fairly young, the overall impact of their experiences is still not known. It remains a chapter that is unwritten and one that could bring difficult circumstances.

Another category of victims comes in the form of those who will speak of themselves as if their lives had never experienced any kind of disturbance and that they had a normal upbringing. They do so, however, knowing well it is not true. This is why they seek help in finding their biological mothers; they are aware that they have been living in an imaginary world. That is perfectly acceptable. Perhaps it is a defense mechanism they have learned to utilize to better survive the days without the torture that comes along with those familiar questions so many victims around the world are asking themselves every single day: "Who am I and where is my family?" It is a curiosity in these victims that has on more than one occasion brought a tear to my eyes. Having been brought up in an amazing family unit, I found it very difficult to relate and this frustrated me more than anything I have ever researched or written about before. For these victims, I will continue the fight to bring some closure to the Elsa Cuellar part of their life.

We should never discount those involved in this case as victims as well. The emotional anguish, disgust, and psychological discomfort the Elsa Cuellar case brought many of the law enforcement officers and school employees involved merits consideration. One official who did not wish to be named told me a story about how one tribe of Native Americans would tie their enemy by their limbs to four separate posts. They would use wet leather straps to tie them and place their enemies on a bed of fire ants. When the sun began to dry the leather, it would shrink slowly pulling the enemy's limbs from their body. "That's what I felt like doing to Elsa Cuellar. If I wasn't such a moral person, I may just have done it."

Investigator Alexander Rodriguez continues to work in law enforcement and discusses the case with the bitterness that comes with having so many questions still unanswered. He takes his time when bringing up the case as it continues to make him feel as if somewhere along the way he failed some of these victims. It is difficult to convince him this is not the case. Elsa Cuellar was a master manipulator who precisely calculated the law. With this case, I learned that when ethical people are doing their best to fight the unethical, there will always be disadvantages. The scales of justice will sometimes tilt slightly in the undesired direction.

The number of employees within the United Independent School district who were impacted by this case is too many to count. Somewhere along the way, the educator's responsibilities manifested into much more than teaching. At one point during my research for this case, a parent told me: "I don't know what is wrong with these teachers. My grandfather was a very prominent attorney in Minnesota during a time when there was no technology and today, teachers are having all kinds of problems." My response was: "That is correct. Your grandfather went to school when teachers did not have all these problems." From a time when educators were able to exclusively focus on education to an era where they must serve as teachers, disciplinarians, counselors, social worker, and at the same time be aware of the signs that something is wrong at home, it makes perfect sense that the burdens educators face today are impeding the learning part of education. Simply stated, teachers are being held accountable for too many things that are outside legitimate teaching responsibilities. Some of these expectations are more unreasonable than others; they are unreasonable, nonetheless.

I had the honor of meeting many teachers in my quest to better understand what might be happening in classroom settings. The Elsa Cuellar case's relevancy was to make a point about how a trafficked child can easily go through the education system undetected. She related a story to me about a boy who was technically too old to be in elementary, but his school performance was so poor that there was no way they could promote him to middle school yet. The fear was that he would be set up for failure if promoted before acquiring the skills needed. They hoped to work with him and possibly try to move him at mid-year. Although he had never been a disciplinary problem, the teacher noticed a dramatic change in his behavior. He began to refuse to do his work, began cursing at the teacher, and bullied other students (something he had never done before). Finally, the student reached a level of discipline the teacher could never be prepared for. While trying to get him to understand math, he became aggressive refusing to do it, he picked up his math book and threw it at the teacher's face. The teacher suffered a bloody nose and a bruise on her face.

The boy appeared frightened and did not react like a student intending to injure his teacher would have normally acted. Although not all the details of the case could be revealed to me, it was later learned during a parent conference that the mother had been instructing the boy to behave in a certain way with the teacher. Her motive was to be able to submit the school's paperwork for his behavior to the state allowing her to argue for a specific behavioral disorder that would in turn qualify her to receive a check. As this story was related to me, I thought about Imelda. How can teachers pick up the early signs Imelda was exhibiting at her school when teachers are dealing with scenarios that would by comparison make the little girl seem normal? How can educators focus on educating academics when the level of morality in the parents is intervening? Logically, the child too would be lacking in morals. Theodore Roosevelt said it best: "To educate a man in mind and not in morals is to educate a menace into our society."

Now, with my bags packed and my laptop put away, I made one last stop to eat in Zapata as I prepared to go down Zapata Highway realizing that somewhere in the area I had once been trafficked myself by the Solanos. I realized how easy it was to go to and from Mexico and how challenging border security is to police such a large area. Like teachers, they are held accountable for so much that it almost seems unrealistic. Luckily, people like *El Viejon* have made that transition in their lives to now serve as instruments of learning. I would never have been able to penetrate the society I came to know so intimately without his help, and for that I am grateful. I must admit it is not a venture I care to reacquaint myself with, of course, for the right story, I would probably do it. Today, *El Viejon* is putting his passion for art to great use. He has become something of a local celebrity with his art being showcased in restaurants, city walls, and of course on canvas. He has removed himself from the dark world that at one time had consumed him and now has future projects lined up that will certainly make him a wonderful living. As for me, I can boast about the painting he once did of the elephants on that enchanting property I got to visit. I remember how proudly the Solano I met told me *El Viejon* had painted it. Today, that painting hangs in my study in my house: a gift I will forever cherish. I appreciate the sentiment and look forward to sharing more about him in a future project.

I finished my meal and made my way down that hot highway. As I passed the sign that read "Leaving Laredo," I looked in the rearview

This painting was given to me by El Viejon. His remarkable story will be shared in a future project. Source: Author.

mirror and watched the distant lights from the city become smaller. I looked away for a moment and by the time I checked the rearview again, Laredo was no longer there. With every minute, I left it further behind. I realized that just because I could no longer see it, it did not mean it was no longer there. I got to Houston at nearly 1:00 a.m. As I waited at a traffic light, I saw a police officer speaking to a group of prostitutes. One of them looked fairly young and very uncomfortable. By the time the light turned green, the police officer had let the girls go on their way. Once again, I looked through my review and wondered about the younger girl. I wondered if she wanted to be there or if she even knew her real name. Like Laredo, she was gone from my view in a matter of seconds. Now, she lives in my mind as I can still see the image of her scared face when I close my eyes. I hate closing my eyes now. I can still see the image of Elsa Cuellar like a ghost who followed me east from the southernmost corner of the Rio Grande.

Bibliography

Bales, Kevin, and Ron Soodalter. *The Slave Next Door: Human Trafficking and Slavery Today* (Berkeley: University of California Press, 2009).

Cullen-Dupont, Kathryn. "Human Trafficking." *Global Issues*, 2009.

Ganster, Paul, and Kimberly Collins. *The U.S-Mexican Border Today: Conflict and Cooperation in Historical Perspective* (Lanham, MD: Rowman and Littlefield, 2021).

Gulbas, Lauren E., and Luis H. Zayas. "Exploring the Effects of U.S. Immigration Enforcement on the Well-Being of Citizen Children in Mexican Immigrant Families." *RSF: The Russell Sage Foundation Journal of the Social Sciences*, vol. 3, no. 4, 2017, pp. 53–69.

Duger, A. Focusing on Prevention: The Social and Economic Rights of Children Vulnerable to Sex Trafficking. *Health and Human Rights*, vol. 17, no. 1, 2015, pp. 114–23.

Haynes, Dina Francesca. "The Celebritization of Human Trafficking." *The Annals of the American Academy of Political and Social Science*, vol. 653, 2014, pp. 25–45.

Juffer, Femmie, et al. "II. Development of Adopted Children with Histories of Early Adversity." *Monographs of the Society for Research in Child Development*, vol. 76, no. 4, 2011, pp. 31–61.

Mollema, Nina. "Follow the Leader: Best Practices to Combat Human Trafficking in the United States." *The Comparative and International Law Journal of Southern Africa*, vol. 48, no. 1, 2015, pp. 1–41.

Moodley, Pat. "Inter-Country Adoptions and Child Trafficking: A Fine Line Indeed." *Agenda: Empowering Women for Gender Equity*, no. 70, 2006, pp. 145–48.

Terrell, John, and Judith Modell. "Anthropology and Adoption." *American Anthropologist*, vol. 96, no. 1, 1994, pp. 155–61.

Vance, Carole S. "States of Contradiction: Twelve Ways to Do Nothing about Trafficking While Pretending To." *Social Research*, vol. 78, no. 3, 2011, pp. 933–48.

Wegar, Katarina. "Adoption, Family Ideology, and Social Stigma: Bias in Community Attitudes, Adoption Research, and Practice." *Family Relations*, vol. 49, no. 4, 2000, pp. 363–70.

What Research Tells Us About the Effect of Divorce on Children: https://www.verywellfamily.com/children-of-divorce-in-america-statistics-1270390. Verywell Family (2022).

Zimmerman, Yvonne C. "From Bush to Obama: Rethinking Sex and Religion in the United States' Initiative to Combat Human Trafficking." *Journal of Feminist Studies in Religion*, vol. 26, no. 1, 2010, pp. 79–99.

Index

aborigines, of Australia, 3
abuse symptoms, low-income and, 82, 220
activists, celebrity, 225–26
ad litem role, 212
adoption: psychological impact of, 210–11; screening process for, 145; in South Africa, 55
advertisement: Cuellar, I., as, 94; family photo as, 105, *106*, *107*, *108*
Africans, enslaved, 4
aggravated assault, 134–35
AIDS: of Carlitos, 52; of Nuñez, M., 50; of Ortega, J., 60
Alaniz, Isidro "Chilo," 204–5, *208*
aliases, 179
Almazan, Jose A., 20, 82; on low-income families, 220
Alvarado, Elsa. *See La Pastora*
American society, women in, 21
anti-depressants, 24–25
Arabs, slavery of, 4
architecture, narco, 13–14
Aristotle, 3
Arredondo, Juan, 89
arrest warrant, for Cuellar, E., *33*, 175
artwork, of *El Viejon*, 10, 12, *243*
Asian women, prostitution of, 119

attorney: Cuellar, E., posing as, 58–59, 116–17, 149–50, 151, 162; District, 122, 135, 204–5, *208*; Talamantes as, 129, 130–31
Australia, aborigines of, 3
autopsy report, of Valentine Alonzo, *43*
Ayala, Marcos, 142; Rodriguez relation to, 135–36, 144; Valencia Ramirez investigation by, 136–38, 143, 157
Aztec Empire, Spaniards in, 3

babies, profit from, 131–32
bail bond hearing, 130–31
La Bala Espinoza, 179; De Luna relation to, 186; Mata, T., relation to, 180–81
Bales, Kevin, 118
Basilica de Guadalupe, 168
Bearden, Sandra, 231; child abuse by, 232–33; Cuellar, E., compared to, 233–34; greeting card from, *236*, *237*; vulnerability of, 235
Bible, slavery in, 3–4, 90
birth certificates: of Cuellar, B., 117; of Diaz, 128; fake, 35, *165*, 175; Mata, B., and, 29
birth control, for Cuellar, I., 99
black markets, for organ selling, 88
"Black Pearl of Mexico," 6

bond, of Cuellar, E., 35
border cities, stereotypes of, 103–4
border crossing, vii–viii; false
    documents for, 5; of Flores, S.,
    148–49; illegal, 75, 76, *77*, 87; of
    Maz, D., 71
border culture, of "Los Dos
    Laredos," vii
Border Patrol, US: checkpoints of,
    149; Cuellar, E., relation to, 91; in
    Laredo, 104
Bracero Program (1942), 75
Brazilian jiu-jitsu, 218
budgets, for public safety, ix
Bush administration, 224–25
business: of human trafficking, 6; in
    Mexico, 183; of slavery, 3
Bustamante St., 177

Calle Thomas Urbina, 65, 68
cancer, of Mendoza, J., 167
cannibalism, 219
Cardenas, Julia, 201–2
Carlitos, AIDS of, 52
Catholicism, in Mexico, 55
celebrities: as activists, 225–26; victims
    as, 228; *El Viejon* as, 243
*The Celebritization of Human
    Trafficking* (Haynes), 225–26
certified nurse assistant (CNA), 64
charges, of Cuellar, E., 203
checkpoints, of US Border Patrol, 149
Chiapas, Mapastepec, 206
"chickenpox," 77; of Cuellar, I., 92; of
    Nuñez, M., 51; of Nuñez, S., 47–48
chickens: Cuellar, I., and, 92; at Kearny
    Street, 123–24; in Laredo, 78; in
    Nuevo Laredo, 47; Nuñez, M.,
    and, 53
child abuse, 82; by Bearden, 232–33;
    CPS relation to, 135
Child Advocacy Center, Webb
    County, 176

child behavior: in divorced-parent
    settings, 19; home environment
    relation to, 1
child placement, loopholes to, 81
child pornography, 216
Child Protective Services (CPS): child
    abuse relation to, 135; Cuellar, E.,
    relation to, 35, 161–63; Cuellar, I.,
    and, 101, 160; Flores, P., relation to,
    134; immigration relation to, 212–13;
    Mata, B., and, 23–24, 25; Mendez
    and, 122; Nuñez, M., and, 48–49, 51;
    teachers calling, ix; U.I.S.D relation
    to, 86, 145
children: abuse of, 82, 135, 232–33;
    behavior of, 1, 19; foster care effect
    on, 211–12; immigration status of,
    213; placement of, 81; pregnancy
    of, 87–88; psychological impact on,
    209; rights of, 55; sexual behavior
    of, 145, *146*; vulnerability of, 46
Christian values: evil relation to, 225; in
    Mexico, 55
churches, *56*; *Basilica de Guadalupe*,
    168; *Hermanos del Siglo Neuvo*,
    42, 68–70; *Uncion Fe Y Poder
    Ministries*, 57
Clinton administration, 225
CNA. *See* certified nurse assistant
cocaine, of Cuerno, 139
"El Coco." *See* Ramirez, Luis Alistar
    "El Coco"
Coffield Unit, *El Viejon in*, 9
Collins, Kimberly, 76
Colombian drug cartel, 190
Colonia La Joya, 11
communication, of criminals, 131
El Conejo, 148–49
Contreras, Efrain, 179; at *El Gallo
    Prieto*, 182; Mata, T., relation to,
    180–81; in Monterrey, 183; at *La
    Sombrilla*, 184–85
conviction, warrants relation to, 127
cooperation, with law enforcement, 131

corruption: in law enforcement, 15; in Mexico, 21

Cotulla, Texas, 204

CPS. *See* Child Protective Services

crime rates, in Laredo, viii

criminal justice, ix

criminals, communication of, 131

Cuellar, Arlene Jasmine Elsie Alvarado, 206

Cuellar, Belinda, 117

Cuellar, Elsa, *62. See also specific topics*

Cuellar, Imelda Chavez, 85–87, 89, 93; "chickenpox" of, 92; CPS and, 101, 160; false documents of, 91; grooming of, 94–96; mental health of, 82–83; pregnancy of, 97–98; Ramirez, T., relation to, 159–60; Rodriguez meeting with, 157–59, 163; teachers relation to, 242; at U.I.S.D., 99–100, *102*

Cuellar, Leslie Marie, 1–2

Cuellar, Michael Jonathan Alvarado, 206

Cuellar household, 147–48

Cuerno, 138; cocaine of, 139; Cuellar, E., relation to, 140, 142; El Popo relation to, 141

culture: of Europeans, 3; of Mexico, 19, 179; of victims, 210–11

deceased people, social security numbers of, 175

De La Rose, Carmen, 64–65

De La Rose, Naomi, 64

Del Mar area, in Laredo, Texas, 76, 77–79

De Luna, Sevedres *"El Toro,"* 181; at *La Sombrilla*, 184–86

destitution, in Mexico, 11

Development of Adopted Children With History of Early Adversities (Femmie), 211

Diaz, Bobby, 19–20, 35, 125; birth certificate of, 128; Ortega, J., relation to, 133–34

Dillon Western boots, 191

District Attorney: Alaniz as, 204–5, *208*; evidence for, 122; Ramirez, L.relation to, 135

divine intervention, 221

divorced-parent settings, child behavior in, 19

DNA tests, 36

doctor, Cuellar, E. posing as, 21–22

Doctor's Hospital, North Laredo, 203

domestic setting: of Cuellar, E., 213; manipulation in, 20

Don Felipe, 114–15

donkey show, 188, 199

doors, shower curtains as, 24; in *La Zona*, 189

"Los Dos Laredos," border culture of, vii

drug cartels: Colombian, 190; Cuellar, E., relation to, 5, 53, 87; false documents for, 17; ransom by, 26

drugs, mules for, 189

drug trafficking industry, 16

Dugan, James, 40–42; Rodriguez relation to, 202–3

earning potential, in prostitution, 189–90

Esparza, Yolanda, 123–26

ethnic background, of victims, 22

Europeans, culture of, 3

evidence: for District Attorney, 122; for law enforcement, 81–82

evil, 225

explosion, at *La Sombrilla*, 185–86

Expo-Mex (*La Fiera* festival), 147

factories (*maquiladoras*), 26, 167

fake birth certificates, 35, *165*, 175

false documents, xiv; for Asian women, 119; birth certificates, 35, *165*, 175; for border crossing, 5; of Cuellar, E.,

35, 71, 87, 134, 177, 220; of Cuellar, I., 91; for drug cartels, 17; for Flores, S., 152; law enforcement affected by, 55; of Mata, B., 30, 31; statistics affected by, 46

false pretense, 20

family photo, as advertisement, 105, *106, 107, 108*

FBI, Cuellar, E. questioned by, 142–43

festivals, in Laredo, 147

field training officer, in Laredo Police Department, 215–16

La Fiera festival (Expo-Mex), 147

film industry: human trafficking in, 2; organized crime relation to, 227–28

First National Conference of Human Trafficking, 224–25

Flores, Angelica, 149, 150, 151

Flores, Carlos Nicolas, 63

Flores, Diego, 112, 113–14

Flores, Eddie, 150; Laredo Police Department arrest of, 155–56; Linares relation to, 153–54

Flores, Patricia: Cuellar, E., relation to, 116–18; pregnancy of, 114–15; Rivera relation to, 112–13; Rodriguez meeting with, 134

Flores, Saul: border crossing of, 148–49; ICE arrest of, 152; in McAllen, 150–51

force, in human trafficking definitions, 18

foster care: children affected by, 211–12; for Cuellar, I., 158; for Flores, E., 154

France, Paris, 13

En Frecuencia (blog), 205

Freddy, 216–17

Frum, David, 225

Gallego, Paul, 36

El Gallo Prieto, 182

Ganster, Paul, 76

genetics, in human development, 210

Gomez (Reverend), 169

Greeks, slavery of, 3

Greene, Al, 209, 212

greeting card, from Bearden, *236, 237*

El Grillo. See Mata, Tony *"El Grillo"*

grooming, of Cuellar, I., 94–96

Guerra, Vicente: Cuellar, E., relation to, 41, 139–40; interrogation of, 137–38, 143; Valencia Ramirez kidnapped by, 141–42

"happy trafficking," 21

hardships, for illegal immigrants, 76

Haynes, Dina, 225–26

HEART, 153

Hermanos del Siglo Neuvo, 42; Maz, D., at, 68–70

heroin, 189

Hispanic people, in Laredo, 22, 103

Hobby Unit, in Merlin, 233

home environment, child behavior relation to, 1

Homeland Security, 175

Houston, Texas, 199; prostitution in, 244

human breeding, 29

human development, genetics in, 210

human trafficking. *See specific topics*

Ibarra, Angie, 52

Ibarra, Elizabeth, 52

Ibarra, Ruben, 56, 57

ICE. *See* Immigration and Customs Enforcement

illegal border crossing, 75, 76, *77*; religion relation to, 87

illegal immigrants: Cuellar, E., relation to, 90–91, 149–50, 151; hardships for, 76; Ortega, J., as, 56

illusions: social media relation to, 75, 227; about US, 56

immigration, CPS relation to, 212–13

Immigration and Customs Enforcement (ICE), 206; Flores, S., arrested by, 152; in "Operation Cabbage Patch," 176; Rodriguez relation to, 207

immigration law, 223
immigration policies, of US, 5
implementation, of laws, 226–27
insanity, 234
International Bridge 1, 103, 137. *See also* United States-Mexican border
interrogation, of Guerra, 137–38, 143
IQ: of Cuellar, I., 83; of victims, xiv

Jalapeño Festival, 147
Jehovah's Witnesses, 91
jiu-jitsu, Brazilian, 218
Juvenile Detention Center, Webb County, 217
Juvenile Justice Alternative Education Program, Webb County, 145, 147

Kasdon, Robert, 221
Kearny Street, 122; Rodriguez at, 123–26
kidnapping, of Valencia Ramirez, 141–42

Lake Charles, Louisiana, 7
Lamar Middle School, 39
Laredo, Texas: chickens in, 78; child abuse in, 82; crime rates in, viii; Del Mar area in, 76, 77–79; festivals in, 147; Hispanic people in, 22, 103; Manor Road, 45, 109, 110; Maz, D., in, 72–73; North, 203; organized crime in, 215; San Bernardo Avenue in, 103–4; San Francisco St., 8, 10; *Los Solanos* in, 6; taco stands in, 63; Ventura, L., in, 197; West Bustamante Street in, 139. *See also* United Independent School District, Laredo; United States-Mexican border
Laredo Police Department: Bearden relation to, 233; Cuellar, E., complaint to, 127; Cuellar household and, 147–48; field training officer in, 215–16; Flores, E., arrested by, 155–56; in "Operation Cabbage Patch," 176; Rodriguez relation to, 130, 135–36; Ventura, L., relation to, 197–98

Latin America, 173. *See also* Mexico
law enforcement: cooperation with, 131; corruption in, 15; Cuellar, E., relation to, 36; evidence for, 81–82; false documents effect on, 55; pet products relation to, 7; psychological impact on, 240–41
laws: for human trafficking, 20–21, 46; implementation of, 226–27; manipulation of, 241; rights-based approach for, 46
lice: of Cuellar, I., 94; of Mendez, 121; at U.I.S.D., 47
lifestyle, of organized crime, 13–14
Linares, Yolanda, 153–54
literacy, 3
local news, 133
Las Lomas, 143
loopholes, to child placement, 81
Lopez, Joe, 131
Louisiana, Lake Charles, 7
low-income, abuse symptoms and, 82, 220

manipulation: for child placement, 81; in domestic setting, 20; of laws, 241; of victims, xiv, 220. *See also La Pastora*
Mann, James R., 119
Manor Road, Laredo, 45, 109, 110
Mapastepec, Chiapas, 206
maquiladoras (factories), 26; Mendoza, J., at, 167
Marez, Polo, 179; at *El Gallo Prieto*, 182; Mata, T., relation to, 180–81; in Monterrey, 183; at *La Sombrilla*, 184–85
Martinez Delgado, Pedro, 136–38, 142
Mata, Bidi, 23; anti-depressants of, 24–25; false documents of, 30, 31; pregnancy of, 26, 27–28; Tijerian relation to, 29–30

Mata, B.moros, Mexico, 138, 139

Mata, Tony *"El Grillo,"* 176–77; *La Bala* Espinoza relation to, 180–81; *La Sombrilla* relation to, 183–84, 185–86

Maz, Dolores, 65–67; border crossing of, 71; at *Hermanos del Siglo Neuvo*, 68–70; in Laredo, 72–73; in Nuevo Laredo, 73–74

Maz, Pedro, 65–68

McAllen, Texas, 148; Flores, S., family in, 150–51

medical examination, of Valentine Alonzo, 40

Mendez, Juanita, 121–23

Mendoza, America, 167, 168, 171

Mendoza, Flor, 167–70; in Taxco, 171–72

Mendoza, Joaquin: cancer of, 167; *La Pastora* relation to, 168–69; San Miguel relation to, 170; in Taxco, 171–72

mental health, of Cuellar, I., 82–83

Merlin, Texas, 233

Mexico: Black Pearl of, 6; business in, 183; Catholicism in, 55; Colombian drug cartel in, 190; culture of, 19, 179; destitution in, 11; human trafficking laws in, 21; Mata, B.moros, 138, 139; migrant workers from, 75; Ortega, J., in, 60–61; poverty in, 56; Reynosa, 148; social structure in, 46–47; Taxco, 169–72; Veracruz, 231, 233. *See also* Nuevo Laredo, Tamaulipas

midwife: Cuellar, E., posing as, 57; Don Felipe as, 114–15

migrant workers, 75

Minnesota, Flores, S. job in, 148, 149

minors: printing press effect on, 3; sexual services with, 88–89, 95–96

mobility: human trafficking and, 6; across United States-Mexican border, 16

Monterrey, Nuevo Leon, 14, 182, 183

Morgan, Philip D., 3

mothers: Cuellar, E., as, 45, 207, 209–10; single-parent, 188; of victims, 220–21, 239, 240

mules, for drugs, 189

Muñoz, Sylvia, 158

Muslims, slavery of, 4

narco-architecture, 13–14

Nashville, Tennessee, 199

Natalie: Cuellar, E., relation to, 150; Cuellar, I., relation to, 98–99; Flores, E., relation to, 154–55; Flores, P., relation to, 112–15, 134

North Laredo, Texas, 203

Nuevo Laredo, Tamaulipas: anti-depressants from, 24; chickens in, 47; *Hermanos del Siglo Neuvo* in, 42, 68–70; Maz, D., in, 73–74; Maz, P., in, 65–66; *La Zona* in, 186–87, 188–89, 194. *See also* United States-Mexican border

Nuevo Leon, Monterrey, 14, 182, 183

Nuñez, Martha, 50; chickens and, 53; CPS relation to, 48–49, 51

Nuñez, Samantha, 47–48

Obama administration, 225

Ojeda, Diamantes, 190–92, 193–95

"Operation Cabbage Patch," 175–77

organized crime: film industry relation to, 227–28; in Laredo, 215; lifestyle of, 13–14; profit in, 223; *Los Solanos* relation to, 7–8

organ selling: black markets for, 88; in Latin America, 173

organ theft, 172–73

Origins of American Slavery (Morgan), 3

Ortega, Jennifer: Cuellar, E., relation to, 57–59; Diaz relation to, 133–34; as illegal immigrant, 56; Vargas relation to, 60–61

Ortega, Leslie, 51–52

"El Otro Lado," 19

Palmview, Texas, 149–50
Paris, France, 13
passports, 31
pastor. *See specific topics*
La Pastora: Flores, P., relation to, 112;
    at *Hermanos del Siglo Neuvo*, 68–69;
    Mendoza, J., relation to, 168–69;
    at *Uncion Fe Y Poder Ministries*,
    57–59. *See also* Cuellar, Elsa
pepper spray, 232
Perusquia, Jesse, 20
pet products, law enforcement relation
    to, 7
police officers: Ramirez, L.arrested
    by, 104; at U.I.S.D., 20, 35, 175;
    along United States-Mexican
    border, 19. *See also* Laredo Police
    Department; law enforcement
policies: immigration, 5; trafficking,
    226. *See also* laws
El Popo, 138; cocaine and, 139; Cuerno
    relation to, 141
poverty, in Mexico, 56
pregnancy: of children, 87–88; of
    Cuellar, I., 97–98; of Flores, P., 114–
    15; of Mata, B., 26, 27–28; teen, 118
printing press, minors affected by, 3
probation, sex offenders on, 199
produce stand, of Maz, P., 65–66
profit: from babies, 131–32; in
    organized crime, 223; of victims, 229
prohibition, in US, 187
prosperity, in US, 76
prostitution: of Asian women, 119; child
    trafficking relation to, 228; Cuellar,
    E., and, 125; earning potential in,
    189–90; in Houston, 244; across
    United States-Mexican border,
    187–88; of Ventura, L., 196–97; in
    La Zona, 186–87, 188–89
psychological impact: of adoption, 210–
    11; on law enforcement, 240–41;
    of social media, 228; on teachers,
    241–42; on victims, 209–10
public safety, budgets for, ix

"Radio Mapastepec," XHCSAC-FM
    94.3, 206
radio station, of Cuellar, E., 205–6
Ramirez, Luis Alistar "El
    Coco": aggravated assault by, 134–
    35; Cuellar, I., relation to, 95–96, 97,
    98, 99; Texas Rangers and, 105
Ramirez, Teresa, Cuellar, I. relation to,
    159–60
Ramos, Alicia, 189, 190, 195; Ventura,
    L., relation to, 196, 197, 199
Ramos, Salvador, 109
El Rancho Escondido, 39
ransom: by drug cartels, 26; of Valencia
    Ramirez, 138
rape, statutory, 89, 101
record-keeping, 206
recruitment, for human trafficking, 21
religion: of Bearden, 234; evil relation
    to, 225; illegal border crossing
    relation to, 87; society relation to,
    205, 224; vulnerability and, 169
Religion and Politics (Zimmerman), 225
Resendez family, 154
Reynosa, Mexico, 148
rights: of children, 55; of victims, 46
rights-based approach, for human
    trafficking laws, 46
Rio Bravo, 15
Rio Grande City, Texas, 129
Rio Grande River, 63; in Laredo, 103;
    Mexican culture across, 19; in Nuevo
    Laredo, 65. *See also* United States-
    Mexican border
Rivera, Miguel Alvarado, 31, *32*, 35;
    Cuellar, I., relation to, 92; Flores, P.,
    relation to, 112–13; at *Hermanos del
    Siglo Neuvo*, 69; warrants for, 175
Robb Elementary School, Uvalde, 109
Rodriguez, Alexander, 36, 47, 204,
    241; Ayala relation to, 135–36, 144;
    Cardenas relation to, 201–2; Cuellar,
    E., meeting with, 127–29; Cuellar,
    I., meeting with, 157–59, 163; in Del
    Mar area, 76, 77–79; Dugan relation

to, 202–3; Flores, P., meeting with, 134; ICE relation to, 207; at Kearny Street, 123–26; Mendez relation to, 121–22; Nuñez, M., relation to, 48–50, 53; in "Operation Cabbage Patch," 176; Ortega, L., relation to, 51–52; Talamantes meeting with, 130–31
Romans, slavery of, 3
Roosevelt, Theodore, 242
Ruiz, Brianna Maldonado. *See* Ventura, Lucy

San Bernardo Avenue, Laredo, 103–4
San Francisco, sex labor in, 119
San Francisco St., Laredo, 8, 10
San Ignacio, Texas, 8
San Miguel (Doctor), 169–70, 171–72
La Santisima Muerte, 65, 73
Santos, Myra, 121–22
S.C.A.N., 11
school safety, at U.I.S.D., *111*
screening process, for adoption, 145
security, for border crossing documents, 5
sex labor: in San Francisco, 119; Victims of Trafficking and Violence Protection Act to fight, 20. *See also* prostitution
sex offenders, on probation, 199
sex slave, 140
sexual abuse, 219; sexually transmitted diseases in, 88; of Ventura, L., 198
sexual assault, 219
sexual behavior, of children, 145, *146*
sexually transmitted diseases, 101; of Mendez, 122; in sexual abuse, 88
sexual services, with minors, 88–89, 95–96
shower curtains, as doors, 24; in *La Zona*, 189
single-parent mothers, 188
slaveholders, human traffickers compared to, 118

The Slave Next Door (Bales and Soodalter), 118
slavery: in Bible, 3–4, 90; definitions for, 118
social characteristics, human trafficking relation to, 2
social media: human trafficking on, 2; illusions relation to, 75, 227; psychological impact of, 228; victims affected by, 229
social security numbers, of deceased people, 175
social services education, ix
social structure, in Mexico, 46–47
social support, viii
society: American, 21; religion relation to, 205, 224
sociology, immigration relation to, 5
Los Solanos, 6, 16; Cuellar, E., as, 18; organized crime relation to, 7–8; across United States-Mexican border, 223–24
Solano Uno, 9–10
La Sombrilla, 176–77, 179; explosion at, 185–86; De Luna at, 181; Mata, T., relation to, 183–84, 185–86
Soodalter, Ron, 118
South Africa: adoption in, 55; human trafficking laws in, 21
Spaniards, in Aztec Empire, 3
Squire, Billy, 201
statistics, false documents effect on, 46
statutory rape, 89, 101
stereotypes, of border cities, 103–4
stories, of victims, xiii
stress, of victims, 211
suicidal ideologies, 100

taco stands, in Laredo, 63
Talamantes, Cuate: Cuellar, E., relation to, 129; Rodriguez meeting with, 130–31
Tamaulipas. *See* Nuevo Laredo, Tamaulipas

TAMIU. *See* Texas A&M International University
Taxco, Mexico, 169–72
teachers: CPS called by, ix; psychological impact on, 241–42
teen pregnancy, 118
Tejada, Andres, 52
Tejada, Rolando, 52
Tennessee, Nashville, 199
Texas: Cotulla, 204; Houston, 199, 244; McAllen, 148, 150–51; Merlin, 233; North Laredo, 203; Palmview, 149–50; Rio Grande City, 129; San Ignacio, 8; Uvalde, 109; Zapata, 63, 91, 239, 242. *See also* Laredo, Texas
Texas A&M International University (TAMIU), vii
Texas Rangers: Dugan as, 40–42, 202–3; in "Operation Cabbage Patch," 176, 177; Ramirez, L.and, 105; Rodriguez relation to, 129
Texas State Troopers, 48
Tijerina, Ricardo, 26, 27–28; Mata, B., relation to, 29–30
Tobias, Rogelio, 41, 137–39, 143; Cuellar, E., relation to, 140; Valencia Ramirez kidnapped by, 141–42
El Toro. See De Luna, Sevedres *"El Toro"*
trauma, 211

U.I.S.D. *See* United Independent School District, Laredo
Uncion Fe Y Poder Ministries, 57–58
United Independent School District, Laredo (U.I.S.D.), xiv, 18–19, *37*; CPS relation to, 86, 145; Cuellar, E., relation to, 109, 127–30; Cuellar, I., at, 99–100, *102*; lice at, 47; police officers at, 20, 35, 175; psychological impact on, 241; school safety at, *111. See also* Rodriguez, Alexander
United Nations, 21

United States-Mexican border, 2; Mata, B., at, 30; mobility across, 16; police officers along, 19; prostitution across, 187–88; *Los Solanos* across, 223–24
United States of America (US): Border Patrol of, 91, 104, 149; illusions about, 56; immigration policies of, 5; migrant workers in, 75; prohibition in, 187; prosperity in, 76; statutory rape in, 89. *See also* Texas
Uvalde, Texas, 109

Valencia Ramirez, Juan, 135; Ayala investigation of, 136–38, 143, 157; kidnapping of, 141–42
Valentine Alonzo, Juan, 39, 46, 144; autopsy report of, *43*; medical examination of, 40; Rodriguez investigation of, 135–36
Valerie: Cuellar, E., relation to, 150; Cuellar, I., relation to, 98–99; Flores, E., relation to, 154–55; Flores, P., relation to, 115, 134
Vance, Carol S., 227
Vargas, Lazaro, 60–61
Ventura, Ana, 188, 189; Ojeda relation to, 190–92, 193–95; Ramos, A., relation to, 196
Ventura, Lucy, 188, 189–90, 195; Laredo Police Department relation to, 197–98; in Nashville, 199; Ramos, A., relation to, 196
Veracruz, Mexico, 231, 233
Very Well Family, 19
victims: as celebrities, 228; culture of, 210–11; ethnic background of, 22; in family photo, *107, 108*; IQ of, xiv; mothers of, 220–21, 239, 240; profit of, 229; psychological impact on, 209–10; rights of, 46; social media effect on, 229; stories of, xiii; vulnerability of, 45
Victims of Trafficking and Violence Protection Act (2000), 20

El Viejon, 6, 8, 13, 186, 242; artwork of, 10, 12, *243*; as celebrity, 243; in Coffield Unit, 9
Villa, Pancho, 187
vulnerability: of Bearden, 235; of children, 46; in Laredo, 215; religion and, 169; of victims, 45

warrants: conviction relation to, 127; for Cuellar, E., *33*, 175; District Attorney relation to, 122
Webb County: Bearden in, 231; Child Advocacy Center in, 176; Juvenile Detention Center in, 217; Juvenile Justice Alternative Education Program in, 145, 147

Wegar, Katerina, 210
West Bustamante Street, Laredo, 139
White Slave Traffic Act (1910), 119
women, in American society, 21
World War II, 75

XHCSAC-FM 94.3, "Radio Mapastepec," 206

Zacate Creek Park, 10, 15
Zapata, Texas, 63, 91, 239, 242
Zapata Highway, 8, 15, 242
Zimmerman, Yvonne, 225
La Zona, Nuevo Laredo, 186–87, 188–89, 194

About the Author

Roger Rodriguez is an American author born in Houston, Texas. He is the author of *The Long Way to Mexico*, which won an International Latino Book Award (2022) and a Silver Book Fest Award (2022). In 2008, he was featured in the Discovery Channel for his work *The Grass Beneath His Feet: The Charles Victor Thompson Story*, which highlights the escape of death row inmate Charles Victor Thompson. Later, this work was translated into French, German, and Italian.